False Security

False Security

Greed & Deception in America's Multibillion-Dollar Insurance Industry

Kenneth D. Myers

 Prometheus Books

59 John Glenn Drive
Amherst, New York 14228-2197

Published 1995 by Prometheus Books

99 98 97 96 95   5 4 3 2 1

Library of Congress Cataloging-in-Publication Data

Myers, Kenneth D.
     False security : greed and deception in America's multibillion-dollar insurance industry / by Kenneth D. Myers.
          p.   cm.
     ISBN 0-87975-928-3
     1. Insurance crimes—United States—Case studies.
2. Insurance—Corrupt practices—United States—Case studies.
I. Title.
HV6769.M94   1995
364.1′68—dc20   94-40533
                                                               CIP

Printed in the United States of America on acid-free paper.

Dedication

This book salutes the two groups most grievously harmed by the frauds and failures within the American insurance industry.

First, it is dedicated to the innocent victims—the policy-holders and shareholders whose companies failed, leaving them uninsured and wiping out their annuities and invest-ments. They deserved better protection from the system.

Second, it is dedicated to the honest, hard-working in-surance professionals in every part of America. While selling quality insurance products for a fair price, many were nearly ruined by unscrupulous price gougers. The reputation of the entire industry was unfairly damaged by the illegal actions of a few.

Contents

Acknowledgments

During the three years of research for this book, scores of persons from coast to coast contributed generously to the project. They ranged from victims who recalled their own experiences and media personnel who shared their notes and observations, to state regulators as well as prosecution and defense lawyers involved in the cases, who provided documents and insight.

To mention each important contribution would require a chapter all its own, but the following individuals were particularly helpful:

New York State: State Insurance Commissioner Salvatore R. Curiale and staff members, the *New York Times*.

California: Staff members of State Insurance Commissioner John Garamendi, Deputy Receiver of Transit Casualty Company in Liquidation Burleigh Arnold, the *Los Angeles Times*, the *Sacramento Bee*.

Florida: Patricia King Eicher, staff members of State Insurance Commissioner Tom Gallagher, the *Miami Herald*.

Texas: State Insurance Commissioner J. Robert Hunter and his staff, the *Dallas Morning News*.

Washington, D.C.: *Roll Call,* the *Washington Post,* staff members of the U.S. House of Representatives Subcommittee on Oversight and Investigations of the Committee on Energy and Commerce, staff members of the U.S. Department of Justice assigned to insurance fraud prosecution, Rep. Billy Tauzin, D-La., Rep. Bob Livingston, R-La.

Louisiana: David Czernik, then of the Louisiana Consumers League; State Insurance Commissioner James H. Brown, Jr., and his staff members Winston Riddick (chief deputy), Allan Pursell, and Ms. Pat Hill; Baton Rouge attorney Steve Irving; the late Sheldon Beychok, Ph.D., then a Baton Rouge attorney; District Judge Joseph Keogh; Baton Rouge attorney Michele Fournet; Louisiana Inspector General Bill Lynch; Covington attorney William R. Alford, Jr.; former U.S. attorneys John Volz, Harry Rosenberg, and Robert J. Boitmann; Daniel J. De Noux of International Securities and Investigations, Inc. (Metairie); Frances Pecora, Paul Ironmonger (Baton Rouge); Robert Bernard, assistant Federal Public Defender (New Orleans); Al Pappalardo, Jr., The Pappalardo Agency (The Travelers Insurance Company, New Orleans); Robert Kuswa of Tomorrow, Inc. (Mandeville); and former State Insurance Commissioner Sherman Bernard.

Finally, this book would not have been published without the advice and persistence of my agent, Henry Berry.

1

Pirates in Pinstripes

This is a story of real people and real pain. It is the chronicle of how Americans from every state lost more than $10 billion and their faith in a great national institution, the insurance industry. One great decade of despair, 1983 to 1993, saw the virtual collapse of a half-trillion-dollar industry, and it all took place in that dark spot in the soul of commerce where greed converged with incompetence.

The concept of insurance is by no means uniquely American. So far as we know, Jonah, in the belly of the biblical whale, had neither health insurance nor protection from loss of income, but a good seventeen centuries before the birth of Christ ancient merchants had devised an informal tax on the populace to make up any loss from robberies. At the height of the Roman Empire, soldiers of the legions pooled their savings in burial societies to create a kind of group funeral fund. In the 1600s, Edward Lloyd of London began an informal network of "shared risk" in which fluctuating layers of investor-underwriters paid to buy shares in the potential loss or profit from individual oceangoing ships. The Lloyd's of London syndicates, which were never really an insurance company at all, would be at the heart of international insurance commerce and intrigue for the next three centuries.

The thrifty Puritans brought with them to America the concept of insurance protection. No less stellar a figure than Benjamin Franklin created the new country's first fire insurance company in 1752, carefully tripling the rate owners of frame structures paid over those whose buildings were built of sturdy, colonial brick! That company, originally named Philadelphia Contributorship for the Insurance of Houses from Loss by Fire, exists to this day.

The growing nation embraced a simultaneous expansion in the products offered by insurance companies. Our westward push may have been fueled by adventure but, in their hearts, the pioneers really sought safety and security for their families and that was at the heart of what insurance companies said they were selling.

The concept of accident insurance came across the seas a century later when Hartford, Connecticut, businessman James G. Batterson and some associates went to London to study its experience in that field. Soon after his return, Batterson encountered a banker who asked how much it would cost to insure himself against an accident until he got home for lunch. Batterson quoted a two-cent fee and the Travelers Insurance Company was born, opening for business April 1, 1864. The original two pennies are still on display in the Travelers' Museum.[1] The original policies covered personal injury or loss of life. They specifically excluded injury or death by dueling, or while traveling in any state or territory in rebellion against the U.S. government—an important consideration since we were then in the middle of the Civil War, and soon, "any injury or loss of life caused by Indians" was added to future policies. And thus was born the first accident insurance policy with fine print and loopholes!

It was, of course, inevitable that owners of the new "horseless carriage" would want insurance protection and the Travelers opened that market as well. In 1897, Gilbert Loomis of Westfield, Massachusetts, paid $7.50 to buy $1,000 worth of coverage on a car he built himself. For sixty years, until his eighty-fifth birthday, Loomis was a Travelers customer, after which he turned in his driver's license and cancelled his policy. The Travelers probably holds the record for the longest string of claim-free years in the automobile insurance business—three. The company paid the nation's first automobile claim in 1900.[2] It was not a collision loss but one due to death by fire, occasioned when policyholder Hieronymous Meuller of Decatur, Illinois, tried to fill his gas tank while smoking a large cigar. It would have been a marvelous opportunity to introduce the nation's first "nonsmoker discount," but that came much later.*

And so it went for almost another century, from the transnational insurance companies to the little "mom and pop" insurance brokers who often operated in only one city or one state; total sales reached $400 billion by the mid-1980s. In general, the industry enjoyed a solid reputation

---

*While it is true there are nonsmokers discounts for life insurance there are, in several instances, similar discounts available in automobile coverage for persons who do not smoke, who are within certain age brackets, who have taken drivers' safety classes, who have certain specified equipment and a whole host of other available discounts, many of which consumers fail to request even though they are entitled to certain of the discounts.

for security and prudence. There were occasional failures, to be sure, but they were small and sporadic.

The theory of insurance is deceptively simple. It requires a contract (the insurance policy) between an insurance company (the carrier) and the insurance buyer (the insured) whereby the company, in return for an agreed premium, agrees to compensate the buyer for loss on a specified subject by reason of specified perils. The subject might be health and the peril restricted to the occurrence of cancer, in a cancer policy. In the case of an automobile policy, there might be many specified perils such as uninsured motorist coverage.

There are literally scores of specialties and subspecialties in terms of types of insurance ranging from automobile policies where there are millions of buyers to highly technical chemical and industrial policies in which there may be only a handful of major buyers.

Despite these differences, most insurance companies operate along similar structural lines. They have salespeople (producers) who sell the policies to the general public. They have underwriters and actuaries who determine what the premium should cost (using complicated formulas including the buyer's age, accident or injury history, occupation, location, and type of insurance, among many other factors.) They have a claims department to receive and pay the cost of accidents, injuries, or other claims against the policy. Many companies have loss prevention and fraud departments to work with major customers, putting in place safety programs to prevent injuries or investigating claims that the company believes may be fraudulent. Most companies have auditors who review policies to make certain that buyers and their employees are properly classified according to occupational and other codes. (It costs more to insure a truck driver than an office worker so the company wants to be sure persons insured as office workers actually *are* employed inside the operation and not in some more hazardous area of the business.) The companies also have accounting, marketing, legal, and human resources departments, among many other job descriptions.

The front line of every insurance company is its sales force. Some companies only sell policies through their own agents. Others are represented by "independent agents" who sell for many competing companies.

There are no national requirements for persons wishing to become insurance agents; each state has its own rules. Most states require that a prospective agent be sponsored by an insurance company. The would-be agent must then pass one or more written examinations. There are some two dozen possible insurance licenses for which an applicant may take a specific examination, depending upon what type of insurance (usually called the "product") he or she wishes to sell. Some types of licenses include life, health, and accident; industrial; credit life; credit hospital and burial service; travel, health, and accident; fire, casualty, fire and casualty; vehicle; physical damage; title; industrial fire; fidelity (bonding); baggage; and automobile club.

The licenses are administered by the insurance department in the state where the applicant intends to live and work. Each examination takes as much as a half day, at a cost of $25 to $500. Some states, such as New Jersey, also require a Federal Bureau of Investigation background check, and most states now also require that each agent complete a certain number of hours of continuing education each year in order to keep the license current.

There is no one national insurance agents' license that

allows a person to sell insurance throughout the country; each agent must either take the examination in each state where he or she wants to sell insurance or must be licensed through a reciprocal agreement between one's home state and the other state(s) where one hopes to sell. In most states, the most difficult license to obtain is an "agency license," which allows the holder not just to sell insurance for a company but to "hang out his own shingle" as an independent businessman. Those licenses usually require the applicant to prove financial stability in addition to passing the examinations.

For the most part there are no federal requirements and few state guidelines for the other positions in the insurance industry, although some positions, such as actuaries and some legal and medical positions, do require certifications and licenses. Many others, such as underwriters and claims examiners, simply worked their way up through the company ranks, learning through experience. Nowadays, most insurance companies require that new employees have formal insurance education at a college or university school of business, an accounting degree, or some other specialized education or college degree.

The same lack of consistent requirements is present in terms of gaining approval to purchase or start an insurance company; here, too, each state sets its own rules. Generally, getting into the insurance company business requires demonstrated background and education and a substantial amount of paid-in capital, but the specific levels vary widely from state to state. In virtually every instance, the state department of insurance is supposed to conduct an exhaustive examination of the proposed company and its owners before allowing it to open for business. As you will see, in some states the examination consisted only of filling out the basic application form and making a generous contribution to the state insurance commissioner's re-election fund. Increased public scrutiny in the aftermath of the $10-billion-dollar insurance failures of recent years has led to more stringent review in most cases.

Why is there no federal licensing for companies or agents? That is the legacy of the National Association of Insurance Commissioners (NAIC), the old-boy network of state insurance commissioners. One of the prime missions of this assembly is to protect the turf of elected state insurance regulators from encroachment by the federal government, which also prevents national uniformity in regulation or enforcement. This crazy-quilt pattern historically led to unscrupulous insurance company operators "shopping" to locate in states where the insurance commissioner was known to be a person of easy virtue or where regulation was known to be haphazard and ineffective. The NAIC accomplished this dubious feat through passage of the federal McCarran Act, which exempts insurance companies from antitrust enforcement so long as they are regulated by individual states. The operative section of the act is 1012, which says, in part, "The business of insurance, and every person engaged therein, shall be subject to the laws of the several states which relate to the regulation or taxation of such business." In theory, it was a states' rights issue; in practice, it became a license to steal.

No more glaring example of that operational deficiency exists than in the state audits of insurance companies. Every three years, a handful of overworked, underpaid state insurance department bureaucrats arrives to attempt to conduct a full-scale audit of millions, sometimes billions, of dollars of insurance written by that company since its last review. In the case of an insurance company teetering on the brink of insolvency, such a review is frequently too little, too late. Some states conduct selective "desk audits," interim reviews of company paperwork done at the state insurance commission headquarters, but such cursory samples are often inadequate to establish any kind of "early warning system."

In these triennial audits, state regulators try to look for the three warning signs of impending insolvency: the over-stating of assets, the underreserving of liabilities, and outright fraud.

Overstating of assets occurs when a company deliberately misrepresents the value of its holdings. Since stocks are valued at their current market price, this is not usually a problem. Some cases have occurred in which a company arranges a "sham trade" of certain stocks it holds in order to create the illusion of demand and value when, in fact, the stocks—except for the fake, inflated activity—were worthless and demand for them was nonexistent. That was one of the assertions against the ownership of the Southshore Holding Corporation. A more frequent problem is the inclusion of bonds at their amortized value assuming they will be held to maturity. Obviously, if the company fails in the meantime, that will not be the case. In fact, most insurance companies' bond portfolios are now overvalued by as much as 25 percent.

The *underreserving of liabilities* is quite different. Reserves, the "rainy day contingency" of insurance companies, are divided into two sections. First is a reserve for unearned premiums. That is a calculation of how much the company would have to refund if it cancelled every policy on its books.

Loss reserves, on the other hand, are designed to ensure enough money is set aside from premium income to cover all potential losses. When insufficient loss reserves are established, which happens with alarming frequency, the policyholder surplus (the difference between total assets and total liabilities) can be wildly misstated. This problem is very difficult to detect and represents the single most important aspect of the audit.

Fraud is the final element of the audit. A careful audit can usually pinpoint the most glaring examples of fraud but the long period between audits often spotlights such abuses too late to save the company.

To its credit, the NAIC has established a national "watch list" of property and liability companies considered to be outside established norms. It has also designed a uniform set of ratios within which companies should operate, as part of the NAIC's Insurance Regulatory Information System (IRIS).

How It's Supposed to Work

In the decade leading up to 1984, of the thousands of insurance companies operating across the United States, only about one failed each year and nobody noticed. The perfunctory government regulation by antiquated insurance departments operated by each state was quietly clerical and virtually unknown to the insurance-buying public. In 1984, insurance company failures rose from two the preceding year to ten, an ominous but incipient trend.

Then came 1985, the year the industry's very foundation collapsed and the roof fell in. During the preceding decade, almost every state had passed legislation requiring all employers to provide workers' compensation insurance and all drivers to acquire at least a minimum amount of automobile insurance. Many states provided stiff fines and sometimes criminal penalties for failure to comply. Who was affected? In the main, it was businesses and drivers operating at the margins, those who either wanted to avoid or could barely afford the purchase of insurance. The new laws uncovered a vast new insurance market in which almost every sale was decided on the basis of cost. Most states offered government-operated workers' compensation funds and assigned-risk pools for otherwise uninsurable drivers. The problem was that these policies rapidly priced themselves out of the volatile market. A dual phenomenon occurred. Almost overnight, new, aggressive insurance companies appeared, virtually on every street corner, marketing low-cost auto insurance for high-risk drivers. Second, old-line, existing companies from other segments of the industry saw the vast new markets and decided to take the plunge as well. Many were ill-equipped to underwrite the new business at a profitable rate. Others had no idea of the size and cost of the claims management operations these kinds of insurance policies required. The sleepy, little, state insurance regulation staffs, which operated almost literally with lead pencils and green eyeshades in the age of computers, were simply overwhelmed. The best state operations were swamped as new insurance company applications to operate within their jurisdictions first doubled and then doubled again. The worst of the regulators were, if not married to the very applicants they were supposed to regulate, surely living in sin with them. In insurance commissioners' offices, there was rampant figurative neck strain from repeatedly looking the other way. First to suffer were the many responsible insurance companies and their agents who sold policies at a rate that made a profit and generated sufficient reserves to pay their claims. Next to suffer were the consumers who bought low-cost policies that proved to be worthless. Deals that looked too good to be true usually were.

The first of the major nationwide companies to fail was Mission Insurance Company of California. For years it had been a successful operator in the workers' compensation field—operating in every state and the District of Columbia. But it was unable to resist the lucrative underwriting of major commercial liability policies, a field in which it had very limited expertise. Huge losses in 1984–85 went largely undetected until the scheduled triennial regulatory examination, which concluded on March 25, 1985. To their horror, examiners discovered Mission had $900 million in unpaid claims and a $169 million shortfall in its reserves. The company entered conservatorship on October 31, 1985, where it remained, essentially brain dead, until February 24, 1987, when it was ordered liquidated.[3]

A similar fate soon befell Transit Casualty, once a sleepy Missouri insurer of bus lines and taxicabs. By then located in a palatial California headquarters, the company plunged into commercial liability coverage in every state, insuring some of the biggest losses in world history, and collapsing spectacularly in December 1985 to the estimated tune of $2 billion—the largest single failure in the American insurance industry.[4]

On the other coast, New Jersey's Integrity Insurance Company failed just eighteen months later. When it fell, in March 1987, the estimated losses were $300 million, a figure which soon grew to $1 billion, with customers in every state.[5]

By 1985, major failures had grown to twenty-one

companies in liquidation. By 1989 that number was forty-eight. Liquidations peaked at one hundred three in 1991.[6] The total cost of this generation of greed would eventually total more than $10 billion. That may prove to be an inadequate estimate, as the industry "rides the long-tailed tiger." Insurance is called a "long tail" business because, in many kinds of insurance—workers' compensation being a prime example—the final cost of a claim cannot be known for many years.

Some observers have taken comfort from the fact that the insurance industry's collapse, at $10 billion, has done less damage to the nation's economy than the $150 billion savings-and-loan debacle, but that is an ill-fitting comparison. When the savings-and-loan industry fell on hard times, optimistic regulators put the price tag at $5 billion to $7 billion. Only when the lingering damage was tallied was it clear that the total was thirty times the initial estimates.

In the savings-and-loan failures, any person whose account contained $100,000 or less was repaid in full by the federally backed insurance fund,* bolstered by emergency congressional appropriations.

The same was not true in the insurance collapse. If you were a shareholder in a mutual insurance company that failed, you lost everything.

The biggest losers were insurance consumers. Some were big-name figures like San Francisco 49ers quarterback Joe Montana, victimized by a scam that sold phony insurance against injuries. Most were just average Americans whose lives were often ruined by inept or unscrupulous insurance kingpins. There are hundreds of thousands of stories:

---

*Federal Savings and Loan Insurance Corporation (FSLIC).

Families that paid thousands of dollars in health insurance premiums on policies that did not pay, leaving them to face hundreds of thousands of dollars in medical bills; drivers who paid for insurance with companies that later failed, forcing them to absorb the loss of unpaid claims and buy new, more expensive policies, sometimes from companies that soon failed as well; innocent victims of accidents caused by drivers whose policies proved to be worthless, often leaving them with years of payments remaining on demolished vehicles and no way to collect. Most settled with their state's insurance guaranty funds for pennies on the dollar. Many have yet to receive a cent.[7]

State insurance guaranty monies come from a percentage of premiums paid by each insurance company operating in the state. This essentially resulted in contributions by the good companies going to pay for the excesses of the bad ones. Since the state assessment for the fund was very small, when the state guaranty funds were weighed against colossal failures on a scale no one could have imagined, they were almost immediately overburdened. Several state funds became temporarily insolvent; numbers of them had to suspend compensation to victims until their resources could be built back up or supplemented by increased assessments. Individual companies routinely increased the rates their policyholders paid in an effort to cover this added expense. At the same time, the companies were allowed to deduct their state guaranty fund assessments from their taxable income, meaning state tax revenues were reduced, with the state's taxpayers making up the difference.

The funds settled claims for a fraction of their value to conserve the fund's inadequate resources; almost no one was totally compensated. The victims came from every state in America; they, or the person at fault, bought insurance from companies licensed and approved by their state's insurance commission and, in case after case, their finances were wrecked and their lives were ruined.

How could it have happened, often and everywhere, in a business supposedly so well regulated? How could one industry have attracted so many thieves and incompetents? Can any insurance buyer ever again be safe and secure? Is anything being done to make certain this national plague will never be repeated? These are the stories that comprise an American tragedy.

Notes

1. Information supplied by The Travelers Insurance Company.
2. Ibid.
3. Report of the Subcommittee on Oversight and Investigations of the U.S. House of Representatives Committee on Energy and Commerce, February 1990.
4. Ibid. Also, Transit Casualty Company Insolvency and Liquidation Report, September 1993, and interview with Burleigh Arnold, Esq., Deputy Receiver, Transit Casualty Company in Liquidation.
5. Transcripts of hearings held by, and the report of, the Subcommittee on Oversight and Investigations of the U.S. House of Representatives Committee on Energy and Commerce, April 1989.
6. Transcripts of hearings held by, and the report of, the Subcommittee on Oversight and Investigations of the U.S. House of Representatives Committee on Energy and Commerce, February 1990.
7. Transcripts of, and report by, the Subcommittee on Oversight and Investigations of the U.S. House of Representatives Committee on Energy and Commerce, April 1989, and February 1990.

2

Mission: Bells Tolling

It should have been a warning. It was the earliest failure of a company that operated in every state. It established a pattern for most of the failures which followed. By the time the raging current of collapse had sputtered to a stream a decade later, 332 pages were required just to list the 479 names comprising the cavalcade of corporate corpses. The dimension of its failure should have been impossible; no company with $240 million in capital surplus should have been allowed to cause $1.5 billion in losses.

The warning bells tolled at Mission Insurance Company for a very long time, but no one was listening. The company operated from handsome headquarters in Los Angeles, with all the trappings of success. It was the flagship of the Mission Insurance Group, a holding company traded on the New York Stock Exchange. The enterprise is best thought of as a carefully constructed triumvirate consisting of Mission Insurance, Sayre and Toso, and Pacific Reinsurance Management Corporation, usually called "Pacific Re." The latter two were agencies that wrote large amounts of business for Mission and other insurance companies across America.

Mission Insurance Group's 1982 audit, for the period ending in 1981, was a happy little document with only some minor housekeeping recommendations. Three years later, California regulators took the lead in a six-state routine audit that found a $169 million reserve deficiency and $900 million in unpaid claims. Hoping against hope, the California Insurance Department placed Mission into conservatorship on October 31, 1985. Conservatorships are designed for troubled companies who need a little "hands on" help from regulators to get their management houses back in order. In Mission's case, the claims total soon passed $1.5 billion, revealing a crisis more complex than any simple recovery system could cure. The entire operation was placed into liquidation on February 24, 1987.[1]

It did not require a Harvard MBA to discern the difficulty with Mission's operations. First, its losses were mounting exponentially and second, its reinsurance companies, which were supposed to pay for most of the losses, wouldn't or couldn't. Reinsurance is supposed to be a fairly straightforward enterprise in which an insurance company with a substantial block of potentially costly business sells off some of that insurance coverage, "ceding" it to another insurance company. The new company thus picks up the policies and payments, while the original company receives a commission or fronting fee for the transaction. It is vaguely similar to the local bookmaker who "lays off" part of his bets with an associate bookie in order to reduce his risk in the event of loss. In the insurance business, reinsurance agreements, called "treaties," are only as good as the reinsurance companies who participate in them. Assuring the financial stability of the reinsurance companies is the business of the original company because, by federal law, it must ultimately stand behind the insurance contracts if the reinsurer fails.

Mission wrote reinsurance for other companies and bought reinsurance for policies it initiated itself. In the end, more than six hundred reinsurance companies were picking up Mission's direct policies, coverage that represented about $2.5 billion in paper assets for Mission. Sadly, a half billion of that was impossible to touch because the reinsurance companies responsible for it had either failed or lacked sufficient funds to pay their obligations to Mission. Mission caused the same situation with the business it reinsured for other companies; they had to stand behind $180 million in paid losses that should have been reimbursed by Mission.

Mission wrote its way into bankruptcy with alarming speed. Just five years earlier, it had a solid reputation as a regional workers' compensation carrier and a rating to match from A. M. Best, the most widely known of the several groups that rate the soundness of insurance companies around the nation.

The eager Mission management branched out aggressively, trading on the company's previously unblemished reputation to write big-volume, commercial property and casualty insurance. The chief kinds of business Mission now undertook were high-risk automobile policies and "commercial multiple peril" policies. Those are "basket" policies in which all manner of possible commercial perils are combined into one premium that is lower than the total of all those policies if written individually. In the case of Mission, peril was certainly the operative word.

Power of the Pen

Mission wrote this business by naming Sayre and Toso and Pacific Re as managing general agents, "MGAs," for it and its various reinsurers scattered around the globe. The MGA operation was to become a familiar formula for failure. To a very large extent, an MGA has the "power of the pen" for the insurance company it represents, with all of the rewards and none of the responsibilities of the company in whose name it acts. The MGA decides what insurance policies to sell, to whom, and for how much. Many of the MGAs were trusted to collect the premiums for the policies they had underwritten, and they frequently handled claims under the policies as well.

In theory, an insurance company's use of managing general agents dispersed throughout the country made perfect sense. It allowed the company to achieve much greater geographic penetration in much less time. It also lowered the company's cost of sales since it was relieved of the cost of supporting individual office locations as well as the cost of layers of support personnel in billing, underwriting, claims management, and the like. The downside to the MGA arrangement was that the company also simultaneously surrendered its ability to control—and frequently even to know about—the levels of risk it was assuming since those decisions were now allowed to be made in the field by the MGAs without permission or supervision from the corporate office. Prompt receipt of premium payments also became an acute problem under many of these arrangments. Since these MGAs were not, strictly speaking, "insurance companies," the actual liability for the MGAs' misdeeds and actions fell squarely on the shoulders of the insurance company each represented—a burden many companies were financially unable to bear.

Mission's two MGAs used Mission's name to write a mammoth volume of policies that they immediately reinsured with others. The problem was that the reinsurers were frequently unlicensed carriers who could not write business in their own names and thus needed Mission to "front" for them so they could do business. Unlicensed reinsurers are required to post letters of credit showing their ability to make payment on losses. Time after time, these letters of credit went unchecked and unchallenged, by both the insurance company writing the business and by regulators. Frequently, the letters of credit proved to be worthless. One simple rule of retail is that every check is good until it is presented for payment.

There is no prohibition against an insurance company using an unlicensed carrier for purposes of reinsurance. Similarly, there is nothing to preclude such an unlicensed carrier from accepting this reinsurance as ceded, provided the reinsurance company has posted a "letter of credit." Had reinsurance carrier(s) in question wished to be licensed, they would have had to submit to the admitted assets and other capitalization tests required in various states, rather than simply the formality of the letter of credit. In many cases, these unlicensed carriers were simply the original companies themselves, doing business under another name, siphoning off levels of risk so they could write more business at the same time as they made substantial profits on the reinsurance commissions involved in the process.

This vast network of sometimes-shady reinsurance companies, often ensconced in exotic locations like the Cayman Islands or the Isle of Man, based their letters of credit on loss reserves that often proved to be inadequate or non-existent. Foreign banks, which were supposed to honor letters of credit immediately and without question, refused. From one end of the United States to the other, the reinsurance thicket proved to be a liquidator's nightmare, costing millions to chase and collect.

Meanwhile, Mission was already living on borrowed time. It had become best known as a big regional writer of workers' compensation insurance. During the early 1980s, in state after state, workers' insurance companies were failing, often paying $1.25 or more in claims for every $1 they collected in premiums. Oblivious to such dangers, Mission fueled its workers' compensation business by deep discounts, premium rebates, and cash incentives for its agents. Had Mission never entered the automobile insurance or multiple peril business, the "long tail" of workers' compensation claims would inevitably have caused it to fail; the collapse simply would have taken longer and cost less.

Sayre and Toso took in a 6 percent commission from Mission for writing large, direct commercial liability policies. Less than 5 percent of those policies were retained by Mission; the remainder were passed off by Sayre and Toso to reinsurers, for which they earned another 15 to 25 percent commission. Since Sayre and Toso was wholly owned by Mission's holding company, the deals resulted in as much as 31 percent total commission while retaining very little of the risk, which would have been brilliant had the reinsurance agreements been worth the paper they were written on.

It is important to understand how such lucrative arrangements work. Mission needed to sell large, commercial liability policies as a matter of generating profit and cash flow. It made at least a paper profit (prospectively) in selling, for example, a policy that generated a million-dollar commission. Much of that revenue was eventually upstreamed to Mission's holding company. The holding company also owned Sayre and Toso. Thus, it made an additional profit when Sayre and Toso got 6 percent commission on the million dollar premium ($60,000) for actually selling the policy. The holding company rang the register again when Sayre and Toso charged the reinsurance company as much as $250,000 commission for passing through the ceded reinsurance to them. Until the claims came in, the holding company was doing very well indeed.

Pacific Re, also wholly owned by the holding group, took in 6 percent commissions from Mission and others for managing reinsurance pools, joint ventures among the participants in which Mission carefully limited its exposure to 10 to 20 percent of the risk.

Many of the Sayre-Toso reinsurers were American companies not licensed in and therefore unregulated by California. Three-quarters of the reinsurers were headquartered outside the country. Pacific Re put together Mission reinsurance agreements with seventy-eight companies, fifty-six of whom were either not admitted in California or located outside the United States. The selection of these far-flung reinsurers had nothing to do with a sense of global interaction. Rather, the MGAs knew that foreign reinsurers would likely be less familiar with the substantial risks they were undertaking and seldom audited the reinsurance agreements they were acquiring. Keep in mind, there was nothing illegal in either Sayre and Toso or Pacific Re passing along this business to foreign or offshore reinsurance companies not licensed in the state so long as the company in question had posted a "letter of credit" as previously explained.

It was a highly profitable short-term arrangement; the reinsurers took in hundreds of millions in premiums while Mission grew fat on the fronting fees. When the house of cards inevitably collapsed, each side blamed the other, leaving only victims and taxpayers to shoulder the cost.

No Control at Mission Control

Mission's management, almost as if it sensed the imminent collapse of this kind of poor underwriting, severe underpricing, inadequate reserving, and misleading accounting, seemed bent upon selling as much as possible as quickly as possible. When the end came, management tried its best to look arrogantly innocent, blaming everyone else involved for causing the debacle.

E. Richard De Rosa, Mission Insurance Group's president and chief executive officer, called himself a "hands on" manager during his twenty years at Mission's helm. He might better have said "hands on the throat," because he was present at the creation of this crisis and clearly in charge of causing the catastrophe. That's not how he told it. He blamed Mission's failure on a six-year cycle of depressed insurance rates that he had expected to turn upward after the third year. None of this, he said, was his fault. Mr. De Rosa retired comfortably in early 1984 just as the big losses resulting from his management actions were becoming apparent. He sold 116,000 shares of Mission stock on January 9, 1984, in a corporate-guaranteed transaction that provided him a large profit and 41 percent premium over market value just weeks before Mission declared a $37.2 million loss for the fourth quarter of 1983. He denied he violated federal insider trading laws but conceded his sale might be considered "an extremely fortunate business decision." He was not, so far as I have been able to learn, charged or convicted.[2]

Associating themselves with De Rosa's innocence were his chief lieutenants, chief operating officer Louis J. Marioni, and chief financial officer Michael Mulholland. Each purported to have had no knowledge of the financial shenanigans that sabotaged the company. One was reminded of the cartoon in which occupants of a wrecked vehicle tell the patrolman, "Nobody was driving officer; we were all in the back seat singing." Company officials were carefully shielded by directors and officers' insurance coverage; nobody went to jail, everyone just took the money and left the scene. Mission's executive compensation program provided stock options and bonuses tied to the company's financial performance compared to the insurance industry as a whole. That kind of incentive offers no reason for an executive to slow down uncontrolled growth.

Marioni and Mulholland departed Mission in the company's waning days in 1985, soon reappearing as principals of Superior National Insurance Company, which they acquired from the royal family of Kuwait. It was a shell corporation but it had one invaluable asset: it owned an insurance license and the boys were back in business, as, of course, they had every legal right to be. About one-third of the financing for the deal came from former Mission agents.[3]

It was at Pacific Re that much of the mischief occurred. Ronald Bengston and Robert Marsh, who had owned stock in Mission, sold it before the true condition of Mission was known. They left to form their own reinsurance intermediary company, which managed to contribute mightily to the subsequent demise of Integrity Insurance Company (more about Integrity later) before sinking from sight.

Bengston reportedly abandoned the insurance industry. Marsh, in an ironic twist of fate, climbed on board the receivership of Transit Casualty. Since that enterprise presumes to last until well into the next century, Marsh could conceivably complete his career looking into the misadventures of others connected with the Transit failure. When asked about the appropriateness of retaining Marsh, Transit's deputy receiver Burleigh Arnold said there were a lot of shady operations requiring investigation in the Transit failure and "it takes one to know one."[4] He defended Marsh in general, quoting one of the Mission examiners as saying Marsh was "either one of the best liars or the stupidest insurance executives" he had ever encountered.

Both Bengston and Marsh professed to be uninvolved in the Mission failure, Bengston said it was "unfortunate" but not the fault of anyone at the top. Marsh joined in to say it was the fault of "many, many factors." To believe that assertion, you must believe that senior management lacked the competence to detect a remarkable pattern of internal deception. The company routinely understated its necessary loss reserves, which provided wonderful financial statements if you could overlook the time bomb they ultimately represented.

No single factor so well demonstrates the inept reserving at Mission as the "incurred but not reported" reserve formula. The IBNR is a category designed to protect against truly unpredictable claims that arise every day and that must be prudently allowed for. Mission invented a simple formula that was never tested for accuracy and never reviewed by an actuary. Under the fanciful Mission formula, INBR reserves were set by a simple five-year declining balance. After the fifth year, no further reserves were provided at all, despite the clear knowledge that it was after the fifth year that such losses statistically snowballed.

More guesswork was involved in the reserve system for property claims, which do not have an INBR category. Here, the company simply decided that if a policy looked like it was more than 50 percent property coverage, the whole policy would be coded as property with no INBR reserves at all. If it looked to be more than 50 percent casualty, the inadequate INBR reserve system was applied to the whole policy. Since most claims turned out to be casualty claims, it was a "lose/lose" formula.

When those horse-and-buggy procedures were insufficient to hide Mission's worsening condition, the company simply "cooked the books" to provide false reports to regulators and business associates. This allowed Mission to continue its downhill slide during its final three years, when it was already, secretly, insolvent. By the time these problems came to light Mission had collapsed. The alleged misdeeds were referred to federal law enforcement and regulatory officials by the subcommittee.[5] No final determination has yet been made with respect to the individuals responsible. The misleading data also enabled Mission, with an actual 1984 operating loss of $88 million, to declare a $13 million dividend, paid to the holding company. The dividends in question were paid prior to the establishment of the operating losses. One of the problems in the insurance industry is that such dividends are almost always upstreamed before operating losses are declared later in the year.

Putting a happy face on Mission's disastrous financial

condition required special gimmicks like the ultrasecret "discretionary reserve fund," which was used as a kind of slush fund to statistically prop up various faltering reinsurance pools. All income from annual reinsurance pools was lumped together so new business income would camouflage the mounting losses from business already on the books. The outside reinsurance companies relied upon the validity of such reports in setting their own reserves.

Pacific Re had established reassuring guidelines for its reinsurance partners, setting out eight specific, risky types of business it would not accept. Then, Pacific Re ignored the guidelines, writing huge amounts of the forbidden business and telling brokers it would accept individual risks far in excess of its agreed limits.

Sayre and Toso simply "double counted" Mission's participation in one reinsurance pool as being an investment in numerous separate pools. The result was that Mission's risk was extremely limited but the hapless reinsurers were secure in their belief that Mission had a much bigger dollar stake in the enterprise. This tactic works as long as the culprit can keep various groups apart and at arm's length. In fact, the method worked so well that Bengston and Marsh repeated it when they created Continental Reinsurance Company to work with Integrity. Bengston and Marsh each owned half of Continental.

Mission was coincidentally abetted in this deception by the superficial audits conducted by Coopers and Lybrand, which trustingly took Mission's documents at face value and relied upon file information about reinsurance transactions without independently confirming much of the data. There was no independent audit of Pacific Re during these years because Bengston believed the staff could audit itself. Upon examination, no significant audits could be found showing that Pacific Re had examined the procedures of those primary companies whose policies it was reinsuring. Files showing such prudent audits were inexplicably missing when requested by congressional investigators.

Thus was created a classic case of greed combined with incompetence. Only one outcome was possible but by the time regulators had figured out the formula, the terrain was littered with the remains of similar insurance operations throughout America.

Mission went into conservatorship October 31, 1985, and into liquidation February 24, 1987. The liquidator is suing to recover whatever he can. Guaranty funds in all fifty states and the District of Columbia are paying (at dimes-on-the-dollar percentages) claims against Mission. Transit's situation is thoroughly discussed in chapter 3. Integrity went into liquidation March 24, 1987. The insolvency is now estimated to be in excess of $1 billion with claims liability in excess of $2 billion. Early access distribution of $32 million was paid in 1992. The guaranty funds in each state and the District of Columbia are paying compromise settlements the same as in the Mission case above.

Notes

1. California Department of Insurance. See also, Report of the Subcommittee on Oversight and Investigations of the U.S. House of Representatives Committee on Energy and Commerce, February 1990. There was also a published report in the *Los Angeles Times*.

2. Report of the Subcommittee on Oversight and Investigations of

the U.S. House of Representatives Committee on Energy and Commerce, February 1990.

   3. Ibid.

   4. Interview with Burleigh Arnold.

   5. Transcript of the Subcommittee on Oversight and Investigations of the U.S. House of Representatives Committee on Energy and Commerce, April 1989.

3

Sic Transit Gloria

Transit Casualty Company's receiver would later call it "the *Titanic* of insurance company insolvencies," with estimated liabilities of $4 billion that may take until 2012 to liquidate. Transit's failure is a world-class example of how inept, greedy, and unscrupulous management can take a small, sleepy company to international prominence and then watch it perish.

Transit Casualty began as a modest Missouri operation born at the close of World War II. For many years it enjoyed solid, if moderate, prosperity writing commercial property and casualty insurance for city buses, charter buses, and long-haul trucking companies. By the mid-1970s it had been acquired by Beneficial Standard Corporation and its executive offices relocated to California, although it remained a Missouri-chartered corporation.

Beneficial Standard was a holding company with subsidiaries in the life insurance, property/casualty insurance, and real estate businesses. While nominally a public company, traded on the New York Stock Exchange, the real control was exercised by the Mitchell family, which owned

35 percent of its stock. Through president and chief executive Joseph N. Mitchell, the family ran Beneficial for its own benefit. Arbitrage magnate Ivan Boesky also owned a combination of stock amounting to 6.9 percent. Mitchell later heatedly denied running Transit into the ground through reckless operations and irresponsible conduct; much of the record seems to refute that blithe denial. Certainly Mitchell had the background to know better. Beneficial Standard Life Insurance Company had been founded by his father. Young Joseph Mitchell joined the company fresh from World War II service in France. He started in the file room and worked his way up to Beneficial's presidency in the 1950s. He hit upon the scheme of insurance mass marketing through Diners Club, oil companies, department stores, and automobile manufacturers.

Along the way, Mitchell became a major player in Los Angeles society: chairman of the National Conference of Christians and Jews and head of fundraising campaigns for the Los Angeles Music Center and the United Way. An advisor to Los Angeles Mayor Tom Bradley, Mitchell later served as executive committee chairman of Cedar Sinai Medical Center. Mitchell had all the right contacts with which to build a major, international, insurance organization.

To run Transit's day-to-day activities, Mitchell selected George P. Bowie, who would eventually serve as both general counsel and chief executive of the company.

By the end of the 1970s, the transportation business, Transit's backbone, was becoming increasingly competitive and only marginally profitable. The choices were clear: to tighten the corporate belt and ride out the cut-throat competition, or to take a profound leap of faith and bet the farm on a new, unfamiliar end of the insurance business. Mitchell made that bet and then doubled it by assuming ownership of part of the local insurance agencies that sold Transit's policies. Had Transit taken time to develop the tedious but crucial internal controls to manage the business prudently, the double dipping might have proved brilliant. Mitchell and Bowie, however, were in far too big a hurry to be bothered with planned growth or management systems.

With the dawn of the 1980s, they hastily slapped together a new Transit operation, the Risk Management Division. Its assignment was to run the risk management and the mercantile multi-peril programs that would ultimately ruin the company.

To kick-start the new enterprise, Transit concocted a national network of managing general agents. Soon operating in every state, it was a scheme destined to boldly go where no insurance executive with a eye for long-range planning would have dared to go. The intrepid Mitchell-Bowie team believed there was only minimal risk for Transit because they intended to rely primarily on the commissions or "fronting fees" from the MGAs, which were supposed to have the real risk underwritten by reinsurance companies around the globe. It was yet one more instance of the power of the pen, as free-agent MGAs eagerly assembled a motley crew of no fewer than nine hundred reinsurers. Transit lacked the ability to make sure each of the reinsurance companies was credit-worthy, even though Transit itself bore the ultimate liability for each claim.

Many were, in fact, completely unknown to Transit's management. Certainly the MGAs had no reason to verify the soundness of their reinsurers, for their hands were firmly on the controls of a marvelous new money-making machine, an apparatus that had no brake.

In a matter of weeks, it was literally raining cash at Transit's handsome headquarters at 3700 Wilshire Boulevard. It was not that no one there was worried about the *nouveau riche* mind-set within the organization. One senior executive marveled that it all seemed "too good to be true." Eleanor Leary, who would later become Transit's chief financial officer, went one step further. In 1982, she wrote a thoughtful, ten-page memo detailing her concerns. She said, in part, "The Company's biggest disadvantage, I believe, is that we are a carrier without a vision of where we are going. Further, we are a small carrier, saddled with an expensive manual processing system, with too small a book of business to justify automation at this time, and a staff who lack the necessary expertise to service the more sophisticated customer and program." She warned, "The Company's lack of written procedures, lack of managerial controls, and lack of expertise in setting up new operations jeopardize any smooth transition into high-volume processing operations. . . . We cannot continue to wildly diversify into all directions at once only to be buried by unsupportable expenses and a logistical nightmare. If Transit is going to grow and prosper in the 80s, we are going to have to develop a battle plan for competing in today's competitive insurance marketplace. I feel the current direction of our company is too unfocused and lacks any real competitive strategy. We must identify a direction, based on competitive advantage, and then stick with it, or ten years from now we will be nowhere."[1] No one at the top was listening, and it did not require ten years for Leary's fears to become reality. Three years later Transit was seized and insolvent, and by the time the receiver arrived Leary and most of the experienced staff were gone, leaving only eighteen clerical workers to help sort through the remains.

From the outset, Mitchell and Bowie opted to ignore the time bomb the small army of unknown reinsurers represented, and they were simply swamped by the tidal wave of transactions produced by the MGAs. Theirs was a company set up to handle five hundred to eight hundred transportation insurance policies a year sold by two hundred independent agents around the country, policies they understood well enough for management to recite them in their sleep.

Suddenly, in their first year of expansion, the sacks of mail contained thirty-seven thousand policies sold by seventeen MGAs and a thousand subagents. Many of the policies were complicated, high-risk policies of the kind Transit management had never even seen, let alone managed, although Mitchell later claimed the company had considerable expertise in underwriting such risks. Overnight, Transit was writing big-volume policies in exotic product lines like fire, marine, medical malpractice, auto liability and property, aircraft, surety, toxic waste, satellite launch, liquor liability, taxi drivers, race horses, and reinsurance assumed from other insurance companies as well. The policy records were soon stacked to the ceiling in 256 locations. By the time they were assembled by the receiver, they stood eight feet high over an area of twenty thousand square feet.

Transit went from writing $93 million in 1979 to $227 million in 1984. It reinsured premiums written by other companies as well; that business grew from $5 million to $51 million in the same period. All of that was backed by Transit's statutory capital of just under $44 million, and even that inadequate amount was inflated by fanciful accounting.

By the time regulators realized what was happening, there were a half million outstanding claims against Transit from around the globe. They included people dying from asbestosis and cancer; and suffering from use of the Dalkon Shield; scores of medical malpractice claims; nursery school children covered by Transit's Kinder Cover program; deaths from the Union Carbide disaster in Bhopal, India; and many, many more. Real people in real pain suddenly found their insurance protection to be illusory.

Transit, in its rush to write new business, neglected to produce underwriting guidelines for its rapacious MGAs. Their income, of course, was directly tied to the volume of business they produced, so they weren't complaining. It took six to eight months for premium reports to reach Transit's headquarters from the scattered subagents and MGAs, so at any given moment Transit had absolutely no idea where it stood or whom it was insuring. In any case, by the time the truckloads of premium reports arrived Transit was completely incapable of handling them. Such was Transit's level of greed that cartons of prenumbered policies were simply shipped out to agents; there was no master list of policies at Transit and no way for Transit to match payments to individual policies.

By the time Transit was examined for the three-year period ending December 31, 1983, it was already late 1984. That examination, conducted by Missouri, Delaware, Georgia, and California regulators, was released in April 1985 and Transit was ordered to stop writing new policies. The company was in rehabilitation by November. Just weeks later it was scheduled for liquidation. The regulatory order was cited in both congressional hearings and in the September 1993 Insolvency and Liquidation Report issued by Burleigh Arnold, Special Deputy Receiver for Transit Casualty Company in Liquidation. This was a Zone Audit, supervised by the Missouri Department of Insurance, where Transit was domiciled and that department issued the order. Transit was placed into receivership and an amended order of liquidation was issued on December 3, 1985. The order was signed by Judge Byron L. Kinder, Circuit Court, Cole County, Jefferson City, Missouri.[2]

Everyone agreed that the "power of the pen" had been primarily responsible for the failure, for each of the MGAs had been allowed to function, in reality, as a separate insurance company, deciding whom to insure, issuing policies, placing reinsurance, adjusting and paying claims, collecting reinsurance recoverables, and handling cash and investments. The MGAs alone decided which reinsurers to use and the amount of security each needed to post, and they were supposed to make sure the proper letters of credit were on file. Through the magic of reinsurance accounting, every time a Transit policy was reinsured, it disappeared from Transit's books, meaning it was then free to write more business, until the whole pyramid collapsed of its own weight.

Transit was certainly not the first or the last company to be undone by hired-gun MGAs. In 1979, an ARMCO Steel Corporation subsidiary named Bellefonte Insurance Company lost millions because its California MGA wrote aviation reinsurance at cut-throat rates. Once the company got wind of the crisis, Bellefonte tried to terminate the errant MGA. It proved impossible to do. It seemed that virtually every MGA contract provided for at least six months notice before termination and, during that period, the MGA continued to write even more underpriced business in Bellefonte's name and the company was powerless to prevent it.

Ranger Insurance, with just $50 million in capital surplus, lost $22 million from business produced by an MGA in Huntington, Long Island. When terminated, the MGA sued for breach of contract and it took Ranger another $2 million to buy its way out of the expensive litigation.

Transit's MGA experience was not unique, but it was particularly spectacular in its scope. Transit quickly obtained an interest in some 22 MGAs and subsidiaries, in addition to the totally independent MGAs around the country. It owned 40 percent of Group Management and Merchandising, Inc., New York, an MGA for auto-truck rental and leasing business; 29 percent of DMT Financial Group, formerly Delaney Offices, Inc., New York, a reinsurance brokerage firm that, in turn, owned 100 percent of Donald F. Muldoon, Inc., New York, which brought in the infamous Carlos Miro; 100 percent of Pace Associates Insurance Services, Inc., Los Angeles, an independent insurance broker; 20 percent of E & S Intermediaries, Inc., New York, a reinsurance firm; 37.5 percent of National Underwriting Agency, Inc., Chicago, which issued massive volumes of Transit excess and umbrella liability insurance; Russell Reinsurance Services, Inc., of Detroit, an MGA; 100 percent of Trans Re Co. Ltd., Bermuda, a reinsurance captive company; 100 percent of Sutherland-Page Inc., Boston, a claims management operation; 100 percent of Glacier National Life Insurance Company, Canada, a life insurance company later acquired by Beneficial Standard; 100 percent of Insurance Company of Maryland, Baltimore, a property and casualty company; 34 percent of Lancer Financial Group-Lancer Syndicate, New York, which wrote property and casualty business, 100 percent of Mid-Pacific Claims and Engineering Services, Ltd., Hawaii, which handled Transit's Hawaiian claims operations as well as other subsidiary operations in Bermuda, Boston, Los Angeles,

Connecticut, Minneapolis, and Chicago. Transit also jointly owned ABA, Ltd., Bermuda, which it operated with the American Bus Association to benefit that group's members, and American Guaranty Insurance Company, Bermuda, with DMT Financial to underwrite that group's business.

For a company that operated with the practical equivalent of a lead pencil and green eyeshades, it was inevitable that this sprawling conglomerate would get out of hand. Two of these subsidiaries were particularly deadly to Transit's existence.

The Muldoon-Miro Connection

In January 1981, Transit signed an MGA agreement with Donald F. Muldoon and Company, New York. Muldoon, a former Travelers Insurance employee, was now operating a captive fronting operation owned by Delaney Offices, in which Transit already had a stake. In the insurance industry, Muldoon was thought to be a whiz at arranging insurance with offshore "captive" companies, generally located on Caribbean islands with minimal regulation. "Captive insurance companies" sound unusual and exotic until one understands that scores of major American corporations routinely employ them. The captive company provides the corporation with equity ownership, tax-deductible premiums, and absolute control of the company that writes its commercial risks. Many of these captive companies enhance their income by reinsuring business for other insurance companies as well.

Muldoon had Transit's authority to do business in its name and to name subagents to do the same, the familiar "power of the pen." He quickly sold a substantial block of reinsurance business to Dallas's Carlos I. Miro, who represented a group called Southern Oil Insurance, Ltd., a pool of businesses located in Louisiana. One year after bringing the SOIL business to Muldoon, Miro actually became a Transit subagent. Miro was then a twenty-six-year-old prodigy, a former Alexander & Alexander executive who had worked on some of the largest insurance accounts in Dallas. He was a genius with figures who liked high living.

Miro's deal with Transit was that he could write insurance up to $10 million risk per occurrence with no constraints on the type of business he could write. Miro devised a complex system of interlocking companies that managed to drain money from each Transit transaction at every step along the way. His fledgling empire, with a staff of forty, soon included Miro and Associates of Dallas, a London office through which he arranged reinsurance with Lloyd's of London, a holding company and reinsurance company on the Isle of Man, and a New Orleans, Louisiana claims supervision office. Miro now says that Muldoon never cared what Transit business Miro wrote or at what price he wrote it so long as each marine policy was reinsured by Lloyd's of London, which Miro handled through the Wigham-Poland agency in London, and nonmarine policies were reinsured elsewhere.[3] Miro particularly favored workers' compensation and general liability insurance, from which he got a 6 percent commission. He then paid Muldoon and Transit each a 4.5 percent fronting fee for the use of their name and promptly reinsured the business, first through SOIL, later through Lafayette Re in Bermuda and its successor, Lafayette Re on the Isle of Man. Miro was a busy man; using Transit's authority, he wrote $8 million in 1981, $20 million in 1982, $30 million in 1983, and $40 million in 1984. Having his own captive reinsurance company allowed Miro to keep another 65 percent of the premiums Miro and Associates collected in Transit's name. In theory, Lafayette Re was supposed to pay the first $100,000 to $250,000 of every claim filed against Transit under such policies. In practice, Lafayette Re was run from Miro's Dallas office without even a separate bank account. All of this occurred with Muldoon's knowledge and compliance.

Throughout these months, Transit's nationwide sales were bolstered by its excellent A. M. Best rating, its licensing in every state, and its reputation (largely due to Miro's efforts) for having policies ultimately protected by the mystique of Lloyd's of London. Miro's agreement with Transit was that Lloyd's would pay $20 million on any claim beyond Lafayette's share and $1 million total if the accumulated first-level Lafayette claims threatened its ability to pay.

Transit's eventual auditors believe Miro sold $102 million in the years 1982–84 but only reported $60 million to Transit and Muldoon. The audit found that he paid $32 million in claims, $10 million in reinsurance fees, and $21 million in fronting fees and commissions. The auditors are still looking for the remaining $45 million but, since Miro is now in prison after pleading guilty to federal fraud charges in 1994 and receiving an eight-year sentence and says he is broke, that sum has proved hard to find. In any event, Transit's own records were so haphazard that no accurate assessment will be possible.

For his part, Muldoon audited Miro in 1983 without adverse comment. Miro maintains that Muldoon knew he was selling policies "off the manual," a question that arose in the dramatic case of Miro's handling of the Wal-Mart account.

Miro wrote workers' compensation policies for Wal-Mart employees in eighteen states in 1983 and 1984. He charged Wal-Mart $3.5 million per year, about half the reasonable rate for such coverage, and guaranteed there would be no increase in the rate. Miro maintains to this day that much of the large coverage in America is written in the same manner, largely due to the hot competition for such accounts. He says that large-account coverage is taken at the proper manual rate and then jacked up to cover high anticipated losses or discounted to allow for low loss predictions. The true policies are given to the customer and then fake policies, showing the proper manual rate, are filed with state insurance commissioners to give the appearance of compliance with the law.[4]

Miro added what he called the "chicken clause" to each underpriced policy, allowing for rate adjustments "subject to all State rates, regulations and guidelines." That simply meant if he found additional premium was necessary to cover the claims, he had some language to support his asking for it. Otherwise, he just waived any additional premium that came to light in a post–policy period audit.

Miro says the Wal-Mart premium was based on false loss figures supplied by Alexander & Alexander's claims management subsidiary for self-insured clients like Wal-Mart. Miro claims the figures were based on a fraudulent computer run that led him to make the lower premium pricing.

When a subsequent audit revealed Wal-Mart owed another $6 million in premiums, Miro proposed a novel solution. Wal-Mart would pay the $6 million to Miro and Associates and it would be refunded the same day as a dividend from Lafayette Re. Miro claims the repayment was supposed to be subject to any additional claims payments needed before any refund. But that is not what the trial judge found. He decided the only purpose of the transaction was to fool Transit into believing the additional premium had been properly collected. Further, Miro declined to even negotiate with officials at Wal-Mart on an additional $8.5 million that should have been demanded, saying they had paid all they were willing to pay. In any event, Wal-Mart officials, Alexander & Alexander, and Miro all signed off on this sham, which failed to materialize only because Transit revoked Miro's authority in the meantime. The outcome was that Miro received something like $400,000 in commissions from the Wal-Mart sale while Transit was stuck with $22 million in Wal-Mart losses. Transit, Wal-Mart, and Alexander & Alexander all sued one another; everyone blamed Miro; no one sued Miro. There were hardly ever criminal charges in cases such as this. Here we have a Missouri company (Transit) insuring an Arkansas company (Wal-Mart) relying upon information from a Texas consultant (Alexander & Alexander), which was legally headquartered somewhere else. The only possible level for criminal action would have been in federal court on mail fraud charges, and such cases were very rare at the time. No state was able to assert or assume jurisdiction in such a convoluted case.

Miro negotiated a complex maneuver the receiver called a "looping procedure," in which Miro's reinsurer covered Transit, after which Transit, in effect, reinsured the reinsurer against loss. In plain language, that meant Transit was insuring itself, a highly questionable way to run a major insurance company.

Miro still believes he has been a convenient scapegoat for Transit Casualty and Donald Muldoon. He points out that even the entire $80 million Transit sued him for was only 2 percent of the ultimate $4 billion price tag for the company's failure. While Transit sued for $80 million it settled for $9 million in a roundly criticized compromise. Miro's Dallas lawyer, Al Kroemer, in-house attorney David Vaughn, and London solicitor Mel Stein all recommended that Miro spend considerable time in the home he had recently purchased in London, the better to avoid personal service in the suit. Miro moved his stash of capital from London to Switzerland. Miro divided his time between the London home and his vacation home in Marbella, on the south coast of Spain. The case against Miro was only able to move forward when Transit lawyers happened upon him during one of his furtive New York forays, whereupon he was promptly served with the subpoena for the suit. Miro's assets were still beyond Transit's reach. The truth was that $9 million was the limit of Miro's own insurance protection. The receiver could have refused to settle for that and taken the case to trial, but only at great risk. Had Miro been found guilty of fraud before the trial, his insurer would have paid nothing, because fraud was specifically excluded from Miro's policy. In the receiver's case, discretion seemed the better part of valor, so he took the money and ran.

Power of the Pen—Again!

The message from Transit had consistently been "Write on!" The Muldoon-Miro team had taken the advice to heart, but it remained for Chicago's National Underwriting Agency, NUA, to carry the charge from the sublime to the ridiculous. NUA served as an MGA for Transit from 1979 until Transit failed in 1985. Its job was to write excess and surplus lines of insurance for *Fortune* 500 companies. Basically, that means NUA was supposed to write coverage for classes of business that could not obtain such insurance through the normal, direct market. Insurance was unavailable to those companies not because they were small or unknown but because they were engaged in high-risk enterprises. NUA insured drug companies, asbestos manufacturers, hospitals, and similar clients who were sued on a regular basis.

NUA did not write such high-risk insurance on a cautious, limited basis. Rather, in the six years it had the power of the pen, NUA put Transit on the line for $31 *billion* of direct liability and property insurance and reinsurance for policies written by other companies. Because NUA concentrated on a few, high-risk industries, a catastrophe in any one industry would impact Transit much more significantly than it would an insurance company that had spread its risk around many industries. NUA's fondness for writing asbestos, environmental pollution, and product liability policies is a perfect example of this risky business. Further, it is nearly impossible to predict the total eventual cost of policies like environmental pollution and product liability, meaning the Transit receiver must be prepared to pay claims for many years to come. The receiver finally projected NUA's blow to Transit at about $2.4 billion in losses, or 60 percent of the total Transit failure.

Some Transit executives subsequently portrayed NUA as a "rogue agent," a loose corporate cannon operating beyond their knowledge and control. That was not quite the case. Similar to the Muldoon experience, Transit actually owned 37.5 percent of NUA; both Mitchell and Bowie were on the NUA board of directors. The remainder of NUA stock was owned in London by Henry S. Weavers; Weavers's Holding Company, London United Investments; and the agency's managing director. Everyone involved made colossal commissions, as the "Weavers Stamp" eventually comprised 20 percent of Transit's entire reinsurance business. Weavers, now in liquidation itself, was a wholly owned subsidiary of London United Investments. The "Weavers Stamp" consisted of a band of twenty-seven individual reinsurance companies that passed the business along one more step to other reinsurers, a process known as retroceding.

The British Department of Trade and Industry says $51 million was spirited out of H. S. Weavers Agencies, Ltd., into Liechtenstein agencies controlled by former Weavers auditor Graham Smith. Smith isn't saying anything to anyone, but former London United Investments chairman Peter Wilson says the money represented legitimate commissions and, in Illinois, NUA's Richard Foss says he thought Smith was Weavers's reinsurance broker.[5]

The scheme came to light when Munich Re, one of Weavers's principal reinsurers, discovered all premium payments were processed through the Smith companies without its knowledge or approval. Following the money trail, one finds that one of the Smith companies put up $10,000 for shares of Russell Reinsurance Services, Inc., an American company in Detroit, Michigan, half of which was secretly owned by Weavers, Wilson, and Charles Ronald Driver, another former London United chairman. Another 23 percent was owned by Transit, the remainder by Russell executives. The true ownership came to light as part of the KWELM companies' liquidation in the United Kingdom and Bermuda.

Only in late 1988, when Russell Re tried to sell itself

to London United Investments for $1.6 million, was it discovered that Wilson, Weavers, and Driver secretly owned half the enterprise. The three then protested that they were just holding the shares for LUI's benefit. Since it was stretching the point, even for these insurance moguls, to sell LUI $1.6 million worth of something it already owned, LUI consequently gained Russell Re for free.

In the meantime, five of the Weavers Stamp companies, Kingscroft, Walbrook, El Paso, Lime Street, and Mutual Re, went broke themselves. All but Mutual Re, a Bermuda operation, were British companies. That group has come to be known as the KWELM group. Weavers was an underwriting agent and manager, writing original business and reinsurance business on behalf of Weavers Stamp companies, receiving premiums, settling and paying claims, and holding monies on deposit in both its name and those of the individual companies. The KWELM companies mostly wrote general and product liability insurance for pharmaceutical and other manufacturers; officers' and directors' liability policies; professional indemnity insurance for accountants, architects, engineers, and lawyers; hospital and medical malpractice insurance; as well as reinsurance for Transit and many other North American insurers.

The KWELM companies are being wound down through a process known as a "scheme of arrangement." Such an arrangement between a company and its creditors allows the insolvent company to run off the business according to terms mutually agreed upon. (In theory this is the opposite of a shut-down and liquidation.) This system requires agreement by creditors representing 75 percent of the value of total KWELM claims. It is thought that this method provides the quickest and greatest return for creditors, unlike a standard liquidation, which takes much longer and costs more. Neither system is fast; both can take fifteen to twenty years to complete.

The administrator of a scheme of arrangement can be held personally liable if he distributes assets too quickly (thereby leaving too little money to handle "long tail" claims that take years to evolve), so the scheme obviously proceeds with great caution.

No such vehicle is available in the United States, which relies solely on the standard liquidation process, although State Sen. Tom McCarthy of Missouri introduced a modified plan along the lines of a scheme of arrangement in that state. Without a major national overhaul of insurance procedures, state-by-state action would be necessary to achieve this quicker, cheaper system of compensating creditors in the United States.

The $400-million suit against Transit's officers and directors was settled out of court. It was one of the first such suits in American brought under the RICO statutes,* previously reserved for drug running and organized crime cases. The one criminal action resulting from Transit's collapse, tried in Jefferson City, Missouri, proved very difficult to explain to a country jury and resulted in a not guilty verdict. Joe Mitchell retired from the insurance business and George Bowie resurfaced as president and chief counsel for Lancer Insurance Company in Oregon.

Both men, in heated appearances before the congressional

---

*RICO is an acronym for Racketeer Influenced and Corrupt Organizations, a federal law that allows the government broader leverage to bring conspiracy charges and to seize property connected with federal crimes.

subcommittee on oversight and investigations of the Committee on Energy and Commerce, denied being in control of Transit's activities during these turbulent years, although the record speaks to the contrary. Mitchell complained that he had personally lost $13 million in the failure. Mitchell told the committee, chaired by Rep. John Dingall, D-Michigan, that the actual losses would be even less than the $156 million first predicted by the Transit receiver. As the long-range losses from environmental insurance and other claims become known, however, the receiver now thinks it will be a $4 billion loss; the two are clearly on different pages. Bowie protested that he was primarily concerned with performing legal work for Transit and should not be held accountable for the collapse.

That is not what other Transit employees told the committee. They portrayed Mitchell and Bowie as the driving forces behind the MGA network and cited their own warnings about the great risk the company was undertaking through that system. The executive vice president of risk management said, as early as 1982, "We are entering areas where we don't belong. We have picked up programs which have historically been unprofitable industrywide, and provided coverage where most companies wouldn't participate. We really don't have the background or experience in some of these areas and, frankly, it scares me."[6]

Transit's reinsurance audit firm underscored that warning. Norman Reitman's 1983 personal letter to Transit management, accompanying his report, concluded, "In summary, I am very worried, since the Transit policies are up front, the captives, in some instances are undercapitalized, and controls are practically nonexistent." One of Transit's own MGAs wrote Bowie in August 1983 warning that

Transit could soon lose its MGA network because of a ratings drop by A. M. Best and the problems caused by Muldoon and others. He said, "I feel it is my obligation to do everything I can to keep everything running well here, even if it means writing a letter I wish I didn't have to write. By this letter it is my hope to persuade you to do something *now* to change the course of things."[7]

The independent audit firm Touche Ross and Company pointed out administrative and control deficiencies each year, finally threatening to qualify its audit opinion for Beneficial Standard, since Transit's operations could not be adequately measured. Bowie's response? He dismissed the Touche Ross and other complaints as the unqualified viewpoints, suggestions, and concerns of persons who lacked his keen understanding of the insurance industry. After thirty-one years with Transit, he said, he was clearly better qualified to render a decision on the health and well-being of the company than these opinionated outsiders.

Bowie's actual performance demonstrated otherwise. In 1984, he fired the first head of the Risk Management Division because he could not manage the MGA and reinsurance operations. He then named a replacement who he admittedly believed was incapable of handling the same operation.[8]

Wallpapering over Termite Damage

The commission-rich reinsurance operation was Transit's cash cow. If it was in deep trouble, the Transit solution was cynically cosmetic, the operational equivalent of putting wallpaper over termite damage.

First came an "aggregate stop loss agreement" with

Clarendon Insurance Company. A move that provided no real transfer of risk, the transaction was actually prohibited by most states.* Nevertheless, on December 28, 1983, Clarendon agreed to put $23.5 million in trust to cover future Transit losses. In return, on January 25, 1984, Transit gave Clarendon a $16.8 million premium that it was free to invest until the anticipated loss payments might occur. The deal allowed Transit to inflate its net income and statutory surplus for 1983 by $4.6 million just three days before the year ended. The result of this lessened risk was to allow ledger transfers on the part of Transit to show the $23.5 million in trust purportedly established by Clarendon thus increasing Transit's net income and surplus since the premium to compensate for the $23.5 million was only $16.8 million.

Cosmetically, the deal was perfect. It kept Transit's 1983 capital surplus report at $43.7 million, compared with $43.9 million the preceding year. Officials at Beneficial Standard, well versed in the criminal penalties for filing false Securities and Exchange Commission documents, opted not to utilize the "transfer" on its 1983 10K Report, admitting no significant economic risk had ever been transferred to Clarendon. The whole transfer had been done only to placate increasingly suspicious state regulators. Three states questioned the transaction but it remained on Transit's books.

That took care of 1983, but conditions worsened in 1984, so the two companies undertook an even more daring move. Transit paid Clarendon $8 million for a "surety bond agreement," for which Clarendon guaranteed a $23.8 million

---

*A stop loss agreement is one in which a reinsurer agrees to assume all risk above a certain, stipulated level, thereby reducing the initial insurer's exposure to liability for payment.

shortfall in letters of credit required from Miro and other unauthorized reinsurance carriers. This transaction enhanced Transit's 1984 capital surplus report by $15.8 million. Transit needed to have letters of credit in hand from various unlicensed reinsurers, especially in light of impending audits. They had failed to demand such letters in advance and many were not now available. That meant Transit might be required to stand behind the entire amount of insurance liability, not just the amount it had retained after the transfer to the reinsurance companies. It lacked sufficient capital to cover itself for such exposure. Therefore, it obtained a $23.8 million guarantee from Clarendon for which Transit paid an $8 million premium, in the form of a "surety bond agreement." The difference between the large amount of new protection and the lower amount of premium was shown by Transit as surplus.

Events were now unfolding too rapidly for even a pretense of propriety. New York State, one of the jurisdictions which had to approve the arrangement, had outlawed such agreements as of December 1, 1984. Transit hadn't even signed the agreement until April 1, 1985, but simply backdated the signature to November 15, 1984, to circumvent the deadline. In March of 1985, Transit reduced Clarendon's risk to $9.8 million but continued to show the full $23.8 million protection in its report to Missouri insurance officials. If the true size of Transit's exposure, once Clarendon's protection had been significantly reduced, had been known to regulators, the Transit seizure and shutdown would have been vastly hastened.

The net effect of those two transactions was that 93 percent of the $21.9 million capital surplus Transit showed in 1984 was fake. With receivership weeks away, Transit voided both deals and released Clarendon entirely. Clarendon repaid the premiums but avoided the substantial claims liability the receiver would otherwise have been entitled to collect.

Was Clarendon an innocent victim too? One wouldn't think so, inasmuch as: (1) one of Transit's officers served on Clarendon's board of directors, (2) there had been prior business dealings and stock ownership, and (3) key Transit officers and directors had been routinely employed by Clarendon during the period in question.

A Beneficial Arrangement

Missouri, where Transit was chartered, has a law that provides an insurance company may only declare dividends "from the surplus profits arising from their business." Yet Transit paid Beneficial Standard dividends of $6.5 million in 1982, $5.2 million in 1983, and $4 million in 1984, even though there were no actual profits in those years. With the Mitchell family owning 35 percent of Beneficial, it was certainly a beneficial arrangement for the Mitchells.

With the end game ominously in sight, more beneficial transactions came to pass. In May 1984 Beneficial's shareholders voted to dissolve the holding company within one year to gain favorable tax treatment. In June, Beneficial announced it would cease all insurance activities, selling its life insurance subsidiary for $130 million. No one wanted Transit, which meant state regulators could tie the two together by taking over Transit. The solution was quick and simple. Beneficial just wrote off its $47 million book investment in the corpse of Transit and offset that against its gains from sale of the life insurance company. That provided significant tax benefits for Beneficial, even as it left Transit twisting in the regulatory wind.

It was also, presumably, a big relief to Touche Ross, which had conducted years' worth of audits of Beneficial without ever raising the spectre of Transit's imminent financial suicide. To be sure, Touche Ross knew of the problems and clearly communicated them to both Beneficial Standard and Transit but never to regulators or the public.

Fortunately, the Missouri receiver was able to create, on the scene in California, a competent, professional team to sort out the financial debris following Transit's spectacular fall from grace. This was a daunting task, in view of the fact that only a handful of generally befuddled Transit employees remained in the California headquarters when the receivership was created. Named special deputy receiver was Missouri native Burleigh Arnold. He had been assistant Missouri attorney general, executive assistant to Missouri Gov. John Dalton, an associate circuit judge, a bank officer, and chairman of a Missouri life insurance company.

Arnold's administrative and insurance industry experience were invaluable in creating, almost overnight, the effective equivalent of a major insurance company, charged with the responsibility of defining and classifying liabilities, collecting and commuting receivables, and distributing the proceeds to creditors situated throughout America.

The receivership was a costly creation; it took $200,000 just to locate a staff of two hundred, and $34.1 million to get the receivership up and running. So far, Arnold's operation has recovered $456.6 million. About a third of every dollar collected has been spent on the receivership, consuming a total of $142.9 million by mid-1984, including start-up costs, with no end in sight. Since it is projected to last until 2012, this project may represent the sunset of many of the receivership executives' careers.

That may be small comfort to Transit's 200,000 claimants, any one of whom would presumably be happy to settle for either the $647,000 Bowie took when he left or Mitchell's $1.3 million, payments achieved by sympathetic accelerated stock options from Beneficial Standard.

Notes

1. From a May 17, 1982, internal memorandum from Ms. Leary contained in the transcript of hearings, Subcommittee on Oversight and Investigations, U.S. House of Representatives Committee on Energy and Commerce, April 1989.

2. Report of the Missouri State Director of Insurance, 1993. See also, Transit Casualty Company Insolvency and Liquidation Report, September 1993, and interview with Burleigh Arnold, Esq., Deputy Receiver, Transit Casualty Company in Liquidation.

3. Transcript of testimony of Carlos Miro before the Subcommittee on Oversight and Investigations, U.S. House of Representatives Committee on Energy and Commerce, May 19, 1993.

4. Ibid.

5. Investigation by the Subcommittee on Oversight and Investigations, U.S. House of Representatives Committee on Energy and Commerce. Interview with Burleigh Arnold, Special Deputy Receiver, Transit Casualty Company in Liquidation.

6. Report of the Subcommittee on Oversight and Investigations, U.S. House of Representatives Committee on Energy and Commerce, February 1990.

7. Letter included as exhibit, attached to transcript of testimony of the Subcommittee on Energy and Investigations, U.S. House of Representatives Committee on Energy and Commerce, April 19, 1989.

8. Testimony of George Bowie before the Subcommittee on Oversight and Investigations, U.S. House of Representatives Committee on Energy and Commerce, April 19, 1989.

4

Other Winners and Losers

Why Did They Call This Place "Integrity"?

Integrity Insurance Company emerged in 1957, the first year of the second Eisenhower term. In keeping with the tone of those quiet years, Integrity spent two decades as an affiliate of a group of private financial services companies, serving institutional lenders from its headquarters in Paramus, New Jersey, from which it provided customers with insurance policies backing loan collateral and the principals who took out the loans.

By the late 1970s, Integrity's management had been infected by the same "go-go" growth craze that had swept the rest of the American insurance industry. By then licensed in every state,* Integrity decided to diversify by offering commercial property and casualty insurance.

---

*A company must go through the exhaustive process of submitting its listing of admitted assets, paid-in capital, operational capability, the names of officers and directors and their education and experience, and proposed rates to each state's insurance regulators. There follows a comprehensive examination and review and payment of a substantial fee, sometimes as much as a million dollars, as a kind of security deposit in return for being allowed to do business in a given state.

It soon became what its receiver would call "the quintessential MGA operation," as its hurry-up offense strung together a network of eighty managing general agents spread around the nation. In the same pattern that marked the demise of so many other, formerly prudent insurance operations, Integrity's MGAs were independent operatives, mini-insurance companies using the familiar power of the pen to commit Integrity to monumental risk.

They wrote such uncoordinated, unstructured kinds of coverage that the receiver likened them to "twelve insurance companies rolled up into one." Their coverages on behalf of Integrity included excess and umbrella liability, commercial vehicle programs, hospital professional liability, personal automobile coverage, residual values, commercial fire, inland marine, commercial special multiperil, and general liability. Integrity suddenly found itself writing surety programs including Small Business Administration systems, contract and financial guaranty surety, and numerous, unique, special lines like workers' compensation and yacht insurance. Integrity also assumed reinsurance from other companies on a bulk and per-case basis.

These were complex coverages presenting great risk and requiring skilled underwriting. Old-line insurance companies with experienced underwriting professionals approached this kind of business with great trepidation, if at all. Integrity just plunged in.

The excess and umbrella business was very broad and soon became Integrity's largest single source of premium income. Almost overnight, previously unknown Integrity became one of America's largest carriers in this volatile area,* insuring some three hundred of the *Fortune* 500 corporations, not to mention government operations from sea to shining sea. Knowing next to nothing about how to manage this far-flung empire, Integrity soon wound up with a piece of the Bhopal disaster, the MGM Grand fire, the space shuttle Challenger, Love Canal, Agent Orange and toxic shock syndrome. It required the courage of Lassie to undertake even one such high-risk policy; Integrity seemed to wind up with its share of all of them.

But not to worry. The enterprising MGAs were busily passing off the risk to reinsurance companies, leaving Integrity with as little as 1 percent of the coverage. Integrity's grand design was to prosper and grow rich not by writing insurance but by getting a commission from each reinsurance transaction as the business marched onto and off its books.

By 1982, Integrity's path had crossed those of the West Coast wizards Bengston and Marsh, who had abandoned the sinking ship at Mission and Pacific Re and created Continental Re for themselves. They were no longer salaried employees, as they had been at Pacific Re; at Continental

---

*Excess or umbrella coverage in which an insurance company assumed potentially billions of dollars of risk for high-risk chemical manufacturers and the like is a very high stakes game. There are substantial premiums, to be sure, but the premium income pales in the light of the potential for loss if a large-scale accident or injury takes place (e.g., the Alaska oil spill or the chemical leak in Bohpal, India). Determining how much such an accident or series of accidents might cost requires careful, skillful underwriting. Most established companies simply concluded the premium profit was not worth the potential liability. Many of the new, hard-charging companies chose to ignore the long-term risk in favor of the short-term cash flow.

Re they each owned half the action. Since they were not an insurance company, only a reinsurance intermediary, they needed no regulatory approval to start writing business.

The collaboration of Integrity and Continental Re may have been a marriage of convenience but it was a wonderful match. Integrity relied almost entirely upon MGAs to write its business but it lacked an assumed reinsurance arm, which was a necessity for such an arrangement. In addition, each side knew the other because Bengston and Marsh had insured much of Integrity's direct business when they were still affiliated with Mission and Pacific Re.

In fact, Mission acquired $28.6 million worth of Integrity's business through its Pacific Re arm, high-risk coverage that would result in losses to Mission well in excess of $50 million.

Integrity officials attended the very birth of Continental Re, loaning Bengston and Marsh a half million dollars on their signatures with no collateral, a transaction that took shape at the 1982 regulatory convention of the National Association of Insurance Commissioners in Miami, even though both men were still technically Mission employees at the time.[1] It is generally considered a breach of etiquette for one insurance company to fund the desertion of key employees of another company.

With their new-found nest egg, Bengston and Marsh settled into plush Pasadena, California, offices; signed a management agreement with Integrity; and began writing business in mid-1983.

Bengston and Marsh were, apparently, not very quick learners, for they simply repeated the fatally flawed old Pacific Re five-year formula, resulting in seriously inadequate reserves. With Integrity's management a whole continent away, they were totally in control of their own destiny, producing a book of business easily as inept as in their old days at Pacific Re.

That included sheer fraud and cooking the books on a familiar scale. The inevitable outcome of this enterprise was that the reinsurers would almost unanimously allege fraud by Continental Re in refusing to honor Integrity claims losses. Integrity's receiver verified the instances of fraud and was forced to settle with the reinsurers for dimes on the dollar. Surviving insurance companies through state guaranty funds, insurance-buying consumers, and the taxpayers will eventually make up the difference.[2] It is impossible to tell how much individual state guaranty funds will finally wind up paying, since not all claims are settled, and the ultimate cost to taxpayers is impossible to compute.

For example, Continental Re assured reinsurers that the company would write no more than $6 million in premiums in 1983, knowing full well that one transaction alone would exceed that limit. Bengston and Marsh projected total premiums of $21 million for 1983–84 when actual premiums were almost three times that amount. This greatly increased the exposure of reinsurance pool participants without their knowledge.[3]

Continental Re promised never to write previously reinsured business, yet it immediately began writing large volumes of such coverage. Bengston promised to limit Continental Re's percentage of risk on specific treaties, then assumed 100 percent of the risk on large-volume business, resulting in staggering losses when claims were filed. Continental Re even devised a system in which Integrity wound up reinsuring itself.

Much of Continental Re's business was written for Reinsurance Agency, Inc. (RAI), of Chicago, which was headed by Bengston and Marsh's friend Paul Davies. In a six-year association covering both Pacific Re and Continental Re, the three transacted large volumes of high-risk business with only the most negligible review. Over $73 million or 18 percent of Pacific Re's business came from RAI.[4] A third of Continental Re's business, $28 million, was generated by RAI, its largest broker.

Continental Re arranged for most of Integrity's reinsurance to be assumed by foreign reinsurers and syndicates of the now-failed New York Insurance Exchange. Integrity was the leading creditor of two such syndicates, settling its claims in 1988 for a quarter on the dollar. RAI did handsomely, generating $2.7 million from business Davies placed with his friends Bengston and Marsh in their six-year association. In congressional testimony, Davies stoutly maintained that a broker has no responsibility to determine whether the business it markets will be profitable to the company that accepts it.

When it came to the hapless Integrity Insurance Company, apparently integrity existed in name only. The enterprise only collapsed when Integrity failed in December 1985, after which Continental Re, now without the power of anyone's pen, was forced to close after three years of running wild in the industry.

When Integrity's receiver reached the scene of the disaster, it was the same scenario as Mission and Transit: Integrity had depended on 350 full-scale reinsurance treaties and thousands of individual agreements, concluded with more than 500 reinsurers, many of whom had serious solvency problems of their own. Integrity never attempted to develop a management information system capable of tracking its large volume of business and was, thus, statutorily insolvent a very long time before anyone noticed or cared. There were apparently plenty of folks on hand to count the cash but no staff actuary and no one with the skill to set reserves. Even the cash managers were eager but inept. Seventy-five percent of the premiums received were immediately paid out to reinsurers, yet no adequate system was ever developed to collect monies due from reinsurers. Integrity was unable to collect at least $75 million lost in the Mission failure, caused through Mission's reinsurance of Integrity policies. Premiums due from MGAs were chronically late and past-due balances mounted to gargantuan proportions.

After three months of unsuccessful rehabilitation efforts, Integrity was humanely placed into liquidation on March 24, 1987. The basic insolvency was $1 billion, with eventual claims liability of twice that amount. Every state's guaranty fund was involved.

The receiver blamed management and also cited Touche Ross, which performed the same independent audit functions at Integrity as it had at Transit. Similarly, the receiver sued to recover $300 million, part of which was represented by a $12.9 million dividend Integrity paid to Yegan Holding Corporation, its parent company, at a time when it was insolvent and should have paid no dividend at all. Creative bookkeeping was again apparent, as Yegan showed a $15 million surplus for Integrity, its only subsidiary, when Integrity was actually $142 million in the red. Yegan voluntarily deregistered with the Securities and Exchange Commission in 1987, and at this time the receiver is still attempting to collect from Yegan in civil court.

Integrity's last regulatory report, in 1985, claimed a net worth of $20 million. However, under statutory accounting principles, it had been insolvent since the end of 1981.

Biting the Bullet

The outcome at Omaha Indemnity was very different, but only because Mutual of Omaha Insurance Company acted responsibly to save its wholly owned subsidiary from its excesses.

Omaha Indemnity has served since 1967 to offer homeowners and automobile insurance as a way to introduce customers to the entire Mutual of Omaha line. That system worked well until the Frank B. Hall Company appeared on the scene. Hall, a large international brokerage firm, submitted a fronting proposal in February 1982. What resulted was a complicated international nightmare of unsupervised MGAs, shadowy offshore companies, illicit reinsurance, churning of commissions, and insolvency.

In June 1982, Omaha Indemnity agreed to act as a fronting reinsurer for business generated by World American Underwriters, Inc., a Kansas City, Missouri, managing general agent. The Hall organization was to benefit by brokering reinsurance and underwriting services and by reinsuring 95 percent of the business written through its own subsidiary, Union Indemnity Insurance Company of New York. Unknown to Omaha, Union then reinsured this business with Ocasa S.A.—the abbreviation translates to "society of the anonymous"—a Spanish reinsurer and its affiliates, none of whom had sufficient financial means to meet their obligations.

The whole idea was that World American would write sound business only under strict Omaha Indemnity guidelines. World American was managed by James Wining and Willie Schonacher, two inept but ambitious individuals who eagerly wrote business far in excess of their guidelines and beyond the financial capacity of Omaha Indemnity and its reinsurers. Not content with this arrangement, Wining and Schonacher soon branched out on their own, buying World American to create Royal American Managers, Inc., in September 1983. Reinsurance was soon placed through a network of companies controlled by Kensu Holdings, Inc., their own Delaware holding company. These groups included Interamerica Reinsurance Corporation of New York; Allied Fidelity Insurance Company of Indiana; Fielding Reinsurance Limited of Turks and Caicos, British West Indies; and RAM and AMS syndicates, two impoverished members of the now-failed Insurance Exchange of the Americas, of Miami.

Having essentially found the combination to the safe, Wining and Schonacher soon arranged to be billed for additional brokerage and management fees from Program Administrative Services, Inc., and something called William Alexander Reinsurance Management, Inc. William Alexander actually did absolutely nothing. It was a shell account used only to accumulate the money needed for the creation of Royal American.

The two exercised no underwriting controls and failed to set or accurately report loss reserves. Instead, they inflated their capital surplus; created complicated, circular reinsurance; wrote prohibited business; and finally succeeded in having Omaha Indemnity actually insure them against lost commissions if their MGA agreement was ever cancelled! They constantly cooked the books and carefully disguised the real amounts of premiums being generated, at one time reporting a rental vehicle insurance program as generating $5 million instead of its actual $20 million.[5]

When New York, Missouri, Illinois, and Nebraska issued a damaging examination report in 1987, the pair blustered and stonewalled. They raised sufficient objections that the regulatory authorities were cowed into giving them an additional two years before the final report, plus their objections, was issued.

The negative report stifled by reluctant regulators appears to have been correct. Kensu Holdings and Fielding Reinsurance have been found to have negative net worth. Union Indemnity collapsed. Interamerica Reinsurance is insolvent. So are the RAM and AMS syndicates. Wining and Schonacher went west, forming Laramie Insurance Company, licensed under highly questionable circumstances. Writing business in Wyoming, Louisiana, and Texas, it soon failed, costing the Wyoming Guaranty Fund $1 million. Several civil suits were filed in this matter.

Omaha Indemnity would surely have failed as well, had it been owned by any entity less well-heeled than Mutual of Omaha. Mutual coughed up $250 million to keep its subsidiary solvent and, one hopes, on a shorter management leash in the future. Omaha Indemnity may be comforted by the $225 million arbitration judgment gained against Royal American Managers. Generally, such companies have at least some recoverable assets, sometimes reinsurance treaties, sometimes surety bonds, or other forms of tangible assets that can be levied against or sold to partially satisfy a judgment. It is also possible to proceed against officers and directors of insurance companies for recovery of losses by policy holders.

The $200 million insolvency of Virginia's Fidelity Bankers Life Insurance Company did not dissuade its former chief executive officer from seeking an additional $1.5 million in severance pay under terms of his employment agreement. Following the company's 1991 collapse, the receiver sought

$200 million from an assortment of former officers, charging waste, fraud, dissipation of assets, unjust enrichment, and other misdeeds. Hartford Life Insurance Company assumed the book of business, which included customers in every state but New York.

One of the most complex and corrupt insurance company collapses was that of Maryland Indemnity Insurance Company. The basic company failed in 1977 with liabilities of less than $6 million. The company wrote auto and other liability, workers compensation and surety insurance in Arizona, Iowa, Louisiana, Maryland, Nevada, and New Jersey. Other than the rather strange, patchwork pattern of states in which the company wrote business, at first blush it seemed a routine and minor failure.

Then came discovery of a vast, underground root system, a complex conspiracy with four gigantic waves of additional defendants in 1991 and 1992, as forty-eight more companies and affiliates were added to the roster of rogue companies. Operating from Maryland, these companies wrote medical malpractice, and liability insurance for nurses, hearing aid installers, lounge owners, truckers, underground storage tanks, and guides and outfitters, as well as marine hull coverage. The forty-eight various companies were licensed nowhere but operated everywhere, writing insurance in every state. That simply meant that there was no guaranty fund protection for anyone and apparently no reinsurance either. Estimated claims liability is $50 million.

Maryland Indemnity Insurance became one of the largest international insurance frauds. Thus far, nine persons have been indicted in federal courts in New Jersey and Maryland,

[continued on page 80]

Maryland Indemnity Insurance Company

The company was declared insolvent and placed in liquidation December 16, 1977. All known realizable assets are in the liquidator's possession. There is no litigation in progress. The company wrote auto, other liability, workers' compensation, and surety business in Arizona, Iowa, Louisiana, Maryland, Nevada and New Jersey. As of year-end 1986 the liquidator had assets of $2,211,400 and estimated liabilities were $5,761,358.

The contact person for Maryland Indemnity Insurance Company is Joseph R. Petr, Director, Property and Casualty Insurance Guaranty Association, 332 Chester Building, 8600 LaSalle Road, Towson, Maryland 21204-6304, telephone number (410) 296-1620.

	Court Order Reference
American Surgeons Insurance Company	3
C.A.C.N.M.I Holding Corporation	3
C.A.R.I.B. Holding Corporation	3
Casualty Assurance Risk Insurance Brokerage Company	1
Casualty Assurance Company	2
Casualty Assurance Corporation	3
Chariot Holding Corporation, SA	2
CHS, Inc. (d/b/a Dorsey Hall Health Club)	4
Commonwealth Reinsurance Management Company	2
Commonwealth Risk Management Company	2
Eagle Spirit S.A.H.	4
Elite Holding Company	3
Grand Medical Group, Ltd.	4

International Bahamian Insurance Company, Ltd.	2
International Secretarial Services, Inc.	3
Keystone Holding Company	3
Kyoto Holding Corporation	4
Legal Defense Support Services, Ltd.	2
Legal Liaison Services, Ltd.	4
Medical Liability Purchasing Group, Inc.	2
Medical Liability Purchasing Group, Inc. of Guam	2
Metropolitan Support Services, Inc.	2
MMS Holding Corporation	4
Nationwide Business Consultants, Ltd.	3
Nationwide Business Management Consultants, Ltd.	3
Nationwide Consultants, Ltd.	3
Nationwide Environmental Consultants, Ltd.	3
Nationwide Medical Consultants, Ltd.	3
Nationwide Transportation Consultants, Ltd.	3
New World Bank, Ltd.	3
New World (F.S.M.), Ltd.	3
New World (F.S.M.) Holding Corporation	3
New World (C.N.M.I.) Holding Corporation	3
New World Financial Trading Corporation	3
New World FT&R Holding Corporation	3
New World Financial Trading and Reinsurance Corporation	2
New World Reinsurance Corporation (F.S.M.)	2
New World Reinsurance (CNMI) Corporation	2
New World Reinsurance Company	2
New World Trading Corporation	3
North American Transportation Insurance Company	3
Polaris Holding Corporation	4
Professional Risk Insurance Management Exclusive, Inc.	2
Regency Holding Corporation	2
Royal Viking Holding Corporation	4
Sahl Investment Ltd.	4

TPFSM Holding	3
Trans-Pacific Company	3
Trans-Pacific Holding Corporation	3
Trans-Pacific Insurance Company (F.S.M.)	1
Universal Guardian Insurance Company	3
Umbra Development Corporation	4
Universal Surety & Fidelity Guaranty Company	3

COURT ORDER REFERENCE

1. Company included in order of liquidation dated December 3, 1991.

2. Company included in order of liquidation of additional defendants dated December 17, 1991.

3. Company included in order of liquidation of second additional defendants dated January 21, 1992.

4. Company included in seizure order third additional defendants dated March 9, 1992.

Offices were physically located in Maryland. On December 3, 1991; December 17, 1991; January 21, 1992; and March 26, 1992, respectively, orders of liquidation were entered for these companies. The estimated insolvency is unknown and extimated assets are $3,000,000. These entities wrote medical malpractice, nurses professional liability insurance, hearing aid installers professional liability insurance, marine hull coverage, bar and tavern owners liability insurance, truckers liability insurance, CGL, underground storage tank liability insurance and guides and outfitters liability insurance and were not licensed in any state but operated in all states.

The policy cancellation date was December 3, 1991. The claim filing deadline was December 2, 1992; March 2, 1992 (for the nurses professional liability insurance program and for residents of Guam and Saipan). Policyholders and claimants are not eligible for guaranty fund protection. The estimated claims liability is $50,000,000 and estimated guaranty fund liability is $0.

To date no reinsurance other than reinsurance among the companies in the liquidation has been identified.

These companies are part of an international insurance fraud. To date, nine people have been indicted by the U.S. Attorney's office in Maryland and New Jersey. Seven of these person have plead guilty to various counts including money laundering. One individual has been extradited from Federated States of Micronesia. One of the principals, Martin Bramson is a fugitive. Norman Bramson was arrested wtihin 24 hours after being featured on the television show "America's Most Wanted." A $50,000 reward has been offered for the arrest and extradition of Martin Bramson.

The receivership has identified more than 350 bank accounts opened by the Bramsons as a means of effecting their money laundering. These accounts are scattered throughout the United States and the world. The receivership has recovered more than $5,000,000 from locations throughout the United States as well as Canada, the Caribbean, and Guam. The receivership is working in conjunction with the FBI and the United States Attorney's Office to determine the status of bank accounts in foreign jurisdictions. It is estimated that $10,000,000–$25,000,000 was laundered outside of the United States.

The contact person for these companies is James A. Gordon, Special Deputy Insurance Commissioner and Deputy Receiver, c/o Maryland First Financial Services Corporation, 821 N. Charles Street, Baltimore, Maryland 21201, telephone number (410) 539-8580.[6]

seven pleading guilty to various charges. One person was extradited from the Federal States of Micronesia. One of the principals, Norman Bramson, was arrested within a day of being featured on television's "America's Most Wanted." A $50,000 reward has been offered for information leading to the arrest and extradition of fugitive Martin Bramson.

The busy Bramsons laundered their funds through more than 350 bank accounts in America and around the world. Investigators believe as much as $25 million was laundered outside the country, of which only $5 million has thus far been located.

Apex Placement, Ltd., connected with California con man Robert Campbell, led its affiliate companies over the edge in a spectacular $70 million failure. Campbell created Apex in the British West Indies by simply inventing its list of directors, a small detail that didn't matter much to the California insurance regulators of the 1980s.[7]

The acknowledged master of mischief was Alan Teale, an Englishman of the Lloyd's of London school of scandal. Teale, who operated from Florida but spanned the nation, managed to rip off everyday working people who paid for fake automobile insurance coverage as well as high-profile victims like football players Joe Montana and Jim Kelly, who bought nonexistent disability policies from Teale.[8] Teale and a dizzying network of interlocking accessories and associates took Americans for more than $100 million. Sentenced to seventeen years imprisonment in Alabama, it is a safe bet he'll be back on the streets before the disaster he left behind is entirely understood or repaired.

The Savings and Loan/Banking Connection

It should come as no surprise that familiar names connected with savings and loan and banking failures pepper the pages of this exposé as well. In the main they were not owners of or investors in insurance companies. Usually their banks were sources of emergency cash with which insurance companies maintained the illusion of solvency, often in desperation and always at high cost. Most of these financiers were never repaid; any prudent loan officer should have known the chances of repayment by the drowning insurance companies were exceedingly slender, but in the interim between funding and failure the institutions made giant origination fees and sky-high interest. Many of the financial institutions were themselves to fail as the fast "profit" extracted from insurance companies went on the financiers' wrists, in their driveways, and sometimes up their noses.

The rotund and redoubtable Gus Mijalis, in addition to his myriad insurance interests, led a group that managed Shreveport, Louisiana's Bank of Commerce into a $30 million loss. The Federal Deposit Insurance Corporation sued and won a $28.5 million judgment against the group. Unfortunately, every defendant had filed bankruptcy by the time of judgment and the most the government will get is $87,000. The officers and directors liability insurance carrier wriggled off the hook on a notification technicality as well.

Don't send a care package to Mijalis. He was consultant to his nephew, Sammy Mijalis. The lucky Sammy will make $26 million through the buyout of his stock in a New Jersey gambling company that operates a riverboat casino in New Orleans. On June 15, 1994, Gus Mijalis was indicted on federal fraud and bribery charges stemming from his work on behalf of Carlos Miro. Louisiana State Police immediately wrote Sammy Mijalis, informing him that Uncle Gus must end any role he had with Sammy's Republic Corporate Services, a firm which held a state license to own and distribute video poker machines. That prohibition could be lifted if Gus Mijalis was later exonerated. Republic Corporate Services was allied with Capital Gaming International, an Atlantic City company which won one of the fifteen coveted licenses to operate a riverboat casino in Louisiana. That relationship was the basis for the $26 million buyout of Republic by Capital Gaming. State police took no action with respect to that deal inasmuch as the license had already been granted and the buyout agreement was already in place.[9]

Oklahoma City's Charlie Barazian created CB Financial, which put together limited partnerships in the 1980s with money borrowed from regional thrifts. When it failed, to the tune of $200 million, many remembered his 1978 mail fraud conviction, which stemmed from million-dollar lifetime medical benefit insurance for a start-up cost of $30 plus minimal monthly costs. Of course, at those prices Barazian could not afford to set aside reserves, which led to the demise of his fledgling insurance empire. In the CB Financial case, Barazian turned in his friends, after which his four-year sentence was slashed to four months.

Herman K. Beebe began his career in rural Louisiana. By the time he was stopped, the aging octopus of financial failures had wrapped his tentacles around more than a hundred banks, savings and loan companies, and insurance operations in Texas, Louisiana, Colorado, California, Mississippi, Ohio, and Oklahoma. Beebe used his string of banks to force new customers into his credit life insurance operation, despite the fact that credit life cannot legally be required as a condition for granting a loan.

Navigating among the movers and shakers of the Southwest, Beebe soon linked up with former Texas Lt. Gov. Ben Barnes, once the boy wonder of Lone Star State politics. Beebe and Barnes created a pyramid insiders' network to leverage the purchase of a string of banks.

Beebe had a complicated connection to the late Carlos Marcello, reputed New Orleans Mafia boss. One of Marcello's lawyers, a banker from Metairie, Louisiana, named A. J. Graffagnino, served as one of the Sunbelt Life Insurance Company directors, along with Gov. Edwin Edwards's commissioner of financial institutions. Sunbelt was operated out of Beebe's Shreveport offices.

Beebe was also involved in insurance company businesses with Crowley, Louisiana, banker and thrift operator Judge Edmund Reggie (the future father-in-law of U.S. Sen. Edward M. Kennedy and his long-time confidante), who was later convicted in the failure of Acadia Savings and Loan. Reggie was sentenced to stay at home for 120 days for misappropriation of funds from Acadia, where he had been chairman of the board. After Beebe was twice convicted of bank fraud, the second time through a plea bargain in return for which he received only a year and a day in prison, the Beebe-Barnes empire was largely in shambles. Barnes, who was really talented when it came to locating benefactors, soon tied up with former Texas Gov. John Connolly. A whole new bankruptcy collapsed Connolly's empire as well, the end coming just a couple years before Connolly's death.

Closely connected to Beebe, Barnes, and Reggie was Gene Phillips of Southmark, a Dallas savings and loan, which bought Pacific Standard Life of Davis, California. Phillips was the sole member of Pacific Standard's investment committee. The now infamous Lincoln Savings loaned substantial monies to Southmark, secured by Pacific Standard stock. When Lincoln failed, it meant that America's taxpayers now owned a worthless life insurance company.

The whole arrangement was a familiar, circular one in which Pacific Standard used Lincoln loans to buy junk bonds from its parent, Southmark. In return for the loans, Pacific Standard loaned Lincoln $27.9 million and bought nearly $1 million worth of junk bonds from Lincoln's associate, American Continental Corporation.

Arizona insurance executive James M. Fail bought fifteen insolvent Texas savings and loans with only $1,000 of his own money. He secured $35 million from his own insurance companies. The rest of the needed $70 million Fail got from Southmark's Gene Phillips and junk bond specialist Michael Milken.

California's First Executive Life, owned by Michael Milken associate Fred Carr, had 45 percent of its portfolio invested in Milken's junk bonds. When Milken's junk bonds were decided to be essentially worthless, First Executive Life failed and millions of workers lost their entire retirement savings.

In a score of other instances, creative corruption brought together dozens of the most disreputable figures in banking, savings and loans, and insurance company operations. Apparently larceny, like misery, loves company.

Notes

1. Transcript of Subcommittee on Oversight and Investigations, U.S. House of Representatives Committee on Energy and Commerce, April 1989.

2. Ibid.

3. Ibid.

4. Transcript of Subcommittee on Oversight and Investigations, U.S. House of Representatives Committee on Energy and Commerce, February 1990.

5. Ibid.

6. 1993 Report of National Association of Insurance Commissioners (NAIC).

7. Information provided by the California Department of Insurance.

8. The office of the Florida Commissioner of Insurance.

9. Information provided by the Louisiana State Police.

5

The Champion Chronicles

The dark world of John Marion Eicher, Jr., was starkly divided between his family and a small circle of confidantes, and others—the outside world he alternately feared and disdained.

Inauguration day, January 11, 1988, dawned as a chilly, ominous morning in Baton Rouge, Louisiana, with a sharp wind whipping off the Mississippi River, snapping around the corners of the towering state capitol building nearby. From John Eicher's vantage point, inside the imposing seventh floor private office of the Louisiana Commissioner of Insurance—atop the glistening white insurance building adjacent to the capitol—it was a day of glowing triumph.

Sprawled below were thousands of citizens from all parts of the state, gathered to celebrate the victory of "reform politics" over the putrid politics of the past. Framed against the handsome backdrop of the carefully manicured capitol gardens, newly elected Governor Charles "Buddy" Roemer and the other state officials were about to take their oaths of office.

One of the celebrated "reform" victories of the previous

fall's election had been the defeat of sixteen-year veteran Insurance Commissioner Sherman Bernard by the unknown Douglas Devine Green. Little media mention was made of the fact that the insurance commissioner's campaign had cost Green more than $3 million—more than had been spent in the governor's race—and that almost every penny of that campaign war chest had been furnished by John Eicher through various captive affiliates of Champion Insurance Company.

John Eicher did not mingle with the crowds to watch his protégé take the oath of office; that was not his style. It was enough for Eicher to know, from his imperial position high above the festivities, that the Eichers and Champion Insurance had plucked Green from obscurity, funded his campaign, and enabled his election. In Eicher's feudal mentality, Doug Green was as much chattel as commissioner and the insurance department a kind of expensive annex to Champion Insurance.

In the expensively appointed conference room next door, Eicher had laid out a lavish champagne reception to celebrate the occasion. It was attended by a nervous assembly of outgoing Commissioner Bernard's staffers, Green having named only a handful of replacements at that point. The Bernard people knew who paid for the reception. They knew who paid for Green's campaign. Their conqueror now strode forcefully among them, and many knew their days of employment were numbered.

Eicher paid little attention to the reception; a diabetic who rarely drank, he stayed mostly in the commissioner's executive chair looking down on the inaugural ceremony. Presiding over the festivities was Naaman Eicher, John's son, the stealthy, slender, smoldering crown prince of the Eicher empire. Virtually anonymous, Naaman had quietly become one of the most skilled political operatives in a state in which political intrigue had become an art form.

It was Naaman who first proposed Doug Green for the family's surrogate in the insurance commissioner sweepstakes. Green had not been the first or even the obvious choice. A cadre of higher-profile possibilities had been contacted and each had declined. At one point, Naaman himself had flirted with entering the race, but the conflict of interest had seemed too obvious and its potential political fallout too severe. Thus Green, with the fresh-scrubbed good looks of an aging altar boy, had been the eventual selection.

Green might have been unknown in Louisiana but he was well acquainted with the Eichers' operations. An Arkansas native, he had come to Louisiana in the early 1970s with a degree in business and economics from tiny Hendrix College, located—some later said prophetically—in Conway, Arkansas.

Green enrolled in graduate school, studying statistics at Louisiana State University in Baton Rouge. His professor and mentor was the late Prof. Vincent Cangelosi, who was associated with John Eicher in Key Premium, a company that financed insurance premium payments.

Soon Green was working part time for Key Underwriters, another Eicher company. It was there Green first demonstrated the amoral aptitude and flexible virtue which brought him to the attention of the Eichers. Louisiana law required each driver seeking insurance be subjected to a state-issued Motor Vehicle Report of the applicant's driving record. The results of that report determined the insurance premium cost each applicant must pay.

Green's system was deceptively simple. He would order

the MVR for each applicant and insure him or her at the appropriate rate. Then, Green segregated all applicants whose bad driving histories required a high premium. He cancelled the policies for those drivers and had refund checks mailed to Key Underwriters. He then forged MVRs showing an excellent record, obtained new insurance coverage with another company at a lower rate based on the forged MVR, and paid for it with part of the refund. Key Underwriters pocketed the difference, never informing the policyholder of the switch. Green's forged MVRs were so professional no insurance carrier ever discovered the deception.[1]

By 1975, Green and Eicher were so deeply intertwined that both were named in a suit brought by the Missouri Division of Insurance charging them with misappropriating $146,374 in premiums and commissions owed to Medallion Insurance Company, a failed insurance company in that state. The suit dragged on for years, the files eventually growing to six feet in height. Green was eventually dropped as a defendant. Missouri recovered virtually nothing.

Only the law firm named to handle Medallion's dissolution prospered, taking in over a million dollars in fees in the nineteen years it took to make the final distribution of assets.

The Medallion failure had been a big blow to Eicher's fledgling Louisiana insurance agency and the Missouri suit further complicated his life. He was, however, able to turn adversity to advantage, a trait that would prove useful in the future. Medallion policyholders learned of the company's collapse and believed they had lost all their payments. Indeed, persons with claims against Medallion received only what the guaranty funds in the twenty affected states would agree to pay. Many of the more substantial policyholders had excess policies, an extra layer of insurance providing higher coverage than their basic Medallion policies. These "excess policies" were written by other companies that were not broke by any means, but when Medallion's basic coverage collapsed, the excess policies were automatically cancelled and refunds sent to Eicher, the agent who had written the policies. Most policyholders simply neglected to ask for those refunds and Eicher pocketed the money, enough to get back into business.

Green hid his long and larcenous affiliation with Eicher throughout the campaign. A careful investigator might have discovered that the probate of Eicher's late wife's estate, filed August 17, 1976, disclosed an undivided three-way partnership in an insurance agency ownership among Eicher, Cangelosi, and Green. The order was signed by District Judge D. W. Parker, whose widow Eicher would later marry in prison, after Champion's collapse and his divorce. Fortunately for the Green campaign, the probate order lay undiscovered in the Baton Rouge courthouse throughout the campaign.

During those turbulent, pre-Champion years, the Louisiana commissioner of insurance was Sherman Bernard, a burly, cigar-puffing former house mover from Marrero, a blue-collar New Orleans suburb. In 1971, Bernard had won an upset election over the incumbent, riding into office on the same populist tide that had elected Rep. Edwin Edwards to the governorship. Bernard campaigned as "The Insurance Watch Dog." Every successful candidate for Louisiana insurance commissioner runs as a reformer and watch dog; only the names on the reserved parking places in the insurance department's parking garage seem to change.

The position of insurance commissioner was an afterthought in Louisiana; Gov. Earl K. Long invented it out of whole cloth to seize powers and duties from a Louisiana secretary of state, with whom he was feuding in 1956. He named his friend Rufus Hayes to the office, which Hayes was able to hold for one term on his own. Only four men have held that post since and each wore the reformer's mantle when he ran.

Bernard was unscathed by his reputation for remarkable mediocrity and boorish manners. Academic underachievement is no political liability in Louisiana, where the high school dropout rate often approaches 50 percent. He was not even particularly harmed by his arrest for parking in the emergency lane at the New Orleans International Airport and calling the security officer who told him to move "chickenshit."

Such is the lexicon of Louisiana politics. Pound for pound, Bernard was as popular as any obscure statewide officeholder in the state's history, drawing a monumental black and working-class vote. His campaign committee, "Friends of Sherman Bernard," called early and often on companies the office regulated—usually in the person of John Browne, his chief aide and confidante.

The story inside the insurance industry was that Bernard's fundraising calls always seemed to coincide with the prospective contributor's license application or audit and sometimes the quid pro quo was given voice. It was a constant, recurring irritant to the insurance companies, although Bernard protested that none of the money went to himself; it was all poured into the various campaigns. It was also illegal and six years after his defeat by Green, at a time when he should have been fishing and enjoying his grandson, Bernard was pleading guilty in federal court to charges involving the accepting of contributions for the licensing of insurance companies. He received a forty-one-month sentence and a $75,000 fine. It was just such a campaign solicitation of John Eicher that began the demolition of Bernard's career and, soon thereafter, of Eicher's own empire. Bernard demanded $10,000 from Eicher at a time when Eicher needed him. Champion Insurance had begun as Modern Home Title Insurance Company in Alabama in 1960. It became Champion Insurance Company in 1976. The Eicher family members had no association with Champion in those days. They were scrambling to salvage their own insurance agency, following the collapse of Medallion.

They were building their own political network as well. In 1978, Naaman was named by Gov. Edwards to the Insurance Rating Commission, the panel that approves premium increase requests in Louisiana. Doug Green was another Edwards appointee, as was Frances Pecora, widow of Nofio Pecora, who had been the right-hand man to reputed Mafia figure Carlos Marcello. The Eichers prospered under Edwards, who named John Eicher's wife, Elayn Hunt, secretary of the Department of Corrections in 1972, a post she held until her death from cancer on February 3, 1976. Her brother Ernest C. Hunt, "EC," was a prominent Edwards ally in Lake Charles, Louisiana. When Edwards retired after the two terms he was allowed, he was succeeded by Republican David Treen. Doug Green, all of whose affiliations were casual, simply changed his registration from Democratic to Republican and was promptly reappointed by Treen.

John Eicher, by then, was hard at work acquiring Champion Insurance Company, which he accomplished in 1983 using Champion Capital Corporation, of which he owned 90 percent. The sale was accomplished with a $3 million loan from Whitney Bank in New Orleans, which was later paid off with part of a $6.9 million loan from Allied Bank in Houston. The purchase nearly collapsed when Eicher discovered that $60,000 of listed assets were duplicates, meaning he had to raise enough additional money to replace them on Champion's books. John Eicher, who carried a weighty mental list of betrayals and double-crossings the way a baseball fan remembers World Series statistics, added the name of Champion owner Reggie Kimble to his inventory, along with that of Alabama Insurance Commissioner Tharpe Forrester. Eicher fumed and brooded at every recollection of the deception. That incident alone led to the decision to move Champion to Louisiana. Without it the subsequent political history of both states would have been very different indeed.

Champion was on an immediate upward spiral once it finally reached Louisiana. The state had just passed a compulsory automobile liability law and companies like Champion, which wrote "high risk" policies, grew rapidly as the number of insured drivers increased from 900,000 to nearly two million. Champion wrote $28 million in premiums in 1985, the year it moved to Louisiana. It wrote $52 million in 1986, $91 million in 1987, and $100 million in 1988.

That was not enough. John Eicher's dream was to expand rapidly, blanketing the South. He won the right to operate in Tennessee, Missouri, and Kentucky and planned to enter Colorado. The expansion required a clean bill of health from the home state regulator, Sherman Bernard, so John Eicher requested a voluntary audit. He forcefully declined, however, to correlate that request with a matching $25,000 contribution to Bernard. It was an odd time to become stiff-necked; he had given Bernard contributions on previous occasions, but

Eicher was also equal parts cheap and imperial. He didn't want to part with the $25,000 and he resented being pressured.

Events went from bad to worse. The audit was assigned to Bernard staffer Max Mosley, who had just written, on department stationery, a demand letter asking several hundred dollars more in settlement for an accident in which Champion's insured, Tesa Posey, had hit a car in which Mosley's son was riding. It was an ill-tempered, ill-timed letter that later disappeared from Eicher's files. John Eicher would never pay what he thought he didn't owe, no matter how politically wise or how small the amount, and he denied the demand out of hand, even as he asked Bernard's help in arranging a settlement meeting to negotiate an end to the Medallion suit. Bernard agreed to arrange the meeting provided Champion resolved a disputed claim for one of his friends.

John Eicher, who did not want to be questioned too closely about the financial arrangements for Medallion refunds, sent a staff member to the session. Representing Medallion were one of the Missouri attorneys and Baton Rouge lawyer Paul Spaht. Bernard arrived for the 1:00 meeting at 1:30, having obviously been overserved at lunch. In fact, he dozed off during the meeting he was supposed to chair, leaving Eicher's people to wrangle with Medallion's lawyers. The Eicher faction later concluded that it was largely successful, despite Bernard's being effectively missing in action.

Champion now faced ominous rumblings on two fronts: Mosley, feeling wounded and shabbily treated by the Eichers, was nibbling around the fringes of a much more intrusive audit than the Eichers had in mind. Champion still entertained the hope that he could be called off by Bernard in time to provide a "green light" audit, enabling Champion's regional expansion. On the other hand, E. C. Hunt, brother of Eicher's late wife, was threatening to cause trouble—and he could, since he knew where many of the financial bones were buried! Hunt was a principal in Boardwalk International, the family enterprise that served as a holding company for the acquisition of Champion.

A Lake Charles, Louisiana, lawyer, he was theoretically one of Champion's chief attorneys and drew $16,000 each month in fees. As a major shareholder, Hunt dared to believe he deserved full information about Champion's operations. He persistently badgered Eicher to relocate the corporate offices to Lake Charles, to a downtown office building he had purchased and gaudily decorated in a style reminiscent of Elvis Presley's Graceland mansion.

Eicher called it "Coon-ass Gucci." He had no intention of moving his headquarters anywhere near the watchful eye of E. C. Hunt and undertook a series of legal maneuvers to remove Hunt from any proximity to power.

Despite those complications Champion's fortunes seemed to be rising. Eicher selected his friend Mike Holmes and Holmes's son John to build a large addition to Champion's headquarters. Eicher had earlier obtained the former Baton Rouge Water Works building, a twenty-year-old structure at 4715 Government Street. The purchase had been a typical Champion operation, with Champion absorbing the cost while family members made a substantial personal profit. The same inbred system was at work in the addition project. Holmes had no experience in constructing a building of this kind or in properly estimating its cost. However, he clearly met the "FOJ requirement"; he was a "Friend of John's" and so the contract was let without bidding or evaluation.

John Eicher had an almost obsessive attachment to his small circle of friends. They met early each morning, seven days a week, at a little restaurant called Maggio's, located near the courthouse in downtown Baton Rouge. He liked Maggio's, despite the fact that it looked like a '50s diner, because the owner opened early and always served his special breakfast, usually steak and potatoes in a quantity that could have sustained a field hand.

It was an odd sight, this collection of aging cronies. Without even a pretense of "first among equals," John Eicher was clearly in charge. Tall, wide shouldered, Eicher always wore an impeccably tailored suit and matching tie, in garish contrast to his trademark mismatched socks. His bold, domineering features were planted on surprisingly soft and youthful skin with piercing blue eyes and a steady, direct stare.

Eicher was not a man ruled by the quest for material possessions. His personal expenditures were for things that reflected his personality. They were big, bold but understated, invariably expensive, and always worth the money. The challenge to Eicher was in the making of the money, not the spending of it—with always the haunting fear that it could all end tomorrow. Even at the zenith of his power and influence, Eicher was uneasy, distrustful to the point of paranoia, and remarkably resentful of the other captains of industry and political power brokers in the state's capital city. Eicher's whole life had been marked by incidents and accidents in which he had been brutalized by the fates and by others, often, he thought, just to prove they had the power to do so. The scars on his psyche were deep; the bitterness boiled just below the surface. Prosperity could bring no peace.

Eicher had been born Wallace Hanks, given up for

adoption in his first month of life. He later came to believe
the adoption was part of a "baby selling" scheme concocted
with the full knowledge and cooperation of local political
powers. He later located his birth mother, saw her only once
despite her pleas for reconciliation, resented her abandon-
ment of him, and refused to attend her funeral.

Eicher's adoptive father made and lost a fortune as a
sawmill owner, later beating bad check charges in both state
and federal court. His adoptive mother, a quiet, Quaker
woman, was one of the few gentle influences in Eicher's
life. A poor student, he was a voracious reader, a trait he
credited to her. He had rickets as a child and she worked
each day with her fat, homely baby, managing the painful
exercises that freed him from leg braces just before he entered
grade school. Eicher came to despise sickness and weakness
and, as an adult, even when he was terribly sick from diabetes
and high blood pressure, he struggled mightily never to
appear weak or vulnerable.

As a young man Eicher had been a popular radio
announcer, with a loyal audience. When reporter Elayn Hunt
came to interview him, he urged her to abandon the media
and go to law school, as he himself intended to do. They
married early in their law school careers and Elayn Hunt,
who kept her own name professionally, went on to become
a respected trial attorney and state official. Eicher's legal
career, like so many aspects of his life, was derailed by the
authorities. His law school professor expelled Eicher and
fellow classmate Ossie Brown (who later became district
attorney in Baton Rouge) from law school for cheating on
an exam.

Eicher bitterly denied the charge, compiled damaging
evidence of the professor's own conduct, and threatened to

sue the university. He was eventually readmitted but quit before graduation, an act he regretted the rest of his life.

Eicher's son and heir apparent, Naaman, did not attend the ritual meetings of the breakfast club. That casual camaraderie would have been totally out of character for Naaman. He was as tall as his father but slender, with finer features and the long lashes of a male model. If John Eicher mastered the art of management by intimidation, Naaman specialized in management by intrigue. The two together were a potent combination; through some unspoken, psychic connection they were invariably on the same wavelength, reading each other's thoughts, anticipating each other's actions.

Naaman never held a formal corporate position with Champion or its affiliates but his only office was at Champion's headquarters and he reveled in what Shelly Beychok, one of the liquidating attorneys, would later call "the indicia of authority." Those who dismissed Naaman as a spoiled, truculent, intolerant youth, with his Porsche and multilevel Lakeshore Drive mansion, missed the point. He was brilliantly dangerous and he was very much in charge.

Together the Eicher father and son assembled a remarkable management team comprising some of the most unlikely characters ever to manage a major regional insurance operation. Champion's legal group was "Hunt, Wroten, Kivett, Bouquet, Mackles, and Fuerst"; it was E. C. Hunt's firm, theoretically headquartered in Lake Charles. At Champion headquarters and in de facto charge was Marshall Wroten. "Wiley" Wroten was extremely well connected throughout Louisiana and did most of his settlement work over the telephone. Alvin Rousse was Champion's special agent in New Orleans. Bright, though nearly deaf, Rousse loved bad jokes and hated Jews, including his Jewish son-in-law. Don McCulloch, Champion's accountant, had been a farm boy from near Missoula, Montana. He was called "Rambo" because of his military background and militant attitude. Coming to Champion from its accounting firm, his ability and unswerving loyalty were soon beyond question, until much later when he came to believe the Eichers were hanging him out to dry, after which he helped put them in prison.

A. Freeman Edgerton was the token president of Champion. Tall, silver haired, and courtly, he had gone to law school late in life. He kept a desk in a law office across town and was also president of State National Insurance Company, from which he was named to the Louisiana Insurance Guaranty Fund. A board member of Metropolitan Bank, he served with Eicher confidante Cangelosi until the bank collapsed at the same time as Champion. Edgerton's bad left eye resulted in a disconcerting blink and stare. John Eicher called him "the ostrich" behind his back. Edgerton owned the remaining 10 percent of Champion Capital, through which Champion was created; it was to be his retirement fund.

Naaman Eicher's friend Scott Hullinger was a whiz at premium finance, the real source of Champion's wealth. They had devised a very carefully constructed plan under which policyholders paid a down payment of one-third of the premium and United Financial Services, Champion's captive affiliate and the "cash cow" of the entire Eicher operation, financed the balance at interest rates of up to 35 percent, which could eventually compute to 100 percent. Many companies, probably most, allow the buyer of automobile insurance to make installment payments of the premium cost. In Champion's case, the one-third down payment was a little higher than most but was arguably justified by the higher class of risk. The astronomical interest rate was the real source of Champion's income, through UFS—that and the up-front policy fees, which were pure profit and had nothing whatever to do with the underwriting risk.

Claims were handled by "Fat Jack" Richardson, whose tall, skinny wife also worked for Champion. John Wade, "Dr. John" to his intimates, was a tall, courtly, middle-aged crony of John Eicher who ran the Champion maintenance crew, along with his own outside interests in real estate and rentals. Special agent Ray Hippchen, a seasoned veteran of the insurance industry, was in charge of North Louisiana. Claims adjustment was handled by R. D. "Buddy" Lee, an elderly Eicher associate who owned Pelican Claims Service. His was a positive, always optimistic influence, even in Champion's darkest days. There were a handful of other key operatives, each given a narrowly defined, closely monitored area of authority. Champion operated on a carefully guarded, "need to know" basis. Everybody needed to know a little something in order to make the operation work, but only John and Naaman Eicher needed to know everything.

John was rarely in his own office, raging throughout the building, cleaning his nails with an omnipresent penknife, and bellowing at the terrified clerks; he seemed not just to know everything but to be everywhere as well.

Then there were the Eicher women: Meredith was John's sullen, wide-hipped, acidic-tongued daughter. She never recovered from her mother's death and spent the rest of her time at Champion trying valiantly to earn her father's attention and approval. Ashley, only nine months younger than Meredith, was as lovely as her older sister was plain. A dark-haired, dark-eyed beauty, she seemed to have avoided inheriting the dark cynicism so evident in her brother and sister. Naaman's wife, Tina, was a slender, deceptively innocent-looking Shreveport girl who rapidly proved her unquestioning loyalty to the family.

Last to join the inner circle was Patricia King. She applied for work at Champion in August 1985, just after graduation from law school at Louisiana State University. She was already thirty-nine, married, and the mother of two girls. She was out to carve herself a better life and Champion seemed like a wonderful opportunity. Patricia King had a faint physical resemblance to Billie Jean King and an air of vulnerability and naiveté that was very appealing to John Eicher. In just over two years, she divorced to marry him and claim a seat in the inner circle. The Eicher girls never really accepted or trusted her; Naaman respected her bright legal mind and knew how much her presence meant in his father's lonely life.

King had joined Champion just in time for the Bernard-Green campaign, although she had little personal interest in politics; that was Naaman's consuming passion. In November 1986 Naaman had called on Jim Carvin, a New Orleans political consultant and dean of the state's campaign strategists, to determine whether Bernard was vulnerable. Carvin's investigation revealed Bernard only vulnerable to a candidate with a million-dollar campaign war chest and a method to wrest away his solid black support. Naaman was certain the black vote could be bought, an eventuality for which there is ample evidence in Louisiana political history.

There was the minor annoyance that Champion's anointed choice, Doug Green, was virtually penniless in the face of the million-dollar campaign requirement. Naaman's computer consulting company, Amicom, simply paid Green $2,000 by check each month throughout the campaign and gave him another $2,000 in cash. Amicom also spent $29,500 in campaign plane rental and furnished a car.

On November 25, 1986, United Financial Services, Champion's premium finance company, gave a company called Doug Green and Associates $250,000. Green's company then reloaned the money in small segments to his own campaign to give the appearance of grassroots support. In addition, some forty-two United Financial Services employees each ponied up $1,000 for the campaign, an amount conveniently just under the campaign finance reporting limit. Their generous contributions to good government in Louisiana returned as Christmas bonuses that December.

Naaman ran every aspect of the Green campaign, including the production of his television commercials in New York City. Green was perfect for the cool medium of television: tall, immaculately groomed, with an earnest presence. It was a stark contrast to the sweaty, ham-fisted populism of the embattled Bernard. Had the two owned competitive automobile dealerships, Green would have hawked BMWs and Bernard would have sold Ford trucks. The more desperate the Bernard campaign's financial condition became, the more evident the strain was on the incumbent as he wheezed and wheedled his way through his first serious challenge in a generation. Green's campaign treasury was an embarrassment of riches; it was literally awash in money for the message. The Green message was simple, to the point, and constantly repeated: Insurance Commissioner Sherman Bernard was failing to make sure Louisiana insurance companies were solvent. Ironically, at that very moment, stacks of unpaid Champion claims were piling up on Government Street as $3 million was siphoned off to Green.

Alert to the possibility that he might be accused of bankrolling the Green effort, Naaman took extra precautions. He made a personal contribution to the Bernard campaign and had himself listed in Green's attack ad charging that Bernard was controlled by insurance company interests.

The demand for campaign money continued to grow as Naaman put together the most expensive race in that year's election. United Financial Services loaned Green's brother Donald $150,000, which was promptly reloaned to the campaign. Had the true source of these contributions become public, the transparency of Green's charge that Bernard was funded by insurance interests would have become readily apparent.

United Financial Services was wholly owned by Boardwalk International, which owned 90 percent of Champion Capital. Champion Capital owned Champion Insurance, United Southern Underwriters, Inc. (Champion's Louisiana managing general agent), and Southeast Underwriting Service, Inc. (Champion's Alabama managing general agent). Bernard repeatedly raised the issue but his relations with the media were by then so poor that his charge was ignored. Had the Louisiana media undertaken even a halfhearted investigation of Bernard's claims, the Green campaign song would have become the theme from "All in the Family."

In 1987–88, United Financial Services paid Donald Green's salary as his brother's chauffeur, plus his $775 monthly apartment rent at the Jefferson Place apartments in Baton Rouge. The cost of Doug Green's son's $1,800 tuition and room at Louisiana Tech also came from United Financial Services. It never seemed to end: When Naaman's wife was hospitalized after giving birth prematurely, Green confronted him in the hospital parking lot demanding cash to attend an insurance agents' conference in New Orleans.

The black vote still needed to be bought. Naaman's solution was Sherman Copelin. A prominent New Orleans black politician, he had years earlier acknowledged his involvement in a bribery scheme that destroyed a local family planning clinic, although he avoided being charged.[2] The leader of one of the city's major black political organizations and owner of several controversial businesses, he eventually became speaker pro tempore of the State House of Representatives and a failed candidate for mayor of New Orleans.

Copelin's firm, Marketing Services, got $180,000 and suddenly, the black vote shifted from the old populist Bernard toward the previously unknown yuppie Green. SOUL, Copelin's political group, could put two thousand workers on the street covering 400 of New Orlean's precincts (the heart of Louisiana's black constituency). SOUL runs the most sophisticated computerized voter identification operation in Louisiana—bar none—and a full-scale telecommunications effort which has proven very effective in both instigating and refuting rumors within the black community. While it is less effective when black support is split among several African-American candidates (which led to his defeat in the mayor's campaign), it is decidedly effective in a race in which black support is not diffused. Naaman added another $7,000 for Green's billboards and $6,000 to Joe Walker, political analyst for New Orleans' television station WDSU, for polling services.

The Eichers worried about Green's constant presence around Champion headquarters; some of the newer secretaries thought he worked there. The problem was, Green needed constant attention. Lacking an eye for style, Green necessitated a clothing consultant (the cost, $500), who taught him how to dress for success. Green, a man with no particular core beliefs, managed to endorse tort reform to insurance agents the same day he blasted it before a meeting of attorneys. Naaman gamely located another $5,000 for a behavioral scientist, who helped Green learn to keep his stories straight.

Having long since passed Carvin's $1 million budget, the amount no longer mattered, although Naaman had to scramble to keep the campaign train's financial engine fueled. He asked Kathleen Bailey, a Champion marketing consultant, to make a $100,000 loan from United Financial Services, to be channeled to the Green campaign, with the understanding that it would never have to be repaid. Champion's maintenance supervisor borrowed and contributed another $100,000, later testifying: "I knew if I didn't, my little career was over." When the heat was on, Wade was asked to repay the loan but given a "raise" equal to the payment, making him temporarily the highest paid janitor in America. Numerous other companies with financial dealings with Champion were similarly pressured to borrow and contribute.

The method by which United Financial Services was able to make all these loans is one of the more glaring examples of Louisiana's corrupt political process. During the Edwards administration,* the legislature authorized creation of "limited function financial institutions" (LFFIs) allowing organizations related to insurance companies to operate much the same as banks except that they could not offer checking

---

*Edwin Edwards's terms as Louisiana governor: 1972–80, 1984–88, 1992–96.

or savings accounts. Edwards's commissioner of financial institutions, Fred Dent, in charge of the LFFI charters, issued four: United Financial Services, Automotive Financial Services, Colonial Premium Finance Agency, and Insurance Premium Assistance Company. Each was the profitable "cash cow" of an insurance company and each insurance company was eventually seized by regulators.

The value of the captive LFFIs was not particularly their ability to make political contributions. They served other, major roles. At interest rates that could reach 100 percent, they were often the only profit center for insurance companies selling policies at cut-throat competition rates they knew would result in a loss. Such losses would trigger all kinds of alarm bells with regulators unless the companies found some way to shore up their reserves, and this presented another major role for the LFFIs. The parent insurance company would present its LFFI a sheaf of premium finance notes; the LFFI, in turn, issued "certificates of deposit" in the same amount that the company would claim as an admitted asset to improve its financial statement, thus disguising its steadily worsening condition. It required no financial genius to see that the "certificates of deposit" were worthless, based upon insurance policies that could easily be cancelled, unlike traditional CDs, which financial institutions base on actual cash on deposit.

Champion pioneered a uniquely profitable system of fringe income, hidden profit related to its sales. Every customer was charged a nonrefundable "policy fee" of $25. There was also a $15 charge to obtain the driver's Motor Vehicle Report. That amount should have been a wash since that was the same cost the state charged to issue the report. However, Champion only ordered MVRs on one in four applicants, but charged the $15 to everyone.

With an average of 5,600 applications being written every week in 1987, for example, that was an additional $200,000 in hidden income to the Eichers each week, money that, unlike the premium payment, was not at risk from accident claims. They used this money to make the books balance, in a fund whimsically labeled the "LCS" account; the Eichers called it the "lie, cheat and steal account."

All these financial shenanigans required the mother of all computer systems and, around Halloween 1985, Naaman found just the one he needed—the biggest made by Data General. Naaman scrapped Champion's antiquated Burroughs system and much of the information it contained. His new system ran on "real time," a convoluted data entry mechanism that later frustrated investigators and prosecutors attempting to construct a systematic chronology of crime. Working with Champion's computer whizzes, Scott Hullinger and Valerie Sheen, Naaman soon had the new system massaged and manipulated to a fine point.

The Champion crucifixion can be traced to Easter 1986. John Eicher and Patricia King were in Alabama, ostensibly to reorganize Champion's Alabama operation. They also spoke to Alabama's interim insurance commissioner to investigate the background of Max Mosley, former Alabama commission employee, now Champion's growing nemesis in Louisiana.

The results of that interview were inconclusive but by the time they returned to Louisiana Mosley had struck. In an internal memorandum strongly critical of Champion, he proposed a surprise audit. Mosley's plan of attack was classically bureaucratic, where murder by memorandum is a highly polished art form. From his considerable height, Mosley seemed in every meeting to be surveying the room, looking for the right opening to strike. The Eichers did not underestimate the danger his position represented to Champion.

Champion had added a new attorney, Patrick McGrew, to its legal complex directly across Government Street from corporate headquarters. At the outset, McGrew provided a reasoned, logical approach that had been largely lacking in the Eichers' bellicose relations with regulators. Later, he was inextricably drawn into the vortex of intrigue and deception, nearly destroying his career in the process. The Champion accounting department was further strengthened by the addition of Raymon Nolan, hired away from the company's Lake Charles accounting firm. The Eichers' friend, Jerry Willis, retired as chief examiner in Bernard's office but was replaced by another dependable ally, Malcolm G. Ward, later to be suspended from certified membership in the Society of Financial Examiners for misconduct.

Mosley was still an ominous and persistent presence. In fact, Naaman approached Willis, attempting to persuade him to run against Bernard, a proposal Willis declined. That was one part of the process that eventually led to the selection of Green as the Eichers' candidate for insurance commissioner.

The Eichers managed to postpone Mosley's proposed audit until the spring of 1987, the year of the campaign for insurance commissioner. Until then, they firmly stonewalled Mosley's increasingly frequent letters of complaint. Disputes about claims were answered with rambling, convoluted, contentious replies; complaints about premium financing were simply dismissed with a curt note saying that subject was the business of the commissioner of financial institutions; the Insurance Commission had no business meddling in premium finance disputes at all. In the meantime, the Eichers had gained a certificate of authority to sell insurance in Tennessee, an additional milestone in their quest to build a massive regional presence, and they had managed to remove E. C. Hunt and A. Freeman Edgerton from most Champion corporate positions. Both had gone reluctantly, particularly E. C. Hunt, who knew he would now have virtually no inside information about the Eichers' operations. In order to build a powerful regional insurance company—the Eichers's ultimate goal—it was necessary to become licensed to sell in each state of the region. Without such state-by-state licenses, they could only be "surplus lines" carriers in other states, which meant that local insurance agents in those states could only have sold Champion products if similar coverage was not available through admitted insurance carriers in the state. The difference meant many millions in additional income in each state. Becoming licensed is usually not fast or easy, as we have discussed, although in some cited cases, unscrupulous insurance commissioners granted licenses (certificates of authority) in a matter of days, usually following generous campaign contributions by the prospective licensee.

By early 1987, all the Eichers were enjoying the trappings of prosperity; from Naaman's new Porsche to John's homesite lot on Springview Avenue, regalia masked reality. These were largely happy times. After several years of marriage, Naaman and Tina produced an Eicher grandchild, Lawsen.

Efforts to improve Champion's standing increased on a variety of fronts. A. M. Best, the most widely known firm rating the solvency of insurance companies, was about to issue Champion's first such score—no rating was possible during the first three years of any company's operation—

and Freeman Edgerton flew to Best's headquarters in Oldwyck, New Jersey, to lobby for the highest possible grade.

Brimming with new-found confidence, the Eichers contacted Bernard to express support for and cooperation with the audit, now scheduled for May 7, 1987. In an excess of enthusiasm, they even requested the audit be personally supervised by Mosley.

Dr. Sammy Levantino, president of First National Bank of East Baton Rouge, arranged a meeting between the Eichers and the Edwardses, Gov. Edwin Edwards and his brother Marion. Edwin Edwards was, of course, not unknown to the Eichers, Elayn Hunt Eicher having served as head of his Department of Corrections until her death. But this meeting was rooted in business and politics, not pleasantries, and the use of a neutral, third party to arrange the meeting seemed appropriate.

At the meeting, the Eichers spoke harshly of Carlos Miro, the diminutive, Latin dynamo whose Anglo-American Insurance was rapidly becoming a challenge to their insurance empire, criticism that seemed to offend Marion Edwards. The Miro-Edwards connection—cynics called it the "M-E Generation"—would remain an unconfirmed rumor until seven years later, when Miro traveled from his prison cell to a congressional investigating committee making allegations of malfeasance denounced and denied by Edwin Edwards.

The Champion audit began the first week of May 1987. The audit team seemed ineffectual and nonthreatening. Supervising examiner Myron Hissong was thought to be in no danger of expiring from exertion. He was assisted by Fred Tackett, cautiously easing his way toward retirement. The third member of the team, Mike McCarty, was on his first major audit. He was intense and agitated but seriously handicapped by inexperience. Tackett was a contract auditor, living in Texas. Champion was required to reimburse his cost each week. Bernard, in his typical style of management by mishap, lurched along weeks behind in paying Tackett, who was slowly starving to death conducting this audit. Such an arrangement does not lead to aggressive inspection, a condition the Eichers understood and silently applauded.

So halfhearted was the audit, the team completely missed the fact that Champion operated a secret account, a kind of shadow company, that wrote half again as much insurance as Champion, serenely protected from any troublesome rules about reserves, reporting, and the like. The audit did not bother with any intrusive "Market Conduct Study," a major Eicher victory since it meant the auditors would not be contacting agents or customers to determine how honestly Champion operated or how promptly claims were paid. Such a review might have revealed Champion's cavalier careening toward controversy and collapse. Instead, the auditors took a cursory look at the little pending litigation thus far on file and routinely closed the review by the end of June.

Champion's charmed life continued as A. M. Best, from its headquarters on A. M. Best Road, solemnly bestowed an "A" rating on Champion. While an "A" rating was by no means the highest possible, this imprimatur lent Champion a very useful air of legitimacy that came during the crucial period of the Louisiana audit. A later study criticized Best's review procedures, saying they were often skewed in favor of the industry, pointing to several instances in which Best issued favorable ratings immediately prior to company collapses.

The Eichers further capitalized on their good fortune with a $10,000 contribution to the "Friends of Sherman Bernard," the kind of gift uniformly thought within the industry to result in favorable consideration by the insurance commissioner. Based on a favorable rating, Champion's license to write insurance in Kentucky was issued at the same time and all signals seemed favorable.* Only the addition to Bernard's staff of New Orleans investigator Danny DeNoux seemed a minor irritant.

DeNoux, ex-Marine and former New Orleans policeman, was sometimes dismissed as a surly, trigger-happy thug. The problem was, he actually knew quite a lot about insurance. He was a fearless investigator and would prove to be an implacable foe.

The Eichers happily splashed waist deep in influence when it was to their benefit but bitterly resented any evidence of favoritism toward others. For example, Champion's share of the operating cost of the Louisiana Insurance Guaranty Association (LIGA), the industry-funded state agency that paid claims owed by failed insurance companies, was $600,000 in 1987. A quarter of a million dollars each month was going to LIGA's chief law firm, Matthews, Atkinson, Guglielmo, Marks, and Day, which also drew an additional $125,000 each month in expenses.

The Eichers found it ironic that demand for payment against policies issued by London Guaranty might be disputed by LIGA, represented by the law firm of Matthews, Atkinson et al., while actions against London Guaranty would presumably be defended by the same law firm. They

---

*The Kentucky license required all the formalities previously discussed as to a statement of assets, capital, and qualifications. It also required, in most every case, a favorable rating by the insurance commissioner in the applicant's home state.

saw this as a classic conflict of interest. The Eichers used this information in a particularly damaging television spot charging mismanagement by Bernard. They tried to get the Baton Rouge media interested in the story but it seemed too complicated for local reporters to discover and disseminate.

The Eichers wasted some money on their own, as well. They had spent a considerable amount on private investigators to compile a file on Commissioner of Financial Institutions Kenneth Pickering. An unsuccessful candidate for state treasurer, he had already departed as commissioner by the time the investigation was completed. A lawyer, he went on to represent savings and loans, to serve as consultant to controversial financial transactions of Louisiana insurance companies (like the acquisition of Automotive Bank by the principals of Automotive Casualty, which soon thereafter collapsed) and, finally, as Gov. Edwards's appointee, to head the Riverboat Gambling Commission, the powerful agency that granted highly prized dockside casino licenses throughout the state.

Pickering departed without approving the Eichers' application for Limited Function Financial Institution status for United Financial Services. After the Eichers hastily contacted Edwards's office, his new appointee, Fred Dent, approved the application long distance from Washington, D.C., ordering it signed by his deputy, Joe Chase. Thus was born, hastily attended by political influence, the mechanism that would soon serve to finance the Green campaign against Bernard.

The Eichers had spent $16,000 to cover the insurance commissioner's cost of the perfunctory audit and they were well satisfied with the results. Despite the $10,000 contribution, Bernard—prodded by Mosley—was not. He disputed the thoroughness of the financial portions of the audit and ordered it redone. He also intended to send the national consulting firm of Tillinghast and Company to thoroughly investigate Champion's loss reserves and related financial matters.

John Eicher was outraged. Scornful and bellicose at his best, John now raged and bellowed through the building; employees scurried for cover and cowered before the assault and abuse he uniformly visited upon everyone he encountered. Like most ex-salesmen, Eicher relied more on instinct than either logic or learning and he was very often capriciously incorrect. Within the walls of Champion Insurance, few dared correct him, even in his most egregious errors: the act required consummate courage and the reward was hardly worth the risk. DeNoux, accompanied by Hissong, was undeterred by Eicher's ferocity, calmly delivering a formal letter announcing a "show cause" hearing to revoke Champion's certificate of authority to sell insurance for refusal to assist in a financial examination.

Champion's attorney, McGrew, hastily convened a meeting with John Ales, Naaman's confidante and later Edwards's commissioner of natural resources; Billy Broadhurst, the ultimate Edwards insider who participated in the escapade that permanently sidetracked U.S. Sen. Gary Hart's presidential ambitions; and Russell Schonekas, otherwise best remembered as lawyer for reputed mobster Carlos Marcello. The upshot of the meeting was a court hearing and a hastily drawn temporary restraining order alleging that Bernard's own auditors had already signed off on the six-week, $16,000 review and any new investigation was improper.

Bernard's staff was either uninformed or undeterred by

the restraining order, since Hissong and newly named auditor Jim Lewis showed up at the Government Street headquarters almost immediately to demand financial documents. So hastily had Lewis been recruited from Pennsylvania that he lacked even the required approval by the State Department of Administration to perform work for the insurance commission.

Eicher moved quickly to replace certificates of deposit held by other banks with similar certificates issued by United Financial Services, backed by premium notes, not funds on deposit. Simultaneously, A. M. Best included Champion on its "Watch List" warning of the insurance department's show cause hearing. Best had been informed of the hearing by Bernard's functionary Max Mosley, who faxed the company a copy of the hearing notice, adding his own assertion that Champion was attempting to buy the commissioner's race. Mosley neglected to mention that a court had already vacated the hearing and issued a restraining order. Best did not bother to contact Champion for its version of the incident, a contact that would certainly have revealed the existence of the restraining order, hastily adding an insert to its printed edition of ratings that had given Champion an "A," now showing it on the "Watch List" of troubled companies.

Patricia King had a new, gray Cadillac with gold trim to park in the Champion lot but inside the building a siege mentality was unfolding. The services of long-time Champion sleuth Joe Oster were supplemented by high-tech detective Larry Carroll. He arrived in his Mercedes, accompanied by Oster. Bodyguard Ronnie LaHost suddenly appeared on the payroll. While Champion filed a $55 million suit against Bernard, Oster's new assignment was to investigate companies on Champion's own "watch list," painstakingly assembled by Patricia King. At the heart of the list was a score of insurance companies hastily licensed near the end of the campaign or in the waning days of Bernard's administration. Many were "Lloyd's Plan" companies, a hybrid structure of shared risk allowing an insurance company to be formed under the Lloyd's banner. The Lloyd's Plan was a dream come true for fleet-footed entrepreneurs who wanted to leverage their way into ownership of a Louisiana insurance company. Because the risk was shared, at least in theory, capitalization was set at a mere $400,000 and the investors bore no personal liability if their company failed, as many soon did. In the meantime, each Lloyd's Plan company used the Federal Risk Retention Act to write unsupervised business in other states. This business was based solely on the strength of their hastily obtained Louisiana licenses.

The Eichers believed that Bernard authorized a whole spate of such companies in return for campaign contributions; that, because of their low capital infusion, these companies were able to unfairly compete with Champion; and that they were financially flawed, structurally unsound, and ultimately destined to fail. On at least those points, history proved the Eichers correct. Six years later, almost all of the Lloyd's Plan companies had either failed or were in serious difficulty, and Bernard and Browne had pleaded guilty to federal charges relating to the issuing of insurance charters connected to campaign contributions. Browne would get a nineteen-month sentence. Bernard, sentenced to forty-one months, would protest that no contributions had gone directly to his own use; all were funneled into the campaign. That assertion, if true, would not make his offense any less illegal nor benefit taxpayers who ultimately paid the cost of the wholesale collapse of the rickety Lloyd's contraptions.

Suddenly, Alabama authorities, through chief examiner Paul Raadt, began asking questions remarkably similar to Louisiana's queries. The operative word was "suddenly," not "accidentally," for Mosley was a well-connected former employee of the Alabama Insurance Department. He issued a contract to Carlisle Examiners, an Alabama firm, signing the agreement before Carlisle had even registered to do business in Louisiana. Carlisle then subcontracted with Jim Lewis to do the new audit.

When word filtered into Champion headquarters that the new audit might be short-stopped for an additional $100,000, the Eichers retained Bernard's former chief examiner, Jerry Willis, to assist McGrew in his Freedom of Information request as part of the suit. They arrived at the insurance commissioner's offices equipped with their own portable copy machine, personnel to operate it, and Willis's complex and very specific list of requested documents. The incursion achieved its intended purpose; Bernard's personnel were literally swamped trying to provide the demanded documents. Equally disconcerting was the long series of videotaped interrogatories that subjected virtually all of Bernard's key administrators to days of intense questioning.

The whole matter seemed moot with Bernard's defeat by Green. Relieved and emboldened, Champion booted out members of its law firm who had not cooperated with the campaign contribution scheme and created a new firm, McGrew and O'Neill. Gary O'Neill was a dapper man-about-town in Baton Rouge, a famous local "fixer."

Occupying a prominent position on the new firm's first letterhead but performing no discernible work was Toni Higginbotham, wife of District Judge Leo Higginbotham. She had just been narrowly defeated for a seat in the Louisiana

House of Representatives, losing to Sean Reilly, the son of State Rep. Kevin Reilly. The elder Reilly had abandoned a safe legislative seat to run unsuccessfully for state treasurer. Four years later he would emerge as secretary of commerce in Edwards's fourth term.

United Financial Services had donated $25,000 to the Higginbotham campaign by using her maiden name. Naaman's political activities had become so costly that an additional funding source was necessary. It was devised by using the Champion "salvage and subrogation" account, which became the petty cash fund for fueling various campaign war chests.

Based on the election of Green, their proposed new patron, McGrew and O'Neill moved into huge and expensive new offices—with the aid of a quarter million advance from a Champion affiliate—expecting to represent LIGA and the Patients' Compensation Fund, representation which would have been worth millions in fees and would have immediately made the new firm one of the state's most profitable.

Revenge was exacted on both sides. Bernard's people had figured out that one of Champion's "inside sources" was A. G. Gaudin, chief of agent licensing. The Bernard people were said to have used photographic evidence of Gaudin's relationship with a departmental secretary to stop that leak.[3]

John Eicher, always known as a "hardball player," was unleashed by Green's victory. Mosley, in one of the grand examples of wishful thinking, wrote Green a long letter offering to stay and serve his new administration. Even as he offered, the Eichers' private detective was gathering evidence with which to have him arrested and fired. With Naaman's fine hand just discernible in the background, Mosley was actually arrested twice, once for extortion and again for payroll fraud. The payroll charge had to do with Mosley's charging both the state and the companies he examined for the costs of examination.

He contended it was a longstanding practice, a kind of benign fringe benefit to compensate underpaid state employees. The charges were brought on a warrant signed by Judge Freddie Pitcher, who had received Eicher money for his campaign. The investigation was handled by Eicher's detective Joe Oster, working independently because the Eichers did not believe the attorney general's office would prosecute Mosley. After months of expensive litigation, Mosley would be ordered reinstated but, financially exhausted and physically decimated, Mosley never reclaimed his position. Commissioner Jim Brown would bring him back on a contract basis.

In a separate flush of success, Champion filtered its Lincoln Town Cars down to lower echelon staffers and a new mini-fleet of Cadillacs joined Naaman's Porsche in the executive end of the parking lot.

Champion also feathered its legislative nest with the hiring of well-connected Republican lobbyist Pete Arceneaux and legendary black leader, now deceased, A. Z. Young, both men of unquestioned ability and previously unquestioned integrity.

The week after his victory, Green asked Bernard for a tour of the insurance commissioner's headquarters. Bernard, accompanied by Browne, accommodated Green's request but later remembered his advice to the commissioner-elect. "If you want to survive, admit that Champion financed your campaign. Apologize, pledge to the public that you will do the right thing, cut your ties to Champion. The public is in a mood to like and trust you," the vanquished political veteran told his young victor, "and you can survive if you come clean and start on the right foot now." Green ignored Bernard's advice.

Indeed Green seemed to be a reformer and the public did like and respect him in those early months in office; he brought about changes, giving the Insurance Rating Commission (a notoriously lazy rubber stamp outfit) more latitude in reviewing rate increase requests and demanding more proof before such requests were approved.

In fact, the Rating Commission's senior member, Jimmy Patterson, himself a Lloyd's Plan operator who had not supported Green, was later to say, "I don't know what happened in the Champion matter, but if Doug Green's life was a book and he could tear out the Champion chapter, he could be commissioner forever." Of course, Mussolini loyalists prefer to remember Il Duce as the man who made Italian trains run on time.

A delegation of Champion's Louisiana lawyers joined its new Alabama attorneys in a December 21, 1987, session in Montgomery to answer pointed questions by that state's insurance regulators. The Eichers also pointed out Bernard's resounding defeat to the A. M. Best personnel, trying to repair the "Watch List" rating. Best—pointedly aware of the $55 million suit against Bernard—responded that they were unable to rate Champion objectively so long as any possibility existed that they might also be named as codefendants in the action. The Eichers believed that to be the carrot and the stick, a not-so-subtle form of intimidation designed to force them to promise never to sue Best in return for possible reconsideration of the damaging rating. They played for time, operating in the belief that the upcoming Green administration would soon clear their name in Louisiana and around the country.

By spring of 1988, Green had handled one important item on the Eichers' agenda: the unceremonious sacking of Max Mosley. Meanwhile, the Eichers were operating on a variety of fronts. Secure in their relationship with Green, Freeman Edgerton and attorney John Ales were hard at work laying plans for creating their own offshore reinsurance company, a plan already employed by Anglo-American and a score of other sharp operators.

Meredith Eicher, both her marriage and her special friendship with Champion's computer genius Gary Ethridge having collapsed, now considered becoming a certified public accountant. That possibility was not lost on Champion's CPA, McCulloch, who was well aware that blood was thicker than water and his days might well be numbered. The Eichers' fragile sense of loyalty would later be a major factor in his decision to assist in sending the whole Eicher family to prison, even though it would also mean serving time himself.

The remnants of the Sherman Bernard organization were noisily protesting that they had been cheated out of the election by Champion's money. Little did the Eichers know that as they celebrated victory, Bernard investigator DeNoux had spent two hours laying out the inner workings of the Eicher empire to U.S. Attorney John Volz in New Orleans. Volz had not been DeNoux's first choice to investigate the Eichers, but the U.S. attorney in Baton Rouge, Raymond Lamonica, showed no interest in what DeNoux had to say. Volz was different; he and DeNoux shared a single-minded disregard for the political niceties, although for very different reasons. In fact, Volz's zealous prosecution of political heavyweights would be partially responsible for his removal from the office and his eventual loss of a possible federal judgeship, but the Champion investigation was too powerful and too public to be stopped by political intervention.

These were good news/bad news days for the Eichers. Allied Bank, their reliable source of a large line of credit, had been sold and was now First Interstate Bank of Texas. That change in their previously rock-solid financing connection was soon to become the first domino in a collapsing chain.

On the other hand, A. M. Best agreed to remove Champion from the "Watch List," based on a later, favorable audit. Best, which had been on every side of the Champion issue at one time or another, soon reversed itself again, when it saw a scathing March 19, 1989, internal memo written by Mosley, a document drafted in secret and circulated anonymously one week after Green was sworn in. By the time the damage was known, Mosley was gone but it resulted in Best's being added as a defendant in Champion's suit for an additional $35 million. Green, embarrassed by the Mosley leak, decreed that all future Champion correspondence must go through his deputy, Tom Bentley.

Naaman's confidante and legal strategist, John Ales, was named acting director of the Louisiana Insurance Guaranty Fund, an important asset for the Eichers and, presumably, a dependable ally in the McGrew/O'Neill firm's quest to capture the lucrative LIGA representation. Ales's recommendations about the formulation of Capital Insurance Company, Champion's Cayman Islands reinsurance operation, had resulted in a formal request to Green to issue a license for the company. Green personally supervised the handling of the request, approving it in one day and personally delivering it to Naaman's home at night. Each state handles the issuing of its own "Certificate of Authority" for such reinsurance operations; there's no uniform national standard. In cases where the insurance commissioner was a captive of the requesting company, the standards seemed quite flexible indeed.

A. M. Best was not the only recipient of Mosley's secret memo. On October 12, 1988, Alabama authorities, now smelling a rat, refused to accept the first Champion audit and demanded to conduct their own. Alabama auditors showed up suddenly, without first informing Green, as normal protocol required. Green attempted to arrange either a joint audit with Alabama or a zone audit with Alabama, Tennessee, and Kentucky—to be conducted by Louisiana. No state accepted Green's offer. Finally, Green commissioned his own reaudit by Owen Guidry, a short, dark, bearded, contract employee who was also currently managing the receivership of Louisiana Underwriters. He was now to divide his time between the two tasks through his firm, Consulting Financial Examination, Inc. His upbeat, optimistic assessment of Champion flew in the face of mounting evidence that the Eichers' operations were in deepening financial trouble.

Guidry's hiring did help settle a suit by Louisiana Attorney General William Guste, who had brought a civil action seeking United Financial Services records. Guste alleged that Champion and United Financial Services were conspiring to commit fraud through forgery, artificial inflation of assets, filing false public records, and engaging in false accounting. Judge William Brown ruled against Guste, holding that the United Financial Services records were confidential. Encouraged by the victory, Champion pressed the issue, filing suit against Deputy Attorney General Charles Yeager. Guidry's wife, working under her maiden name, Faye

Duvalier, was reported to have received $100,000 to participate in the liquidation of Louisiana Underwriters.

Guidry himself was proposed by Green to supervise the lucrative liquidation of American Lloyd's in Metairie, Louisiana. When his qualifications were challenged in court by attorneys for American Lloyd's, Baton Rouge lawyer Fredrick R. Tulley, the quintessential insider, testified that Guidry was qualified. By that time, Guidry's fanciful analysis of Champion's well-being was open to considerable question, since Champion was bankrupt. Guidry's appointment was stopped by the court.

Tulley and his powerhouse law firm, Taylor, Porter, Brooks and Phillips, were especially intriguing. The firm had represented every Louisiana insurance commissioner since Dudley Guglielmo. As each commissioner was defeated, new faces populated the commission's offices but Taylor, Porter, Brooks, and Phillips remained, apparently entrenched beyond the reach of changing political winds.

Tulley, his reputation apparently unsullied by his association with Green and Guidry, appeared three times as an expert witness before U.S. Rep. John Dingall's House Subcommittee on Investigations, which was looking into insurance fraud, at least those aspects of it generating headlines in America's daily press. Like a handful of others, Tulley's role as legal strategist for the string of commissioners fell into the realm of "attorney-client" services and his role in the Green administration was never challenged.

Subsequent Commissioner Jim Brown, reportedly after intervention by Gov. Edwards, continued to use Tulley, although in a somewhat diminished role, and Tulley, from some Olympian height, had apparently become immune to challenge or change, protected by de facto tenure and evidently appointed for life.

There is nothing in Louisiana's legal traditions to preclude convoluted representation arrangements. For example, the McGrew/O'Neill firm represented the commissioner's office under Green while still technically suing the same office in a $55 million Champion action left over from the Bernard administration, an arrangement that went entirely unquestioned.

Alabama refused to honor the dubious Guidry examination and continued to demand its own. Finally, in an arrangement brokered by Green, the Alabama auditors were sequestered in Champion's second floor boardroom.

Naaman installed a private line for the room, saying it was so he could bill the auditors for their calls, but every telephone conversation was recorded. He set up an elaborate inventory sign-out system and even had the examiners escorted into and out of the building. It was a thin line, because to simply refuse to allow the audit would have resulted in the immediate cancellation of Champion's Alabama license. For good measure, Naaman also installed microphones in the ceiling disguised as smoke detectors and secret surveillance cameras to make certain no activity by the audit team would go unknown to Champion throughout the investigation, which was to last until February 1989.

The Alabama audit process looked ominous, so threatening that Naaman decided to match Alabama audit for audit by ordering Wilson and Associates of Washington, D.C., to audit the work of the Alabama auditors and by ordering his own audit, done by Reznick, Fedder, and Silverman, a national firm that had an Alabama office. The simple purpose of the outside audit was to answer the central question of the Alabama commissioner's audit: was Champion Insurance solvent or not? It was the worst possible time to undertake such considerable costs; Champion was still reeling from the huge expense of electing Green, the costly headquarters addition, and the accelerated payments required when both of the company's major banks called its notes and effectively shut down its lines of credit. Unpaid claims were mounting; legislators and media investigators were hovering around demanding an explanation.

Nonetheless, an additional layer of whitewash was definitely in order. Unfortunately, Larry Burns, who conducted the Reznick audit, decided to do a consolidated, company-wide "audit for fraud." That was precisely what the Eichers did not want; it smacked of the "single business entity" theory they were attempting to stonewall and it raised the potential that carefully guarded details from the Eichers' intricate chain of related companies might become public. The Eichers decided to use some pretext to fire Burns, even if it meant eating the entire cost of the unfinished independent audit.

The Alabama auditors were expected to scrutinize Champion's bank records carefully. The Eichers had earlier considered buying a bank and installing some figurehead like A. Z. Young to run it, but they had lacked time to complete the deal and sufficient cash to make the purchase. They did, however, own an elaborate printing press, which they now used to print their own AmBank monthly statements. Working late into the night and through the weekends, they were able to produce "bank statements" that were virtually indistinguishable from the real thing. Producing months of statements in a matter of days, working only after hours and on weekends, was a mammoth task, further complicated by the fact that only family members were allowed in on the action, employees being carefully kept away while this ambitious printing project was in progress. Patty King Eicher was later to remember being told that the work was a "trial run" in connection with their possible purchase of First National Bank of East Baton Rouge.

Champion employees were, of course, deeply involved in other ways. From the outset, Don McCulloch had difficulty convincing the Alabama auditors that the United Financial Services-issued "certificates of deposit" were valid. There was no Alabama corollary for such a transaction. The difficulty was not abated even by stacking up $18 million of premium finance notes, each legally assigned from United Financial Services to Champion. Jerry Willis came up with the bright idea of having the certificates rated by the National Association of Insurance Commissioners' Securities Validation Office, which did in fact immediately approve the certificates.* When the Alabama audit uncovered a discrepancy in certificates of deposit, McCulloch simply stepped into the next room, typed up thousands of dollars of new CDs, and returned to tell the Alabama auditors he had "just found" the missing certificates. Unfortunately, the examiners took the list of CDs to the Office of Financial Institutions and discovered that the new instruments were out of sequence. They thought the new CDs were issued to inflate Champion's

---

*The problem was basically that Alabama had no language in its statute books either allowing or disallowing the use of certificates as an admitted asset. Thus the NAICSVO stamp of approval served to "legitimize" the process and defuse further discussion and investigation on the point. Today such questionable CDs would be almost uniformly disallowed because they are backed by premium notes on policies that could be terminated or cancelled.

value and keep it from appearing insolvent. McCulloch argued it was simply to correct an earlier clerical oversight. Guidry agreed to write Green a memo saying the CDs were proper, after some bookkeeping adjustments. The Alabama auditors were unconvinced.

John Eicher's old classmate, former district attorney Ossie Brown, and his partner Johnny Moore were summoned to review the mounting problem. They saw it as a political crisis, not a legal matter, and their view seemed confirmed when Dee Taylor of the attorney general's staff hosted a cocktail party at her home for the Alabama auditors. Moore called Naaman's approach the "all or nothing game," and Naaman responded by effectively cutting them out of the loop. He much preferred the advice of McGrew, O'Neill, and his trusted confidante, John Ales.

Johnny Moore's life would continue to be tied to the insurance turmoil. In 1993 he would be sued for allegedly misappropriating $527,000 while representing the state insurance department in the liquidation of Physicians National Risk Retention Group, which wrote medical malpractice insurance throughout the United States.

Champion's widening crisis even involved Freeman Edgerton, figurehead officer of Capital Bank. His own bank, Metropolitan, failed for which he was under federal scrutiny, and his law firm revoked his free office. Even State National Insurance, where he was chief executive officer, suggested he sever his ties to Champion. Edgerton had already undergone angioplasty; the strain was evident.

Champion fought back belligerently. When the state's ethics commission decided to investigate the Green campaign's funding, Champion attorneys Rolfe and Gallagher had it declared illegal because ethics commission members were appointed by the legislature and enforcement was supposed to be an executive function. (The commission's authority would be resolved only long after Champion's demise and too late for it to play any important role in the investigation.) The Eichers' friend, District Attorney Bryan Bush, convened a grand jury investigation into charges that Attorney General Guste was attempting to ruin Champion.

Naaman Eicher had Alabama auditors subpoenaed, believing he could prove Guste's deputy, Winston Riddick, had been secretly supplying them with confidential United Financial Services records. Shortly thereafter, the attorney general's office began investigating Bush for misuse of office funds. Bush, suffering from a nerve-related ailment, eventually resigned in mid-term. It was small-town, state-capital, political intrigue at its murkiest.

When the National Association of Insurance Commissioners convened in New Orleans in 1988, former Bernard aide Danny DeNoux, now running a kind of "Bernard commission in exile" from the offices of American Lloyd's, flooded the meeting with "Doug Green Backs," Green's face pictured prominently on the dollar bill. "Let's Dump Doug" bumper stickers appeared all over Louisiana. DeNoux's own firm, International Securities and Investigations, Inc., invited attendees to view "The Best Insurance Commissioner Money Can Buy," a television exposé about Green produced by Baton Rouge television reporter John Camp. The Eichers responded with a full-scale private investigation of Camp, seeking to prove members of his family were involved with illicit narcotics.

Champion's money woes caused John Eicher to drop his AmBank loan repayments from $250,000 per week to $200,000 and then to $150,000. Even that was hard to make.

Champion cancelled its Kentucky license and received a million-dollar refund, but that amount made scarcely a dent in its deepening financial crisis.

Two of Champion's key Alabama operatives resigned. The Alabama insurance commissioner's office immediately stormed Champion's Birmingham office. Naaman rushed to Birmingham for a venomous, acrimonious session that probably destroyed what slight possibility for regulatory reconciliation might still have existed.

The Eichers wanted Green to close Liberty Lloyd's, which was in fierce competition with Champion. Green was more interested in toppling American Lloyd's, from which the National Association of Insurance Commissioners embarrassment originated.

By spring 1989, pickets from the Louisiana Consumers League, most of whom were angry claimants and/or policyholders, were led by David Czernik, a former "Nader Raider." They marched in front of Champion headquarters and were prominently seen on evening television news and in statewide newspapers. Many other people who had done business with Champion were complaining to their state legislators, who routinely routed such complaints to Commissioner Green for action. Any chance of sweeping Champion's claims backlog under the carpet disappeared.

The Eichers were in international trouble as well. The Caymanese management firm required for Capital Bank to operate in the Grand Cayman Islands withdrew, citing the yearlong delay in providing the proper documentation. Patricia King Eicher was later to blame Naaman's friend John Ales for the failure, in a dispute that nearly wrecked her tenuous marriage to John Eicher. Clearly, emotions were frayed and relationships were coming apart throughout the Eicher empire.

In the meantime, both General Motors Acceptance Corporation (GMAC) and Ford Motor Credit (FMC) were assailing Champion over its "total loss" payment system. Ironically, this was one of the few instances in which Champion was probably acting correctly. Both GMAC and FMC were making automobile purchase loans for virtually 100 percent of the sale. When the finance cost was added to the sale price, the buyer wound up owing more than the value of the vehicle. In the event of a "total loss" through theft or accident, Champion paid the book value of the vehicle, leaving the irate owner still on the hook for the remainder of the note on a demolished vehicle. The credit companies quickly—and improperly—passed the blame on to Champion. Relations between Champion and these lenders eventually became so bad that it was virtually impossible to finance a new vehicle through GMAC or FMC if Champion was to be the insurer, cutting further into Champion's market.

Edwin Edwards, who had earlier been retained by Anglo-American Insurance (AAI), arranged a meeting between AAI and Champion. Carlos Miro first proposed buying Champion from the Eichers and, when that scheme was declined, dividing the state into zones in which each company would agree to dominance but allow the other at least a piece of the action.

John Eicher declined, but not because he was concerned about the rather transparent antitrust violation, since state and federal law clearly prohibited any scheme in which two competitors would divide up a state, each agreeing not to compete in the other's protected territory. Neither was he unduly alarmed by Miro's intricate international scheme, which involved moving vast sums of money abroad through a complicated chain of mysterious companies and then surreptitiously back into the country. In fact, Eicher had patterned much of his own "offshore" activity very closely along the same lines.

Eicher's refusal to do business with Anglo-American was fueled simply by his growing belief that Green was secretly conspiring with Miro and Anglo-American behind his back. He was becoming convinced that Green was that most reprehensible of persons, a politician who wouldn't stay bought. A review of Green's final campaign finance statement suggests Eicher may have been correct, as scores of Eicher's enemies appeared on Green's list of benefactors, including many from the hated Lloyd's Plan companies. Green, as a man with no particular loyalties, apparently saw nothing morally wrong with working both sides of the street.

By now, the Champion gossip was galloping all over the small city of Baton Rouge. Until this point, the Eichers had generally been able to deny rumors of impending insolvency, blaming them on dissatisfied claimants who contacted the media, envious competitors, yellow journalists, and political enemies. And then the other shoe dropped. Even as the Louisiana re-audit glowed and glistened, praising Champion as sound and reputable, the dreaded Alabama audit was released.

It was every bit as harsh as the Eichers had feared—and more so. Champion, the Alabama audit charged, was an interlocking group of companies ruled by a "tyrant patriarch." Alabama disallowed the Capital reinsurance agreement and refused to accept certificates of deposit from United Financial Services, saying the certificates were only backed by perilous premium notes signed by policyholders who were buying on credit, policies that could be terminated for nonpayment or cancelled by the policyholders, either of which would make the resultant CDs worthless.

Charging self-dealing, Alabama declared Champion to be "statutorily insolvent." The only saving grace was that until Champion had an opportunity to respond, the Alabama audit could not be completed. It was released, to the Louisiana Department of Insurance and to Champion. It could not be made public until after the "show cause" hearing was decided. So long as the damaging language from the audit could not be published, Champion still had a fighting chance. So it was the matter of *public release* which was central to this debate.

But the show cause order forcing Champion to show why it should not be declared insolvent and closed could be made public and it was. Alabama hired top-flight attorney Charles Crook to represent it in the hearing. Champion hired Brian Espy, a Republican-connected Alabama lawyer, to attempt a negotiated settlement. So angered were the Alabama auditors that little discussion and absolutely no agreement were possible. On the Louisiana front, Edwards and his confidante Billy Broadhurst again met with the Eichers. They later claimed to have paid Broadhurst $50,000 to no avail whatsoever.

There was no serious question about the eventual outcome of the Alabama action; relations between Alabama and the Eichers were sufficiently fractious and Champion's days as an insurer there were clearly numbered. It was one of the first of a series of scenarios requiring "damage control." McGrew was dispatched to surrender the Alabama license to avoid a public hearing at which all of Champion's difficulties might have found their way to the front pages of newspapers throughout the South. Naaman blamed Champion's troubles on a "board of competitors," other insurance company representatives who sat on the Alabama Guaranty Fund.*

The Eichers' Alabama retreat was handled in a typically crass and insensitive manner. The Birmingham office was abandoned after the close of business on a Friday and all records spirited out of the state before authorities could seek a court order to examine them.[4] Naaman said all Alabama claims would henceforth be handled by the Louisiana headquarters—a dubious pledge given the growing mountain of unpaid claims already confronting the Baton Rouge clerical staff—and Champion's Birmingham employees were paid through the hour the doors were closed, with neither notice nor severance. Some did not discover their jobs were gone until they arrived at the empty offices the following Monday morning.

Radical retrenchment (cutting back staff and reducing every expenditure), a financial tourniquet to stop some part of the cash flow hemorrhage, was the order of the day, but additional revenue sources were also badly needed. John Eicher decided to jump whole hog into the workers' com-

---

*Each state, with one or two exceptions, has a guaranty fund. Every insurance company licensed to do business in that state pays a percentage of its collected premium to the fund, which, in turn, uses that money to pay claims against companies that have failed. The various funds are almost always run by representatives of the insurance companies that provide the monies to operate them. It is very rare that a consumer representative is ever named to such funds, which is one of the complaints of consumer groups. In Louisiana, for example, one of the attorneys for LIGA is a shareholder in the company owned by the chairman of LIGA. The whole thing is unconscionably incestuous.

pensation business, requiring employers to carry insurance protection on their employees in the event that a worker is the victim of an accident or injury on the job. Other companies writing workers' compensation in Alabama spent $1.25 in claims for every $1 they took in. The workers' compensation industry was becoming the scene of wholesale failure; as one insurer after another flamed out, it took on the appearance of an air raid gone completely awry. But workers' compensation insurance was an appropriate avenue for the cash-strapped Eichers because of the nature of the business. Workers' compensation insurance generates a cash avalanche up front, particularly with the front-loaded fees the Eichers collected. Of course, virtually all of that money and often more is eventually consumed by the "long tail" of workers' compensation claims, which generally occur much later and can continue for years. The Eichers decided to collect the lush premiums immediately and worry about the claims later.

Their abrupt entry into the workers' compensation market also placed them squarely in competition with their old nemesis Anglo-American in ways they could never have foreseen. Near the end of Edwin Edwards's term as governor, Anglo's Carlos Miro had reportedly concocted a scheme with Edwards insider Gus Mijalis, who would rake in millions as a "consultant" to gambling interests during Edwards's fourth term. Under the Mijalis plan the state would turn over operation of the entire state workers' compensation program to Anglo-American. The program had been defeated by the legislature and Edwards had been roundly criticized for his involvement. The media neglected to note, however, that in an Alexandria, Louisiana, speech, one of his first after defeating Edwards, "reform" governor-elect Buddy Roemer had praised the plan and Anglo-American. Consequently, Miro's scheme was still very much alive as the Eichers leaped into the competition.

Naaman Eicher did his part to raise capital, remortgaging his Baton Rouge mansion for $375,000. Since most of the initial funding for the home had come from Champion affiliates, it was a profitable arrangement for Naaman, who was also the purported "owner" of the Champion headquarters, leased to Champion at a handsome profit as well.[5]

Events were turning ugly and ominous, like the Louisiana sky just before a summer thunderstorm, as Patricia King Eicher, personally embattled by the tight circle of original Eichers and professionally exhausted by the public chorus of controversy, left town. Sunday, May 28, 1989, she departed for Paris to watch her daughter's graduation. The Government Street headquarters was eerily quiet as she prepared to leave; it must have felt like a castle just before the rabble storms the gates. Eicher packed her personal possessions and took them home, knowing the battle would be over and lost by the time she returned.

As the Champion claims backlog increased to $22 million, John Eicher flirted with the idea of suing AmBank for cancelling his line of credit even though his payments were current, thus diverting funds that might otherwise have gone to claims payments. And then the desertions began: McGrew/O'Neill partner Gary O'Neill suggested executing each official investigating Champion—a notion that would be revisited by the Eichers later that year—and then suddenly sashayed out of town for parts unknown.[6] Court documents reveal that O'Neill left behind a letter in which Champion guaranteed Champion Mortgage's credit line (Champion Mortgage being O'Neill's creation, unrelated to the Eicher holdings), to which he forged Patricia King Eicher's name, and a promissory note, to which he forged Naaman Eicher's signature.

O'Neill also left behind a criminal charge for an alleged assault and a series of other pending charges alleging bank fraud, misrepresentation, and misappropriation. The Eichers were in no position to take action against him, however, since he also left behind his friend Meredith Eicher, who took up residence in his Spanish Town home. Toni Higginbotham, whose legislative race had been financed with Naaman Eicher's money, suddenly departed the law firm, which was of limited impact since none of her associates had ever been able to figure out what she did there anyway.

Of course, not everyone disappeared. Green's brother Donald appeared to get McCulloch to prepare his personal tax return and to ask the Eichers to pay the taxes.

On June 5, 1989, it was over. McGrew filed for liquidation of Champion, abandoning the Government Street headquarters and turning the company over to Green's insurance department. Champion left behind 70,000 unpaid claims, estimated to cost $150 million. The failure also stripped insurance coverage from 100,000 policyholders in Louisiana, 65,000 in Alabama, and 10,000 in Tennessee. Every lawyer in Baton Rouge and much of the Louisiana bar had at least one case against Champion for nonpayment of claims. It is the nature of such disputes, though, that once they are in the legal process they take months to settle, even in the best of circumstances. No one little disgruntled claimant out shaking his fist in front of Champion's block-long headquarters would make any impact at all, except, eventually, by the aggregate weight of their numbers. And by then it was too late.

In exile, suddenly bereft of their imposing Government

Street citadel, the Eichers made do with temporary quarters in the jumbled remains of McGrew's decimated law offices and the CPA office of McCulloch's friend John Davis, who had also been Green's campaign treasurer.

One of the consequences of the forced resignation of District Attorney Bryan Bush, whose grand jury, with the Eichers' assistance, had been investigating the state attorney general, was that now the attorney general assumed control of the grand jury and refocused its attention on Champion. McGrew spent Champion's last $200,000 paying judgments so he could cancel the appeal bonds in those cases and end any remaining connection between Champion and Capital Insurance. One of the important assertions against Champion and its affiliates was that it was a sham organization in which each supposedly independent company was really just part and parcel of the Eicher scheme, not independent at all. That was one of the Alabama auditors' assertions. If Capital Insurance had been used as a convenient source of appeal bonds for cases against Champion, that would tend to prove the "single business entity" theory, so it was important to sever that connection quickly. Then Johnny Moore and Ossie Brown, who anticipated representing Champion's officers and directors in any future criminal action, came by to urge preparation for indictments that everyone suspected were sure to come.

Retired District Judge Fred Ellis, appointed liquidator in the case, now operated from John Eicher's palatial personal office. Ellis seized everything in sight, including all the assets of affiliated companies even though they were not in bankruptcy, and all incoming mail, no matter to whom it was addressed. Padlocks were installed, guards hired, and roadblocks established. Government Street took on the appearance of a military camp.

Judge Ellis ended his career with perhaps the most lucrative assignment of his lifetime. At the time when clamoring Champion claimsholders were receiving nothing, Ellis was paid at a senior attorney's rate of $150 per hour. His hourly fee began each day as he stepped into John Eicher's Cadillac at the Ellis retirement home in Covington, over an hour away, until the time he pulled back into his driveway each night. Ellis's fee was the same as an experienced attorney might have commanded, with one highly profitable difference: unlike a normal law firm, Ellis had no overhead. Cynics also pointed out that he did precious little lawyering to earn that fee, functioning mostly as a high-powered business manager, which was probably what the court should have hired to begin with. In the end, Ellis wound up half a million dollars richer for the experience. Not until Insurance Commissioner Jim Brown took office, over two years later, was Ellis's administrative gravy train derailed.

The case was assigned to District Judge Joseph Keogh, a former state legislator. The silver-haired Keogh was absolutely Irish; his chambers looked like the inside of a very high-class Dublin gift shop. In fact, Keogh's great goal was to retire from the bench and move to Ireland, an ambition he was not to achieve. Within the quaint standards of Louisiana public life, Keogh was considered an ethical official. He was also a brilliant jurist, which would come to be very important given the international complexities of the case, and a great gentleman.

Ellis had not been Keogh's first choice but others declined for various reasons and Ellis was reluctantly available. Keogh would later agree that the costs may have been excessive but pointed out that no one knew, in the beginning, that the case would be so time-consuming and complex.

Others came to do good and wound up doing very well indeed. Paul Ironmonger, a business partner of Assistant Attorney General Winston Riddick, received $50,000 for supervising security. Riddick pointed out, correctly, that the Gracie Corporation, their joint enterprise, represented no conflict of interest in this case. Gracie was basically the landlord of several score of generally run-down rental houses in the less-affluent areas of Baton Rouge. Riddick denied he had hidden Ironmonger's business relationship with him, saying he had only "not disclosed" their joint dealings, a fine distinction that was largely lost on disgruntled Champion claimsholders and "good government" advocates. Ellis's friends Denny-Hall Realtors and B. B. Taylor III, realtor, split $120,000 in real estate commissions for "selling" the Champion headquarters from one state agency to another.

Colorful Sheldon Beychok, a portly, bearded, quintessential political insider, was named conservator of Champion's affiliate, Capital Insurance Company. (Known to have a history of heart problems, and suffering from diabetes, Beychok died on June 17, 1994.) He took nothing for that role but earned over $150,000 in attorney's fees in the case, with his law partner getting another $223,509. Beychok, like most everyone else in the case, was appointed by Keogh, his former law partner. He managed to stay around under new commissioner Brown. His recollection of Keogh's appointment of him was refreshing in its candor. Somebody had to do the job. He was available and, in the aftermath of his own personal and corporate bankruptcies, he needed the work.[7]

The appointment must have seemed like manna from heaven to the impoverished Beychok, who truly enjoyed the finer things in life, and he guarded it jealously. In fact, when all other Champion affiliates were judicially joined as a "single business entity," only Beychok's representation of Capital Insurance and his substantial cash flow from the case were left undisturbed by his friend Keogh. Then, with all Capital assets discovered and depleted, Beychok quietly folded Capital into the mix and left the scene.* Beychok, who was said to be able to smell money from many miles away, once turned a deaf ear to one citizen who arrived at his office, a state legislator in tow, purporting to know where millions of dollars of Champion money had been hidden. He neither reported the conversation nor investigated the assertion—which was one of many such theories— because he was by then "off the clock" and had no way to bill for such services.

Altogether, assorted lawyers would take some $2 million in fees to liquidate the Champion collapse, which exceeded $5 million. Less than $15 million ever went to the Louisiana Insurance Guaranty Association (LIGA), which faced some $144 million in claims and claims-handling expenses. LIGA would eventually spend some $20 million in attorneys' fees in the Champion aftermath. Louisiana's total expenditure for failed insurance companies over a five-year period, from the late 1980s to the early 1990s, would breeze past the $500 million mark.

---

*So long as Capital had assets, it was Beychok's insistent representation to the court that it must remain out of the overall liquidation of the other Champion companies and it was the only one liquidated separately. Once it was reduced to a skeleton, leaving Beychok no further means of accruing billable hours for work on the case, that distinction quietly disappeared and it was put into the other Champion liquidation with the other related companies, where it should probably have been placed to begin with.

By mid-1989, the Champion probe was proceeding on a variety of fronts. The United States attorney in New Orleans, aided by postal investigators, was cranking up a serious inquiry, although a grand jury had not yet been impaneled. Judge Ellis's staff, overseeing the Champion liquidation, was primarily consumed with the daunting task of re-creating the company's records, an effort made geometrically more difficult by the Eichers' thorough trashing of evidence and stonewalling of information.[8]

Naaman had stored cartons of printed records in a warehouse on the Government Street property, but he had carefully divided each activity by transaction type so that payments were in one carton, claims in another, with the result that it was virtually impossible to trace any one policy from start to finish. With an intensive understanding of data processing, the Eicher organization knew that data from computer tapes could eventually be re-created even though a tape had been erased. Thus, they carefully overprinted millions of percentage signs over the data on the computer tapes they left behind, then erased each tape twice, obliterating all data and making reconstruction impossible.[9] Some sixty boxes of records were stored at Womack Construction in Port Allen. McGrew revealed their location to LIGA officials but the subsequent "discovery" of the documents made dramatic headlines.

A small mountain of documents was moved to a temporary warehouse across town. A fleet of rented trucks later moved much of the material a second time, to the Holmes's warehouse property, from which it was seized by a state police raid. Some of the most sensitive computer tapes were stored in a locked spare bedroom at Ann Parker's apartment. Other computer tapes were secreted behind a false wall in the home of Champion's printer, Tim Upton, from which many were simply removed and microwaved into oblivion. Other volatile documents were simply burned in the fireplace of John Eicher's home or in a backyard bonfire at Naaman's. The most damaging evidence was hidden in a garbage bag in the trunk of John's car or spirited around town inside a soon-to-be-famous plastic briefcase. None of this was known to the liquidators at the time; they knew only that the Eichers were ignoring their demands for production of documents and that the liquidation was unable to proceed without the records.

Frustrated, Ellis complained to Keogh, who sentenced John and Naaman to one year in jail for civil contempt of court for tampering with Champion records. Keogh delayed the imposition of the sentences and the accompanying $1,000 fine for each Eicher, believing he had exerted sufficient pressure to force cooperation.

Joining Ellis's legal team at each Champion hearing were staff lawyers from the Louisiana attorney general's office and frequently representatives from Alabama's insurance commissioner's office and its attorney general. In fact, since the Eichers, for the most part, assiduously avoided service of subpoenas from regulators and disgruntled claimants alike, it soon became common practice to simply await their next court appearance and serve them in open court, where there was no hiding place.

The attorney general's prosecution team, which had already assumed control of the former Baton Rouge district attorney's grand jury, got off to a rocky and contentious start. By the time the Champion probe began, longtime Attorney General Billy Guste had already privately determined to retire at the end of his term in 1991. Guste, elected

twenty years earlier, had been a state senator from New
Orleans and was one of a small handful of political figures
from the predominately Roman Catholic New Orleans area
who had been able to win a statewide election. Guste was
considered more showman than legal scholar and was held
in particularly low esteem by many on his legal staff.[10]
Nonetheless, he was a formidable political figure and he
assumed, correctly, that the Champion case could provide
the final, crowning achievement of his tenure as attorney
general.

Guste, who was later unavailable to answer questions
for this book about his handling of the case, decided not
to assign the Champion matter to his criminal division.
Instead, he directed both the civil and the criminal parts
of the case to his principal aide and major domo, Winston
Riddick, who was assisted by lawyers Bill Alford and Steve
Irving.

Alford had originally been assigned to prosecute
Republican District Attorney Bryan Bush, a task the ardently
Democratic Alford relished. He had honed his prosecutorial
skills as a top assistant to controversial New Orleans District
Attorney Jim Garrison and later as a seasoned criminal
prosecutor for several rural Louisiana parishes. Alford was
seriously flirting with the notion of ending his legal career
as a criminal prosecutor with the attorney general. When
Bush's resignation ended that case, the Champion prosecution
seemed a tailor-made chance to try the job on for size before
uprooting his family and actually moving to Baton Rouge.

The towering, chain-smoking Alford brought to the team
an unbroken string of murder convictions. He had joined
the attorney general's team on a temporary basis to prosecute
a Baton Rouge police officer for murder, a case District

Attorney Bush had stepped away from. Alford won handily against long odds.

Although some thought him the office radical, Irving was a brilliant tactician with a remarkable ability to piece together the fragmented events of a case into a pattern that made sense for the prosecution. He subscribed to a dizzying battery of sometimes-conflicting conspiracy theories that was occasionally disconcerting to associates. He was also thought to be generally fair-minded and impeccably honest, which was an unusual accolade in the Champion affair.

The result was a major turf war conducted principally by Rene Solomon, the ill-tempered head of the criminal division, who had been consigned to a mere supporting role in the Champion criminal prosecution. Failing in his turf battle, Solomon, a notoriously sore loser, wound up on the staff of Baton Rouge U.S. Attorney Raymond Lamonica, once chief counsel to Republican Gov. David C. Treen, from where they belatedly cut themselves in on a small piece of the prosecution action.

Only three months into the Champion investigation, Alford was in a serious quandary for several reasons. First, the attorney general's office was woefully understaffed to conduct the kind of wide-ranging, worldwide investigation that would be needed to gain a grand jury indictment against the Eichers. A skeleton permanent staff was on hand and a few additional persons were borrowed from the state inspector general but the team was simply overwhelmed by the truckloads of evidence that had to be researched, cataloged, and fashioned into a successful prosecution.

Alford finally came to believe that the best the state could do would be to find some minor charge such as computer fraud, which was fairly straightforward and easy to explain and prove to the grand jury and a subsequent trial jury. He assumed, correctly as it turned out, that Champion's actual collapse was inevitable, after which liquidators could get the resources to delve deeply into the company's operations. In the meantime, with a minuscule staff and no assistance at all from the antagonistic state insurance commissioner—who quite properly feared he might, himself, be a target of the investigation—Alford argued in favor of getting a criminal conviction on the best available charge.

Second, Alford was increasingly frustrated and dismayed by internal dissension within the office. The attorney general's placement of Riddick to head both the civil and criminal teams investigating Champion had caused a virtual rebellion on the part of the existing criminal staff, led by Solomon. The infighting, second-guessing, and competition represented an almost insurmountable roadblock to progress. While Alford had, and has to this day, unswerving respect for Riddick's motives, he found him to be naive, alarmingly unskilled in the necessary elements of criminal law, contentious, and sometimes pompous.[11]

When Riddick confided his intention to borrow a prosecutor from the staff of Jefferson Parish District Attorney John Mamoulides, Alford's suspicions were confirmed. Riddick called him "Johnny" Mamoulides, a casual familiarity that no one who actually knew the proud Greek would have dared employ. Further, it was evident to Alford that Riddick was unaware of the business relationship between Mamoulides and Frances Pecora, herself rumored to be a possible target of criminal investigations into the state's insurance industry. He knew the resulting publicity might be damaging to the attorney general's credibility and reputation for independence, and said so.

Finally, Alford faced personal difficulties. He lived in Covington, well over an hour away. The long hours spent in the investigation soon necessitated his getting an apartment in Baton Rouge, away from his wife and young family. It was a problem compounded by his wife's need to spend considerable time out of state caring for a terminally ill relative. Alford was getting numerous "hang up" calls at his apartment and finally his young son answered one death threat call at the family home, the caller pointing out that he knew where the Alfords lived. Irving was getting the calls as well.

By September, Alford had had enough of the disarray, the dissension, and the fractured family life. He confided his concerns to the attorney general who, typically, was unaware of any lack of cooperation within his own office. Alford declined to discuss the internal problems. He met one last time with Riddick, packed his bags, emptied his office, and went home to Covington.

Alford had one piece of unfinished business before going back to the country and the peaceful practice of small-town law: he called Frances Pecora. With the gracious manners of a southern belle and the business ethics of a barracuda, she was a familiar figure on the fringes of Louisiana political intrigue. He knew her well enough to nickname her "Frank," and had done some earlier legal work on her behalf. For many years she had been the secretary to reputed Mafia boss Carlos Marcello. Her late husband, Nofio Pecora, had been Marcello's principal lieutenant. She had done a stretch in prison for attempting to bribe a Louisiana sheriff to drop drug charges against her son, who went by the original spelling of his father's name, Nofio Pecoraro.[12]

Before going to prison she had been a high official in

the state's agriculture department; the commissioner of agriculture was himself imprisoned for extortion. Subsequently named to the powerful state insurance rating commission, Pecora and her son later formed Certified Lloyd's, one of the notoriously undercapitalized Lloyd's Plan companies, which was eventually seized and closed, whereupon she pleaded guilty to federal charges while Nofio fled the country. Pecora's principal business ally was Jefferson Parish District Attorney John Mamoulides, with whom she owned an office building in the New Orleans suburb of Metairie, a building that appeared, at grossly inflated value, on the schedule of admitted assets of her insurance company. In 1994, the building at 3445 N. Causeway Blvd. in Metairie, Louisiana—by then owned solely by Mamoulides—was foreclosed against by General American Life Insurance Company. Mamoulides owed $5.75 million on the building but General American had previously offered to settle for $3.38 million, which Mamoulides failed to raise. District Attorney Mamoulides, who filed for bankruptcy, was also being sued for non-payment of two bank loans totaling $247,072 and for another loan made to himself and a former assistant district attorney for $287,139. He had previously lost to foreclosure another building in which he was a major partner on historic St. Charles Avenue in New Orleans.[13]

In prison at the time of the Alford meeting, Pecora was still a potent political operative. Alford told her of his intention to resign and why; then he added that if anyone in his family was ever harmed, he was returning to Baton Rouge to shoot the Eichers.[14] The calls stopped immediately. Patricia King Eicher later denied Eicher responsibility for the calls. She maintained the Eichers valued Alford's presence because of his friendship with their legal advisor, Ossie Brown, and considered Alford a possible sympathetic ear during the investigation. Alford denied any close relationship with Brown, suggesting it was a self-serving fantasy on the part of the embattled Eichers.

Pecora had some gossip of her own to offer. She predicted Mamoulides was about to place his own operative inside the state's prosecution, a vantage place from which he would be able to keep informed and protect key Mamoulides allies. No one ever alleged any untoward action on the part of the powerful Mamoulides, but days later he showed up in Attorney General Billy Guste's office, his assistant district attorney, Ronald Bodenheimer, in tow, offering to "lend" his deputy to lead the prosecution team at no cost to the state. Bodenheimer, with the assistance of some newly found emergency money from the state for the investigation, was universally acknowledged to have done an exemplary job in the prosecutions that followed, although the most effective trials and most stringent punishments came in the federal courts, with the state efforts eventually becoming almost an afterthought. When Guste did, in fact, retire, Mamoulides exerted yeoman statewide efforts to make sure unknown District Attorney Richard Ieyoub, not Riddick, won election as his successor.

Bodenheimer's appearance came at a fortuitous time; Riddick had just been rebuffed in his effort to hire former assistant U.S. Attorney Pauline Hardin to manage the prosecution. A seasoned veteran of white-collar crime cases, she would have been formidable, but she had just adopted a child and was unavailable for the assignment. No one remembers Bodenheimer being on the short list for the job, or any list at all for that matter, but suddenly he was in charge of the prosecution of one of the state's most important criminal cases. The attorney general's team, riddled with controversy and jealousy, was finally in place.

Had the Eichers known earlier in the investigation how fractured the prosecution's front really was, with the U.S. attorneys in Baton Rouge and New Orleans openly competing with each other and the state attorney general's team torn by dispute and intrigue, and had their own underlings not struck their deals with various prosecutors, they might actually have been able to prevail or at least seriously delay the ultimate outcome.

Instead, the previously blind loyalty among Eicher employees was beginning to crack. It must have been a difficult time for defense attorney Tommy Damico, who was representing almost the entire second tier of Champion personnel, as, one by one, they began admitting their own roles and implicating each other. Patricia King Eicher had dismissed their longtime housekeeper, Dale Edwards, as much for financial reasons as any other. Soon thereafter, she experienced a kind of religious conversion and told the story of the fireplace inferno that took place in the heat of June, with the burning of Champion records leaving the smell of smoke throughout the house for days.[15] Even Wade, John's old ally, was beginning to sway under the pressure.

Prosecutors raided accountant Davis's offices and seized all records that could be found. Most related to other companies but that was a fine distinction with which no one bothered any longer. Most of the remaining, readily available money from Champion's affiliates, so far not involved with the liquidation, was in a trust account at the Whitney Bank. Much of it was paid to Upton, McGrew, Moore, Rolfs, Damico, and the accountants, preferential payments largely later recaptured by liquidators.[16]

The Eichers reportedly refused to pay investigator Larry Carroll the $35,000 he demanded for the last remaining videotape of the Alabama auditors, despite concern that the tape could be damaging evidence in the hands of prosecutors.[17]

Much of each day was spent raising working capital for the group. Naaman remortgaged his house and sent Tim Upton around town on a secret mission converting the certificates of deposit from the transaction into more liquid bearer bonds. The Champion fleet of twenty cars, worth almost a quarter-million dollars, including Naaman's Porsche, Tina's Mercedes, John and Patricia's Cadillacs, and others, was sold at bargain basement rates to employees or on a Baton Rouge used car lot. John took $100,000 from the sale and the last $18,000 from the escrow account and gave each of the Eichers $16,000 for a new car. The purchases were made just hours before Keogh signed an order freezing their assets.[18]

John and Naaman made a quick flight to the Cayman Islands in an effort to reclaim $100,000 belonging to Capital Insurance and $425,000 held by Orleans Bank. Capital had already given Beychok $270,000, which had been promptly consumed by costs and legal fees.

By September, the liquidators were turning up the heat. All the Eichers and most of their key employees were jailed for civil contempt of court for failure to deliver Champion's records. Tina's friends mounted a full-scale campaign to win her release in order to care for her children. Judge Keogh later set her free.

Based partly on discovery of John and Naaman's trip

to the Cayman Islands, Keogh ordered the entire group to jail for civil contempt, from which there is neither bail nor appeal. John and Patricia celebrated their second anniversary in separate cells in the parish prison, where they remained for one week.

John and Naaman now faced imposition of the previous year's sentence plus a new year each for the ill-advised trip to the Cayman Islands. The night before surrendering, family members signed proxies seeking to arrange the Cayman Islands companies to be liquidated by Cayman authorities rather than Louisiana officials. An enraged Keogh ordered all Eichers to surrender their passports, although no passport is required to go to the Cayman Islands. He also threatened an "international incident" would ensue if Cayman Islands officials did not cooperate with Louisiana authorities in gaining access to Capital Insurance and Orleans Bank monies. It was largely viewed as a harmless piece of Irish histrionics; no judicially manned gun boats were in evidence.

In order to secure their release, family members signed an agreement to allow Beychok to serve as their representative in seeking financial information from Cayman Islands authorities. Beychok found that Capital Insurance had been incorporated with $2 million of Champion's money, after which it became Champion's reinsurer, receiving $8 million in fees. Most of that flowed immediately back to the Eicher family: $1.3 million went to Orleans Bank, which loaned John $425,000 for construction of his house; $3.8 million went to South East Underwriters, the Eichers' Alabama insurance agency; $2.5 million went to Amicom, Naaman's personal company, for unspecified services; and $125,000 each went to Tina, Meredith, and Ashley. All Capital stock was held by Patricia, Meredith, and Ashley, meaning Capital had no money left with which to pay claims, as provided by the reinsurance agreement.

Lake Charles lawyer Karl Boellert later represented the Eichers in the Cayman Islands liquidations. He infuriated Beychok with mountains of motions, delays, and roadblocks. Keogh later called him "the Nazi," because of his imperious, disdainful German manner. It took near censure by the state supreme court to force Keogh to finally allow payment of attorneys fees to Boellert.[19]

By October 13, John and Naaman were jailed for the second time in two months by Keogh, who said they had made "absolutely no effort whatsoever" to help authorities liquidate Champion.

The central element of Ellis's liquidation was the "single business entity" suit, handled by his attorney Lee Kantrow. If it could be proved that all Champion enterprises were, in fact, one big business with cash flowing back and forth among the various subparts, then all assets of the remaining companies could be seized. While John and his advisors believed the claim was of dubious legal merit, they also understood the political realities of the judicial system, peppered with claims from disgruntled Champion policy-holders and persons with claims against Champion-insured drivers. The "SBE Case," as it came to be called, was assigned to Judge Doug Moreau, after comments Keogh made from the bench made it appear he might not be impartial in the matter. Moreau later left the bench to become Baton Rouge district attorney.

John decided the only way to salvage any assets of the affiliate companies was to thrust them all into bankruptcy. Both John and Naaman suffered significant physical deterioration while in jail; Patricia used her lawyer's privileges to gain access to the visiting room, where she could deliver John's medicine. The bankruptcy hearing provided an incongruous bright spot as the year wound its way to an end. Filing the bankruptcy petition halted, at least temporarily, the "single business entity" trial.

The bankruptcy hearings also provided a welcome respite to John's treatment. Federal bankruptcy judge Phillips ordered that John be allowed to change from prison orange to civilian garb for his court appearance and was unswayed by vitriolic charges by Kantrow, Ellis's attorney. Maneuvering their way through the bankruptcy hearing, with criminal charges clearly pending, required considerable skill. The most simple solution was to suffer a sudden and severe memory loss. That was John's assertion when First City Savings Bank's Diane Carney told the court he had recently withdrawn $95,000 from a Champion-related account there. Straight-faced, John maintained there was nothing either uncommon or memorable about his obtaining $95,000 in walking-around money and he was, thus, unable to recall the event. Judge Phillips was consistently fair, sometimes sympathetic. He criticized Kantrow's fees as unconscionably high, noting the deluge of costs and fees that were daily draining Champion's financial corpse of whatever assets might have remained for creditors. He derided the "single business entity" theory, upon which Champion's assorted adversaries based their offense, as fictitious, invented from whole cloth to suit the prosecutors' and liquidators' purposes. Finally, the court approved a negotiated settlement that got major creditors paid. At the conclusion of the bankruptcy hearing, John was back in parish prison, along with Naaman, who had not participated in the case since he had never been an officer of any of the Champion affiliates.

By then, Patricia, frustrated and frightened, had conducted her own personal investigation, searching the contents of the garbage bag in the trunk of John's Cadillac. What she found changed the course of her life and the Champion case in a drastic, dramatic way. In the bag was conclusive proof tying Champion to the business activities of Capital Insurance and Orleans Bank—one of the essential smoking guns sought by investigators in Louisiana and abroad. This discovery presented Patricia with a crucial choice. It was one thing to claim lack of knowledge of key Champion activities or to invoke the Fifth Amendment about her own financial enrichment from corporate funds, which she did throughout the "single business entity" hearing. Prosecutors would have had a difficult job proving that she knew what she claimed not to know, especially in the face of John and Naaman's well-established penchant for secrecy and duplicity.

That was very different from denying the existence of crucial evidence for which investigators were turning every conceivable hiding place upside down, evidence she had seen and handled and which was essentially in her possession. That evidence, coupled with her knowledge of the computer tapes hidden in Ann Parker's spare bedroom—tapes that proved Champion had secretly been operating a "shadow" insurance operation, writing unreported business beyond the limits allowed by its reserves—surely formed the basis of an obstruction of justice charge. For Patricia King Eicher, the time had clearly come to look out for herself.

First, she told Naaman of the evidence she had discovered and about her knowledge of the secreted computer tapes. Naaman, always one step ahead of the law, had an immediate solution to her dilemma. He ordered the ever-compliant Tina to move the tapes to Upton's, where they were first boarded up behind a hastily constructed, false wall and later microwaved in one last, frantic, futile effort at obfuscation by conflagration. The damning evidence from John's trunk Naaman ordered turned over to Tina for safekeeping. By this time, it had become pretty clear to Patricia that the evidence would be stored for safekeeping at the bottom of the Mississippi River or destroyed in one last backyard barbecue. Either outcome would have rendered Patricia an accessory to obstruction of justice, so she hid the evidence anew and went immediately to the offices of Brown and Moore. They hastily confronted John and Naaman and immediately thereafter withdrew from representing anyone in the case, although they did not feel compelled to return the substantial fee they had already collected (and for which they would subsequently be sued by Ellis's own legal staff).

Brown and Moore dispatched Patricia to inform McGrew of her discovery, which she did in a meeting attended by Tina. McGrew faced mounting problems of his own. He had already pleaded with Judge Keogh for permission to withdraw as counsel and he had sufficient inside information to know that the carefully crafted "united front" within the Champion organization was crumbling daily. He told Keogh that the Eichers had no additional funds with which he could be paid and he needed to be freed from the onerous task of representing a group that now seemed likely to end up against one another. Keogh pointed out that McGrew had already been handsomely paid, $110,000, and ordered him to remain. Patricia's information now put McGrew in the position of knowing that the very charges for which the Eichers had been jailed were backed by evidence. McGrew's obvious responsibility was to inform the court of his knowledge in an effort to distance himself from personal, criminal involvement. And that was precisely what he told Patricia he intended to do. He sent her home to await the results of his conversation with the court.

But no conversation took place. McGrew was so tightly bound with the Eichers' activities that he simply alerted John and Naaman of the imminent danger and then did nothing. When Patricia learned McGrew was participating in the coverup, her alarm turned to desperation. Badgered by John from inside the prison and beleaguered by Tina on an hourly basis, she simply handed the whole bag of evidence over to Tina and went back to Brown and Moore to tell them what she had done.

They sent her to see Michele Fournet, one of the city's most respected criminal attorneys. Fournet, a former teacher, came from the little down-river farm community of Poncha-toula. Fournet's gentle demeanor and wispy figure belied a bright mind and a bulldog tenacity in court. Delivering herself into Fournet's hands meant the intrigue and collusion was over for Patricia, for Fournet insisted that her representation would be ethical and aboveboard.

That meeting marked the turning point in Patricia's legal life, the point of no return in her already-strained relations with John. Michele Fournet came to represent not only sound legal advice for Patricia but virtually her only source of moral support and encouragement in the dark months to follow. Fournet agreed to take the case on her terms and, fortunately for the virtually penniless Patricia, largely on credit.

With Fournet's guidance, Patricia prepared an affidavit detailing what she knew, a document that came to be known as the "October 24th Revelation." They met with Keogh the morning after Halloween in his chambers to reveal the document, which he immediately ordered sealed for Patricia's safety. Given his knowledge of McGrew's involvement, Keogh told them he would also allow McGrew to withdraw as counsel since he might soon be a codefendant.

The furies of hell were a pale comparison to John's wrath when he learned Patricia had retained Fournet as her personal attorney. He swore she would never see a cent of the monies sequestered in the Cayman Islands, funds with which Patricia had hoped Fournet's fee might be paid.

Each of the Eichers, including Tina, who was guarding the very documents she denied existed, swore to Keogh there were no remaining documents or records. Keogh, by that time, knew better, but after thirty-nine days in parish prison, John and Naaman were processed and released. In retrospect, the contempt charge that removed John and Naaman from their free, daily management of the Champion defense accidently accomplished its purpose. Had John not been in jail, Patricia would almost certainly never have dared examine the contents of the garbage bag in his car and the "October 24th Revelation" would never have occurred. Had Naaman been free, the Tim Upton case could probably never have been built.

Upton, Champion's printer and Naaman's protégé, had been in court during one of the many appearances that took place while the Eichers were in jail. It had been a fairly routine appearance in Judge Doug Moreau's court. He was handling the "single business entity" case after Keogh's comments in open court had necessitated his withdrawal from the case to prevent possible prejudgment of the facts. Following that appearance, a cheap, plastic briefcase was left behind.

Most observers think it was carried by Upton, since

Naaman could not take it back to his cell. The briefcase lay around Moreau's chambers for weeks before a curious secretary finally examined its contents. Inside was evidence clearly linking Upton to the conversion of Naaman's certificates of deposit to bearer bonds and, presumably, some detail of the forgery of the bank statements used in the Alabama audit. Immediately upon the discovery, Upton's tax returns, financial statements, and other Champion-related documents were seized, and U.S. Attorney Raymond Lamonica held a headline-grabbing news conference to announce the pending results of his "six-month investigation," an investigation some other prosecutors believed never took place. Nonetheless, shortly thereafter, Upton struck a bargain with prosecutors in which he agreed to testify in return for consideration of a reduced sentence.

Had John and Naaman been on the street, they could almost surely have managed to reassure the raging insecurities of Don McCulloch, Champion's former certified public accountant. Instead, his contacts with the Eichers were cut off by the prison walls and he became convinced they were concocting a plan to throw the blame on him. Confronted by a thick, three-ring binder of circumstantial evidence tying him to the manufacture of the false certificates of deposit from the Alabama audit and other assorted irregularities, McCulloch began to bargain in earnest with the prosecution team from the attorney general's office.

For their part, Patricia King Eicher and Michele Fournet began the tedious rounds of state and federal prosecutors seeking limited immunity in return for Patricia's testimony. The proposed immunity agreement was an awkward construction inasmuch as it required consensus among all the prosecutors, each of whom was by then competing for center stage in the arena of pubic opinion. It was Patricia's only available option but it was probably doomed to failure from the start. Most of the prosecutors believed she was a central part of the Champion conspiracy, not an Eicher ally solely by virtue of her marriage to John. By the time she was trying to fashion a plea bargain, Upton and McCulloch were just a few sweaty moments from collapsing on their own and turning against the Eichers.

U.S. Postal Inspector Bill Bonney, who died just at the conclusion of the case, was particularly useful to the U.S. attorney's team in New Orleans. Patricia's evidence seemed a classic case of "too little, too late," and her eventual sentence was not significantly less than the rest of the Eicher inner circle of Tina, Meredith, and Ashley, who had participated in the daily direction of the conspiracy. Prosecutors failed to effectively use Patricia's inside information about other insurance scandals, for reasons yet unclear. Her assertions about the deal between Carlos Miro and Gov. Edwin Edwards to create a workers' compensation insurance captive corporation were corroborated, years later, by Miro's own confession and plea bargain, but in 1989 no one would listen.

Rumors of an assassination attempt against Judge Keogh and the state's prosecution team had been swirling around the case for months, beginning with O'Neill's initial suggestion that they all be eliminated. In macabre debates that lasted late into the nights, the prosecutors' opinions were evenly divided between those who believed the end might come when John appeared at their respective homes to shoot each of them and those who thought it more likely the devious Naaman would hire the job out to strangers who would kill them and swiftly disappear from sight.

John and Naaman had once again won release from

parish prison but this time the pair did not leave alone. When they were released, they bailed out a new team of cohorts they had met on the inside. No one pretended Robert Karras, Tony, and "Dog" were insurance experts. Their expertise lay in doing bodily harm to others, with a collective string of assault charges and explosives experience. Parish prison, like every penal system in America, was a gigantic grapevine, with a ready cadre of prisoners eager to deliver the latest gossip to authorities in return for better treatment. Consequently, prosecutors were well aware of the impending release of this new little group of Eicher allies before they set foot in the sunlight.

Prosecutors acted swiftly to prevent release of the fourth and final member of the team, however, because he was different from the others. The final member of the Eicher prison circle was a psychopath and an experienced killer. His release they could not risk, so they devised a scheme in which he was searched and found to be carrying a sharpened chicken bone. On the strength of the discovery of this "contraband weapon," he was detained without bail until the danger was past.[20]

Riddick, Irving, Keogh, and others took the emergence of this gang seriously enough to apply for permits to carry handguns for their own protection. Years later, Keogh still remembers the cold mornings on the firing range that were required for him to qualify for permission to carry the pistol. For the judge and stunned prosecutors, this was a far cry from the straightforward business dissolution case they had thought they faced only weeks earlier. They never anticipated their lives might hang in the balance.

Each of the newly freed threesome was contacted by state and federal authorities who warned them they were under suspicion and pressured them to reveal a death plot. The former prisoners denied any such arrangement but they were under constant surveillance and no one took the threat lightly.

Once back on the street, John and Naaman had to immediately regroup. Their once tight-knit band of allies now ranged from dispirited to disloyal. John and Patricia maintained a frigid truce in separate quadrants of their mansion. Their finances were in shambles, a situation aggravated when a Baton Rouge brokerage firm refused to cash the $345,000 in bearer bonds they had so carefully laundered, claiming lack of proof of ownership. Federal and state grand juries were now reviewing the newly revealed financial records and computer tapes. A new grand jury was impaneled in Montgomery, Alabama, to investigate Champion's business activities there. Orleans Bank was ordered liquidated and its half a million dollars in assets delivered into the hands of Judge Keogh, which meant the Eichers would never see those funds again. Finally, to begin 1990, most of the Eichers received formal notification by the New Orleans federal grand jury that they were official targets of an investigation into criminal wrongdoing. It was an ironic notification for the embattled Eichers, vaguely similar to a drowning man, caught in an undertow, receiving a semaphore signal saying, "Unsafe to swim here"!

The Eichers needed attorneys, except for Patricia, who had her own, and the others were openly hostile to her by now anyway. The Moore-Brown firm, of which Naaman had been openly contemptuous, had already withdrawn and McGrew was busy preparing his own prospective defense. In fact, McGrew's former associates were, at that very moment, making serious charges against him in front of a

Baton Rouge grand jury. Keogh had sent McGrew's entire file to the state bar association for disciplinary action, which was never taken, and he was already being sued for return of the large preferential payment he had received just prior to the bankruptcy, leading to his own bankruptcy in subsequent months. John contacted New Orleans attorney Helen "Ginger" Berrigan, an ACLU-connected lawyer and his former fiancé, who declined to help. She later represented Ashley and Meredith and, a few years later, was nominated by President Clinton to be a United States district judge.

Baton Rouge lawyer Jerry Schwehm declined to handle the criminal cases, although he did sign on for the "single business entity" suit, which was revived and renewed after the bankruptcy hearing ended. Finally, Baton Rouge lawyers Nathan Fisher and John DiGiulio came calling, soliciting business. They offered to represent John and Naaman if they could split a $50,000 fee as soon as it could be retrieved from the Cayman Islands. Fisher eventually received authorization for a $50,000 fee from Judge Keogh for representing John, a payment liquidators blocked, saying it was wrong to spend corporate monies for a criminal defense. DiGiulio, who represented Naaman, wound up holding the bearer bonds, either for safekeeping or as security. Fisher and DiGiulio were reserved for the pending criminal trials.

In the meantime, Judge Moreau set January 11, 1990, to start the "single business entity" trial. When Schwehm failed to appear for the trial, the Eichers asked for a postponement. Moreau refused, saying if they could not find attorneys they must represent themselves. On the other side of Moreau's courtroom was a stunning array of high-priced legal talent representing the liquidators, various prosecutors, Alabama and Louisiana officials, and creditors; the crowded counsel table looked like a regional miniconvention of the American Bar Association. Much of the Eichers' defense was handled by Naaman, who was caustically brilliant and, by most accounts, easily a match for the combined legal firepower arrayed against him. A decision reached strictly on the legal arguments of the "single business entity" theory could have gone either way; there was precedent on both sides of the issue. The political aspect of the matter was quite another thing and worked totally against the Eichers. Even as the hearing proceeded, the state insurance guaranty fund, charged with paying off the costs of Champion's collapse, publicly reported thirty thousand pending auto claims and forty thousand premium refund claims, saying the case had already consumed $23 million and would require another $127 million to complete. Indeed, by the time it was concluded, the Champion case cost more than construction of the New Orleans Super Dome.

John always believed the total should have been no more than $60 million and said there should have been sufficient assets to cover that amount. In fact, just before the bankruptcy, John had turned down an opportunity to borrow all the shortfall from an international investor, fearing publicity about Champion would eventually topple the company.

With all the publicity, the political establishment promptly went into "damage control mode," and the Eichers' defense was essentially doomed from the outset. Naaman's subpoenas to a string of high-ranking officials involved in the matter were quietly but firmly quashed by Moreau. It was no surprise to observers when Moreau ruled that all the Eicher enterprises comprised a "single business entity."

The Eichers' inner circle was thoroughly fractured. Separation proceedings between John and Patricia were underway; McCulloch emerged from thirty hours' discussion with U.S. Attorney Lamonica. John believed McCulloch and Nolan had conspired to loot Champion monies and claimed McCulloch had failed to report the free home he had been given as income. The case of "Eichers vs. Others" had in the public perception become "Others vs. Eichers," with the "others" being the insurance victims. The Eichers had become public pariahs, so their counter-assertions were never thoroughly aired.

Desperately strapped for cash, John and Naaman scraped together enough money to open the blue-collar "Essen Grill" on the outskirts of town. Their need for cash flow notwithstanding, it was an event greeted with dismay and disgust by the hundreds of area residents whose claims against Champion had gone unpaid.

The Eichers were left with precious few cards to play. Patricia asked that civil liquidation proceedings be stopped until criminal actions were completed, claiming her Fifth Amendment right against self-incrimination would be vitiated if information she gave in civil actions was used against her in the criminal cases or if such information laid bare her own criminal defense strategy. Her request was denied, although Keogh pledged to take extra care to protect her position in that regard.[21] John and Naaman asked that a mountain of documents be produced, including tax returns, audit reports, and premium finance agreements, all of which had been seized by the liquidators. Ellis responded that complying with the request would be time-consuming and unnecessary, saying the Eichers had waited five months to request the documents and this was simply a delaying tactic. The court agreed with Ellis.

In the meantime, Gary O'Neill, McGrew's former partner,

reappeared as mysteriously as he had departed. O'Neill somehow got himself named head of the Chicago Board of Ethics, a position he held for only one month before an enterprising reporter tied him to the Louisiana scandal. The resulting publicity was too much for even the jaded Chicago political climate and O'Neill resigned under pressure. Arrested in Missouri on his way back to Louisiana, O'Neill would eventually plead guilty to bank and mail fraud and agree to testify for the prosecution.[22]

In February, Ellis reported he had found no evidence that the Eichers removed money from Champion or its affiliates for their personal benefit. "Even though Champion took in $100 million a year in premiums, at any one time you couldn't find but $2 million in the company. The money goes round and round without rhyme or reason," he declared.[23] Some of the prosecutors, who secretly believed Ellis was overpaid and ill-prepared for such a monumental, specialized task, scoffed at the sparse results of his eight-month investigation. Of course, they were suing to recover millions that Eicher family members had loaned themselves and they were by then knee-deep in review of the Eichers' secret, illegal, $3 million funding of the Doug Green campaign for insurance commissioner.

On March 22, 1990, the long-awaited second shoe finally dropped, as the avalanche of indictments against the Eichers commenced. The first day's coordinated action by federal grand juries in New Orleans and Baton Rouge and state grand juries in East Baton Rouge Parish and Montgomery County, Alabama, totaled 515 indictments, with every indication of more to come. John faced 86 charges; Patricia, 62; Naaman, 97; and Tina, 73. Meredith and Ashley faced 59 charges each. McCulloch and Upton had already pleaded guilty to a single federal charge each in return for their cooperation. O'Neill's plea was just days away.

Word soon wafted in from the land of make believe. Insurance Commissioner Green's spokeswoman's sanguine statement said, demurely, "The indictments really do not affect the Department of Insurance. No one in our office has been indicted and we usually do not comment on this sort of thing until it works its way through the legal system."[24]

Given the political realities surrounding the Champion collapse, Judge Keogh's refusal to allow the Eichers to dissipate their personal funds in their defense, and the prospective testimony of former Eicher associates, there was really only one way this chronicle could conclude. On May 26, 1990, assorted Eichers assembled before U.S. District Judge Polozola to plead guilty to reduced charges. John and Naaman were to receive sentences of no more than forty-six months each and be fined no more than one million dollars apiece. All other Eichers would face only two counts apiece in Polozola's court, serving no more than six months each and receiving fines of less than $500,000 apiece. All of this put a hollow spin on Nathan Fisher's brave assertion, weeks earlier: "The indictments were certainly not a surprise, and we're confident that once we get into court we will be exonerated of criminal wrongdoing."[25]

A familiar voice was heard from the political wilderness; former commissioner Bernard predicted Green's indictment, saying he might well seek the office again. In fact he did, and was unceremoniously defeated the following election, before his own criminal troubles began in earnest. Ever the optimist, Green bravely predicted he would escape indictment. Admitting he had been named a target of the investigation, he insisted, "There is a difference in being a target and being a hit target."[26]

The same day as Green's hopeful assessment of the situation, John and Naaman entered guilty pleas in state district court to charges of forgery and filing false public records.

The subtle difference between being a target and a hit target evaporated the first week in June, as U.S. Attorney John Volz announced that the New Orleans federal grand jury had indicted Green on sixteen counts of mail fraud, money laundering, and conspiracy connected to Champion's campaign of largesse on Green's behalf. "They bought themselves an insurance commissioner," Volz said, "He [Green] agreed to give them aid and comfort and assistance and allowed them to rip off the citizens of this state."[27]

It soon developed that Green was not the only public official to provide assistance in close proximity to campaign contributions. It was soon revealed that the "limited function financial institution" charter issued by Gov. Edwin Edwards's Commissioner of Financial Institutions Fred Dent came on the heels of Naaman Eicher's $25,000 contribution to Edwards's unsuccessful reelection campaign and immediately after intercession by the governor's brother.

Shortly after the announcement that lawyers, accountants, and assorted appointees had already charged $1.4 million to dismantle the Champion empire, Green's trial began in federal court in New Orleans. It was a rocky start for prosecutors. Intellectually waterlogged with the myriad, mundane details of the case, the assistant U.S. attorney thoroughly befuddled the jury with what amounted to a doctoral thesis on the financial workings of the American insurance industry, replete with all the operative acronyms:

OFI, LIGA, NAIC, and the like. The dazed jurors struggled to stay awake, let alone to comprehend the arcane litany.

Green's attorney, diminutive Risley "Pappy" Triche, was miles better. In his opening argument, Triche was unfailingly polite. He was funny, he was well-prepared, and he was understandable.

This case, Triche said, was all about politics as usual, the way Louisiana elections have been waged since anyone can remember. Champion Insurance, harassed by Commissioner Bernard, just wanted a "level playing field," and that was all Green promised in return for the Eichers' assistance. Once elected, Green, too, was betrayed and deceived by the devious Eichers.

At the conclusion of each day's proceedings, Green appeared in front of the federal building to tell the assembled reporters he was securely confident that when his side of the story emerged he would be resoundingly acquitted. Reporters thought it a brave, if curious, daily performance, as Green, whose tall, stately wife, Linn, gamely clutched his arm in a death grip which became tighter with each passing day, blithely bubbled about the good times to come.

Inside the courtroom all was not so sanguine as Champion officials confirmed that they handpicked Green to run, giving not just millions in campaign funds, much of it concealed by fictitious "loan agreements," but an additional thousand dollars each week in "walking around money." They admitted providing Green's car and airplane, driver and pilot. They commissioned his polls, hired his campaign consultant, designed his advertising, even hired one consultant to help Green keep his campaign stories straight, and another to teach him how to dress.

On the day it was revealed that the Eichers' consultant

had instructed Green to dress only in a conservative blue suit and red power tie, both Green and his lawyer were wearing that same garb. The Eichers admitted that they demanded "buckets of whitewash" for their audit by the commissioner's office and demonstrated their notion of a "level playing field" with a dramatic sleight of the hand. They testified that they had continued their financial assistance to Green and his brother long after the election was over. It was, they intoned, Green who personally approved licensing Capital Insurance Company, Champion's Cayman Islands affiliate, one day after the application had been received, personally delivering it to Naaman's home at night, unusual service by any bureaucratic standard. Each day, more jurors moved from the defense premise of "politics as usual" to the prosecution position of "graft in general."

Even the hapless figurehead contributors, whose names had been used on fictitious loans funneled from United Financial Services directly to the Green campaign, took the stand to say they had been told that the $100,000 notes they had signed would never be collected. Lawyers for the Champion liquidators filed suit to recover the $100,000 "loans." On that night's television news, Green bravely surmised that the unwitting intermediaries might yet somehow be repaid by campaign committee fundraising events following his acquittal.

The Eichers admitted wiring $250,000 into the account of Doug Green and Associates, from where it was periodically disbursed into the campaign to create the illusion of grassroots support. Several dozen Champion-related employees admitted being pressured to give a thousand dollars each for the Green campaign and being repaid in the form of Christmas bonuses. Naaman best described the surprise selection of the previously unknown Green to make the race by saying, "I wanted someone who was flexible, with a certain moral casualness, I guess you would say."[28]

Green, by now facing a total of thirty-six federal counts, was even rocked by out-of-state testimony from another state's insurance official. Alabama Deputy Insurance Commissioner David Parsons said he told Green, in a September 1988, Michigan meeting of the National Association of Insurance Commissioners, that complaints about Champion were mounting in Alabama and he was concerned about the company's loss ratio. According to Parsons, Green replied that Champion was not in the business of making money in insurance but of getting money into its premium finance business. A representative of A. M. Best said Green gave Champion a clean bill of health in April 1988 based on its 1987 annual financial statement, which he called "a joke."

When the prosecution concluded its presentation, Green said outside the courthouse, "I don't think they've proven their case. I've never not felt confident."

Green, testifying for days in his own defense, claimed he had done no wrong. When asked what he had done to earn the thousand dollars each week from Naaman's Amicom Corporation, he said, "I really couldn't point to any one thing." Green claimed that he discovered that the $150,000 contribution by his brother really came from a Champion affiliate only after the fact. It was a bold assertion since his brother had been on the Eichers' payroll throughout the campaign and virtually totally dependent upon them for his existence.

In his summation, Triche told jurors it was not illegal to spend a lot of money or to spend other people's money. The assistant U.S. attorney responded, "The Eichers purchased some insurance. The insurance they purchased was that man," pointing to Green.

One day short of his third anniversary in office, Commissioner Doug Green was convicted of three counts of money laundering, one count of conspiracy, and twenty-seven counts of mail fraud. U.S. Attorney Harry Rosenberg asked U.S. District Judge George Arceneaux, Jr., to immediately remove Green from office. "I think that once a public official in Louisiana is convicted of thirty-one separate criminal counts in an indictment, it is time for that public official to be totally removed from public office," he said.

Some six weeks later, Green, his wife, and brother pleaded guilty to state court charges after being told they would receive the maximum sentence allowed by law. One week later, Green was arrested for trial in Alabama on theft of property charges related to Champion's operations in that state.

On June 12, 1991, Green was sentenced to twenty-five years in prison by Judge Arceneaux, who called him "amoral." Arceneaux declared, "God knows how much incalculable harm your lack of regulation has visited on the people of this state." Soon thereafter, Green received a concurrent ten-year sentence in state court in Baton Rouge.

The Eichers were left to complain of one more example of unfair treatment in the dark conflict between Eichers and others.

John Eicher received a forty-six-month sentence from U.S. District Judge Frank Polozola. Not to be outdone, Judge Arceneaux matched the forty-six months in his own sentence but did not credit John with the nine months already served before his sentence was handed down, meaning John could actually serve fifty-five months in all. Naaman felt similarly misused. DiGiulio claimed Naaman received a fifty-eight-month sentence from Arceneaux because he did not want to be upstaged by Polozola. Attorneys for both men claimed neither received consideration from Arceneaux for their testimony against Green or their cooperation with federal investigators during the nine months between the Polozola and Arceneaux sentences.

The final irony for the Eichers came months later, when both were transferred, for medical reasons, to the Elayn Hunt Correctional Facility, named in honor of John's late first wife, who had been head of the Louisiana Department of Corrections.

Green was succeeded, in the 1991 election, by former Louisiana Secretary of State James "Jim" Brown, who brought an air of urgency and integrity to the office. One of his first acts was the naming of Winston Riddick as his chief assistant; many of the Champion prosecutors soon appeared on the Insurance Department rolls. In his first two years as commissioner, Brown averaged about one insurance company collapse per month—even temporarily seizing the state's Blue Cross insurance operation—before claiming the worst was over and his department might soon be back to the business of rebuilding.

Even as Brown spoke, a major Louisiana insurer was reputed to be dangerously nonliquid, owing millions to its reinsurance companies, heavily invested in mortgages, and buoyed up only by the generous value assigned to its out-of-state properties. Owned by a prominent political figure and substantial contributor to Insurance Commissioner Brown's campaign, the company was said to have received lenient treatment from Brown when it came to allowing the properties as "admitted assets," which some experts thought imprudent, and extra time to build up the company's value before undergoing the required audit. When asked to comment on the charges, Brown's spokesman said they were raised by disgruntled former employees or dissatisfied would-be employees. Brown's position is that he halted a previously approved sale of the company, after which its asset-base was considerably enhanced by the original owners and the company is now in much more sound financial condition. Many believe, despite the lengthy period Brown allowed for internal improvement by the company's ownership before completing the audit, it is still in precarious condition and the next Champion-type insurance collapse in Louisiana is only just around the corner.

Notes

1. Naaman Eicher's federal court testimony in *U.S.* v. *Douglas D. Green* (1991). Information was also secured from interviews with Patricia King Eicher, the U.S. attorney's staff, and the Louisiana Attorney General's staff.

2. Copelin admitted his involvement in various published and broadcast interviews during the mayor's campaign, and these facts are part of the trial transcript in the original federal criminal case. It had to do with taking thousands of dollars in a meeting in a men's room.

3. Based on interviews with Patricia King Eicher and Danny DeNoux, a former Bernard employee.

4. Interview with Patricia King Eicher. In addition there were many published reports in the media.

5. Information obtained from state and federal court transcripts and from interviews with Patricia King Eicher.

6. Naaman Eicher's statement to prosecutors; also federal court testimony of Naaman Eicher and Gary O'Neill.

7. Report of the Liquidator of Champion Insurance Company. Information was also obtained from an interview with Sheldon Beychok.

8. Most of this information can be found in the court records. Additional information was obtained by interviewing Patricia King Eicher and her attorney, Michele Fournet, assistants of the Louisiana attorney general and the U.S. attorney, as well as Judge Joseph Keogh.

9. Ibid.

10. Interviews with staff members of Attorney General Guste.

11. From interview with Bill Alford.

12. Federal court transcripts and previous conversations with Frances Pecora and Nofio, Jr., on several occasions.

13. Based on federal court records.

14. Based on an interview with Bill Alford.

15. Interview with Patricia King Eicher. Also, interviews with assistants to the Louisiana attorney general, along with information from published reports.

16. Information provided by Patricia King Eicher, and from published reports.

17. Ibid.

18. From federal court transcripts; also from interviews with Patricia King Eicher, assistants to the Louisiana attorney general, and Judge Joe Keogh.

19. Based on interviews with Sheldon Beychok and Judge Joe Keogh.

20. Interview with Judge Keogh and with Winston Riddick and Steve Irving, former assistants to Louisiana's attorney general.

21. Interviews with Patricia King Eicher and her attorney, Michele Fournet, as well as Judge Joe Keogh.

22. Federal court transcript.

23. From published wire service reports based upon the insurance liquidator's report.

24. From a news release issued by insurance commissioner spokesperson Carolyn Blue Mykal.

25. Television interview, which aired on various Louisiana stations on May 26, 1990, following the announcement of indictments.

26. Ibid.

27. Federal court transcripts.

28. Ibid.

6

The Rise and Fall of Carlos Miro

"My God, I'm prosecuting children," thought Assistant U.S. Attorney Robert Boitmann when he entered the New Orleans federal courtroom for the arraignment of Carlos Isaac Miro, July 27, 1992. Carlos Miro did look strangely out of place that afternoon. Weeks short of his thirty-eighth birthday, Miro's slight figure was clad in a blue sports coat and gray slacks, crisp white shirt, and blue-and-red-striped tie. Heavy leg irons gripped Miro's ankles just above expensive loafers that had been buffed to a hard shine.

The final chapters in the remarkable, meteoric rise and fall of Carlos Miro were about to begin. He had been snatched from his Spanish exile, a 5,500-square-foot villa, and hauled unceremoniously back to Louisiana to face sixteen federal counts of mail fraud and one of money laundering for which he faced an eighty-year possible sentence and a $4 million fine.

Miro, accustomed to being surrounded by layers of lawyers and other attendants, appeared alone, telling U.S. Magistrate Ivan Lemelle that only $130 remained of the many millions he had drained from his insurance enterprises in one, short decade. This day, even Miro's appearance had to wait until the court disposed of three detention hearings for narcotics possession and distribution involving Miro's prisonmates, a trio of scruffy black defendants.

Miro's case was much more complicated, involving not just Anglo-American Insurance, the flagship of his enterprises, but scores of allied operations in exotic locales around the globe. Miro's latest caper both began and ended in exile.

Following the collapse of Transit Insurance, Miro had been lying low in London, ensconced in a Hyde Park townhouse he had earlier purchased with the proceeds of his Transit commissions. His London solicitor, Mel Stein, had recommended he stay in London to avoid being served with lawsuits surrounding his Transit activities. But Miro, driven by relentless greed and a high-maintenance lifestyle, chafed in his London sanctuary. By August 1986 he and his longtime associate Sheldon Irion began to spin anew the complicated financial web that had become their international trademark.

First London International was initially created to deal in the securities market. It was soon renamed Anglo-American Securities; then Anglo-American Trust; and finally either Miro-Irion Ventures or Miro, Irion, and Vaughn. Under each of its names it was a British organization. A subsidiary, Anglo-American Holdings, was soon created in Panama so Stein could share in 1 percent of the action. The London operation owned Anglo-American Underwriters, later named Anglo-American Group, a Texas corporation. The Texas company owned Anglo-American Insurance, a Louisiana corporation, which soon specialized in writing workers' compensation and general liability. Miro demonstrated a special skill in schmoozing with public officials, and soon wrote coverage for scores of school boards and other agencies in Louisiana.

Workers' compensation insurance was not the kind of business any prudent company could offer alone; at that moment Louisiana workers' compensation companies were paying out $1.25 in claims and costs for every $1 they took in. The large national companies were abandoning the state despite the fact that workers' compensation was a billion-dollar business in Louisiana. Unprofitable in the long term, that business did present an appealing source of immediate cash flow and an opportunity to earn big reinsurance commissions, however. Miro soon surfaced in the reinsurance field, with dealings spread from Louisiana to Taiwan.

Getting started in Louisiana required the approval of the state's commissioner of insurance, Sherman Bernard. The Louisiana license came at a crucial time for Miro; he had budgeted a quarter million dollars to getting back into the insurance business after Transit and, with Sheldon Irion drawing $10,000 each month, that nest egg was perilously low.

There were, at that time, two ways to get into the insurance business in Louisiana. The first involved the tedious, painstaking process of applying "by the numbers," proving one's liquidity and reserves and withstanding the serious scrutiny of the proposed owners' backgrounds and reputations. There was a second method, a short cut. It involved knowing somebody who knew Bernard and it involved what might charitably be called "front money." It was a method tailor-made for Carlos Miro.

In this case, the somebody was Shreveport businessman Gus Mijalis, a blustering, balding political operative. Mijalis had been on the fringes of Louisiana political influence for years, principally as an associate of Gov. Edwin Edwards. The two had twice been codefendants in a federal racketeering trial surrounding the issuance of hospital licenses, and twice been acquitted. Miro's lawyer, Dallas's J. Albert Kroemer, a former assistant U.S. attorney in the 1970s, gave a cautionary green light to the use of Mijalis to grease the regulatory skids with Bernard. The fee to Mijalis was to be $50,000, cash in advance by cashier's check, if you please.[1] Soon thereafter, Miro, Mijalis, and Bernard convened in Baton Rouge, Louisiana's capital city, and agreed upon the details of the license application. Miro would put up $1.5 million in fast cash capital, more than was required by law, to make the application look good, and he would keep his name off the application, in light of his rather unsavory post-Transit reputation.

For his part, Bernard correctly listed Gus Mijalis as the contact person for the new insurance company application but, thereafter, paid scant attention to the details of the form. Months later, Miro listed himself as president of Anglo-American, which was patently illegal since he was not an American citizen. Miro listed incorporators and directors from Texas and Louisiana, some of whom did not own the required stock to qualify for their position. John Kastner, a former New Orleans policeman who emerged as one of the directors of Anglo-American, later failed on his own at American Lloyd's and has since pleaded no contest in the 24th Judicial District Court in Gretna, Louisiana, to pocketing $2.1 million from an insurance premium payment to his company, G&R Insurance, by Frank's Casing Crew and Rental Tools, Inc., a Lafayette, Louisiana, oil field service company. The policy was never issued. Kastner told the company that insurance had been issued through American Lloyd's, of which he owned 26 percent and where he served as president. When American Lloyd's failed it left behind more than $10 million in unpaid claims. He denies knowing Miro was behind Anglo-American, saying he was approached by Sheldon Irion to participate.

In any event, Bernard proved prompt in getting the new company approved. The process, which customarily takes months, took just thirteen days. The fledgling company's capitalization was promptly raised to $5 million by adding $3.5 million in Florida real estate to the pot in return for a note from the holding company. The scheme was to pay the interest on this transaction by charging Anglo-American Insurance a 25 percent "management fee" from the holding company. This pattern worked momentarily but when Miro brought another $2.2 million to the table, repaid in the same fashion, the state balked. The management fee was cut back to 15 percent and the 10 percent difference made up by creating a reinsurance company to capture that amount as a reinsurance premium.

Mijalis, meanwhile, had cut himself in for a $100,000 annual retainer, which he took in quarterly payments for "research and public relations." The money was paid to the Pelican Agency of Shreveport. This may have been a company formed by Dan Pelican, who was also an earlier owner of National Republic Life of Shreveport, which Mijalis acquired and later sold to Anglo-American as part of their complicated dealings. Part of Mijalis's service in return for the stipend was to convince Bernard to use his influence with the Georgia insurance commissioner to grant swift approval with a minimum of scrutiny to Anglo-American Insurance's license application in that state. This was no small favor, since there is generally a three-to-five-year moratorium on granting a license to any company newly licensed somewhere else. The purpose for the delay is to allow for the first triennial audit to be conducted in the new company's home state before allowing it to expand. In Anglo-American's case, the process did not take three years. In fact, it took barely six months for Anglo-American to be suddenly licensed in Georgia, a feat for which Mijalis charged $100,000. The three—Miro, Bernard, and Mijalis—met again in Kentucky, at the National Association of Insurance Commissioners' convention, accompanied by another $20,000 which Miro brought for Bernard's campaign war chest.[2] Bernard, aware of the regulatory problems with the real estate pledged as security for Anglo-American, suggested that cash be substituted for the property. At this early point in Anglo-American's life, Miro lacked a spare $3.5 million to make this kind of cash infusion, but this revelation brought Mijalis no gloom. He simply arranged for Sam Friedman, chairman of the Nachitoches, Louisiana, People's Bank and Trust Company, which Mijalis had once owned, to make the loan, for which Mijalis charged a 2 percent finder's fee. The proceeds of that loan were supposed to be on deposit to back Anglo-American's letter of credit. However, the loan monies were soon stripped and wired to Barclay Bank in London, leaving the letter of credit with no security.

On June 15, 1994, Mijalis was indicted on fraud and bribery charges related to his actions in arranging the loan. If convicted, he faced 55 years in prison and $60 million in fines. Friedman was also indicted. The indictment claimed that Mijalis received $90,000 for arranging the loan and paid half that amount to Friedman as a bribe. Mijalis was represented by Nashville, Tennessee lawyer James Neal and Gov. Edwards's former counsel Camille Gravel. Both lawyers had represented Edwards in his 1985 federal racketeering trial in New Orleans, which ended in a mistrial.

Anglo-American was freewheeling and fast tracking these days. It went from $6 million in business at the end of 1986 to $22 million in 1987 and then to $32 million in 1988. The revenue from that amount of business, combined with Miro's creative accounting, looping, and layering meant he was soon awash in riches. Conspicuous consumption was Miro's credo and the need to maintain this lifestyle eventually did him in. When he flew, it was by Lear jet. When he drove, it was comfortably ensconced in the back of a stretch limousine. He lived in a $1.5 million, marble-floored North Dallas mansion with chambermaids and servants and a Steinway grand piano nobody knew how to play. It was all for show, engineered by a genius at the art of presentation.

Carlos Isaac Miro y Chavez was born in Havana, Cuba, on September 14, 1954. His grandfather, a dentist, had reputedly cured Spain's King Alfonso XIII of gum disease in 1936, for which he received a large diamond that has remained in the family. Miro's father was a law school classmate of Fidel Castro who fled Cuba when the Communists came to power. The family lived in Florida, Vermont, and Oklahoma before Carlos Miro, Sr., moved to Dallas in the early 1960s to complete a law degree at Southern Methodist University. Young Carlos also proved to be an apt, if easily bored student. By the time he was graduated from Highland Park High School he had amassed so many advanced credits he was able to receive his economics degree with honors from SMU in only three years. That was a substantial achievement for a young man for whom English had been a second language. Typically for Miro, it was not enough. His resume soon boasted further eduction at law school, neglecting to mention he flunked out, and a master's degree from the University of Texas, which he had never received.

Miro's first marriage floundered in his early twenties. His second wife, Becky Garnaas, was an Iowa farm girl whom he met when she worked for one of his businesses. She had never met anyone like the impetuous Miro, who quickly taught her how to live Dallas style. This was a man who thought nothing of chartering an entire coach on the Orient Express for himself and his associates. The theory was always that bigger was better, so the fine house on Glen Albens Circle was traded for the North Dallas mansion on Steuben Court at a cost of $1 million. Miro soon bought a penthouse in the Warrington, one of Dallas's most exclusive apartment buildings, at a cost of $800,000 and spent a similar amount refurbishing it. All those costs came from the company. Miro liked to call the apartment, with its mirrored ceilings in every bedroom, his Anglo Fun House.

Miro called himself "The Weasel," and said, when his first child was born, "The Weasel II has landed." He may have watched too many television episodes of "Dallas," rapidly acquiring both a driver, whom he called his "bodyguard," and a girlfriend, June Lama. She came away with a Rolex watch, a $60,000 Mercedes coupe—a Valentine's Day gift—and a credit card in the name of one of Miro's London firms. By now, Miro was pulling in $600,000 a year in salary and another $120,000 in expense money, in addition to $177,000 from the London operation.

Although he could also be tight-fisted and vengeful— he sued associate Bill Jackson for embezzling $55,000 and despises him to this day, although Jackson denied wrongdoing—in good times Miro and all his friends lived very well indeed, almost always on company money.[3] That largesse included Sherman Bernard. A year and a day after the charter for Anglo-American Insurance was issued, Anglo-

American Underwriters, the parent company, wrote a check for $25,062.50 as a political contribution to Bernard. Although there was nothing illegal at that time about simply sending Bernard the check, Miro made the gift in typical secretive fashion. He cashed the check and had twenty-five sequentially numbered $1,000 cashier's checks issued to Bernard in the names of his employees.

Miro's lawyer, Kroemer, was loaned $550,000 in company money for construction of a house. Another $60,000 went to the former wife of Sheldon Irion. The company pledged a $49,000 certificate of deposit to finance Miro's 1985 Cadillac limousine. Like draining sap from a maple tree, Miro and his associates tapped into the various companies' resources at every step. The $150,000 they had stripped from the bank's letter of credit and shipped to London eventually appeared as a promissory note to Anglo-American Trust, with which they bought Anglo-American Group from themselves. Miro said at the time, "The ultimate objective should be to create some sort of leveraged buyout as regards the insurance company stock by Holding Company A from Holding Company B, essentially the goal being to accelerate five years of earnings for the present stockholders."[4] In simple English, that means he was buying the company from himself and using insurance company money to do it.

Generating the cash flow to keep Miro's lavish life afloat required skillful, creative accounting. The principal instrument was the use of reinsurance companies to drain extra commissions. Even that was not sufficient. In the case of Blackwell-Green, an intermediary Lloyd's of London broker, Miro paid it $1.98 million. The commission for placing the insurance order was supposed to have been 7.5 percent, which should have amounted to $142,000, yet the holding company kept an additional $150,000 as the transaction passed over its desk on the way from Anglo-American to Blackwell-Green.

Miro and his associates were even bolder when it came to the creation of Anglo-American International Reinsurance, which they chartered in Ireland. Anglo-American ceded $5 million in premiums to this reinsurance operation, which consisted of a brass nameplate on a door, and $1,125,000 simply stayed inside Anglo-American Trust as the money went by. And who would complain or become suspicious? Anglo-American was stealing from itself, and only a subsequent international audit—if that ever happened— would uncover the evidence. The Irish company, which no one is certain ever existed, finally faced $4.2 million in reinsurance claims after authorities shut Miro down.

This slippery-footed financial wizardry would surely have come to the attention of regulators, so Miro devised a series of stealthy moves to hide the nonadmitted assets that were keeping the company afloat. On large policies, insurance companies collect a deposit premium that is not a down payment but an educated guess about the total eventual cost of the coverage. It is supposed to be held in a deposit premium account until the final accounting for that policy period, when money is either refunded or additional premium is billed. Such an account is a liability, not an asset. The Miro system was to credit such payments to an "interagency account," a kind of internal petty cash, general ledger fund. Doing so reduced the amount shown as a liability, since the money had been withdrawn from the premium deposit account and, at the same time, reduced the amount of nonadmitted assets by adding real cash to the general ledger fund, which had formerly consisted only of nonadmitted promissory notes. The result was to severely understate the amount affiliate companies owed Anglo-American at the same time as it understated the amount Anglo-American owed its policyholders. This was creative accounting on a scale never before seen in American insurance and pure Miro in its execution.

As the result of Miro's underpricing (offering cut-rate premiums to generate high-volume sales) and overspending began to catch up with him, an additional cash infusion was necessary. The holding company borrowed $12.5 million from a Shreveport, Louisiana, bank, $9.3 million of which soon appeared as an additional capital infusion.* The company neglected to mention that it had also pledged, as security for the loan, all its stock and every receivable and asset. This sudden, new, cash windfall enabled Anglo-American to write considerable additional business but it was terribly misleading, because it omitted the fact that virtually all the new premium income had to be immediately upstreamed to pay the holding company's loan, which soon amounted to $775,000 plus interest each month. The debt service pressure required Anglo-American to write even more and riskier business. The vicious cycle was tightened.

The collapse of Miro's empire was probably inevitable, but it was certainly hastened by Louisiana political events

---

*Lots of banks made such deals, in Louisiana and elsewhere. Most of them failed. The reason for doing such a deal lies in the charging of "points" (a percentage of the loan) by the banks to the borrower. In the short term, the revenue generated through points made the bank's balance sheet look like it was a profitable operation. Only when it was later revealed that the loans were uncollectable and should never have been made did the reality set it. This was the course of nearly 80 percent of the savings and loan and banking scandals.

during 1987. First was the rout and retreat of Gov. Edwin Edwards, a complex and controversial figure. Son of an impoverished sharecropper, Edwin Washington Edwards had grown up with an insatiable appetite for the finer things in life. After a stint in Congress, he had first won the governorship in 1971, wresting the office away from the North Louisiana Protestant establishment to become the state's first Cajun governor. He was to remain for the two terms allowed by law before sitting out the single term of icy, ineffective Republican Gov. David C. Treen. At the apex of Anglo-American's existence, Edwards was well into his third term and seeking a fourth.

Louisianians had a complicated, love/hate relationship with the dapper, charming Edwards. For most of his political career they had overlooked his rather well-established reputation as a gambler and womanizer whose friends had prospered inordinately whenever he held office. Despite continuous hounding by federal investigators, including two, nationally publicized trials at which he was acquitted, Edwards displayed a fascinating ability to stay one step ahead of the law. It was generally accepted that, at best, Edwards was "ethically challenged." It was also undeniably true that he was so fleet of foot he could dance the Cajun two-step on the edge of a dime.

Louisiana has an ill-considered "open primary" law that requires the two top vote-getters to face each other in a runoff if no candidate receives more than 50 percent of the vote. In 1987, Edwards had counted on his opponent being Republican Rep. Bob Livingston, an earnest if uninspired congressman from metropolitan New Orleans. To Edwards's horror, late in the first campaign, the Louisiana press almost unanimously endorsed the diminutive, shrill, and heretofore obscure congressman from North Louisiana, Buddy Roemer. Given last-minute momentum and a brilliant campaign strategy, Roemer placed well ahead of Edwards. Upon counting the votes and considering his suddenly limited options, Edwards abruptly quit the race, conceding the election to Roemer, and leaving legions of lackeys in the lurch.

Gus Mijalis was chief among that number, it being only possible to trade in influence if one actually has influence. To make matters exponentially worse, Miro had bet on the wrong horse in the insurance commissioner's race. One of Miro's chief competitors, John Eicher of Champion Insurance, had put some $3 million in the campaign war chest of challenger Douglas Devine Green. Miro's candidate, incumbent Sherman Bernard, had been unceremoniously dumped. It required no Machiavelli to discern the storm clouds on this political horizon.

With Mijalis about to be on the outside looking in, it was crucial to take advantage of his remaining influence in the waning days of the Edwards administration. For Miro's Anglo-American Insurance, now holding almost $12 million in essentially worthless loans to friends and affiliated companies, the cash flow chasm was becoming acute and apparent.

Miro contended he was approached by Mijalis to construct a three-way partnership with Edwards to pass a bill to create a statewide workers' compensation insurance monopoly. Six other states had similar operations in which the state ran the only allowed workers' compensation program. Miro figured the premium income would be worth at least $500 million each year. The reinsurance commission from those premiums would be worth $7.5 million annually. Miro said he, Mijalis, and Edwards were each to own one-third of the reinsurance action through yet another offshore company, Anglo-American Intermediaries of the Isle of Man, a site Mel Stein picked after considering Gibraltar, Hong Kong, Singapore, and Israel.

Edwards heatedly denies the deal, depicting Miro as a "self-confessed liar and thief."[5] While the record suggests such a person would not necessarily have been excluded from Edwards's inner circle, we do not know the details of the deal. Mijalis, in a business in which silence is golden, had nothing to say about the scheme.

What we do know is that Miro attorney David Vaughn drafted the bill, Miro remained quietly in the background making arrangements for implementation, and Edwards testified in favor of the proposal before the state House of Representatives. Had the bill passed, it would have created an eleven-person board to run the operation. Eight members of the board would have been Edwards appointees, one from each congressional district. Each district would have had a manager appointed to issue policies and collect premiums. Miro says he would have been one of those managers, in addition to handling the reinsurance program statewide. Despite Edwards's lobbying and some kind words from governor-elect Roemer, the scheme was rejected, largely because of united business opposition. A few years later, Louisiana did loan a newly created, private corporation the millions needed to create a statewide workers' compensation corporation, but it was not a monopoly.

So Edwards departed without accomplishing this objective. He may have taken some comfort in his new $75,000 annual retainer from Anglo-American Insurance.[6] Almost immediately thereafter lawyer Vaughn, by then president of Anglo-American, asked the state insurance commission if the company could buy Edwards's Texas ranch and count that equity as insurance company capital. The answer was no. Apparently Miro was not unhappy with the outcome, for he wrote to Vaughn at the beginning of negotiations, "Edwin is trying to transfer an albatross from his neck to ours (remember the $150,000 of debt service and $50,000 minimum expenses attendant hereto) and I would be quite happy to not assume the albatross and pay a $50,000 brokerage fee for the privilege of eating the albatross."[7]

Vaughn's ascension to the presidency of Anglo-American had caused a serious rift with vice president Bill Jackson. Feeling frozen out by the new management, Jackson made various demands, some of which led to his eventual loss in court of a civil suit over misappropriation of funds. Jackson burned his final bridge by going to the new insurance commissioner, Doug Green, with details of the People's Bank loan, the Irish reinsurance transaction (in which Anglo-American had itself posted the required letter of credit supposed to be provided by the reinsurer), and various other sordid details of the Miro operation.

Had Bernard still been in office, such guerrilla warfare could have been easily, although probably not cheaply, deflected. The Green regime, owing Miro nothing, struck immediately, ordering an extraordinary August 15, 1988, audit, barely one year after the last triennial examination. Miro said contract auditor L. D. Barringer offered to "fix the audit" in exchange for the presidency of Anglo-American at $150,000 per year on a long-term contract. No proof of that demand can be found, but the audit sent Miro on an international chase to raise fresh, new money for a capital infusion, the $12 million in internal loans now being public knowledge.[8] Miro offered a mysterious medley of penny stocks and interests in nonfunctioning corporations, none of which was acceptable to Green. The end of Anglo-American was clearly in sight.

By March 1989 Anglo-American was in liquidation, Miro was again in exile abroad, and an international spate of civil and criminal actions was under way. Miro surfaced almost immediately with C. I. Miro & Co., Ltd. in London and opened a Dallas, Texas office, the lease for which was guaranteed by Anglo-American. He later abandoned the handsome Dallas property, sticking the landlord with thousands of dollars in improvements and unpaid rent.[9]

The ubiquitous Mijalis now proposed that Miro purchase Mid-American Insurance Company in Bossier City, Louisiana, across the river from Shreveport, and Miro did considerable work in London to bring about the purchase. He also met with former Anglo-American director John Kastner and his ally, former Bernard investigator Danny DeNoux. Kastner's American Lloyd's had been closed by Green at John Eicher's behest and he had founded Oxford Indemnity, a Wyoming company that would itself soon bite the dust. Miro reentered the United States through Canada and traveled to Louisiana to investigate Mid-American. That deal collapsed when his London banking connection fell apart at the same time as Rep. John Dingall demanded that the U.S. Department of Justice prosecute Miro, Kroemer, Vaughn, Irion, and others.[10]

By the spring of 1990, state and federal regulators were baying at the heels of Miro's remaining American associates, Miro being once again abroad and at the time beyond the reach of extradition. Miro's Dallas attorney, Al Kroemer, effectively stonewalled the investigation, claiming he did not represent Miro, only companies in which Miro owned stock, on the one hand, while asserting an attorney-client privilege about conversations with Miro on the other.

London solicitor Mel Stein, the ultimate insider and essential architect of most of Miro's offshore activities, had jumped ship. It was a dangerous defection because, in addition to intimate knowledge of Miro's activities, Stein had been given virtual total control of Miro's international funds, which he proceeded to freeze. American Express, which had been happy to take Miro's money during his halcyon days, had forced him into involuntary bankruptcy after Stein froze his funds. That act alone sent Miro to Spain where, in considerable financial discomfiture, he decided to open a simple insurance sales agency.

Miro had access only to the remaining $60,700 cash value on his equitable life insurance policy in Dallas. Months of conflicting accounts and chaos ensued as Miro attempted to get his hands on the cash: the money was missing, the agent was missing, the policy was changed, a forgery affidavit was necessary prior to payment. Finally, Equitable in New York ordered him to report to "Expresso Express" in Madrid to pick up the funds, a transparently clumsy concoction that a less desperate Miro would have spurned out of hand. Emboldened by spurious advice from his new, Spanish attorney that he could not be extradited, Miro appeared at the purported "Expresso Express" location. The trap sprung, his next stop was the federal detention facility in New Orleans.

Power of the Pen—Type B

Life looks quite different from the other side of the bars. Entrepreneur-in-exile Miro had peppered the media with a barrage of press releases, mostly generated by Kroemer's Dallas law office, stoutly denying his guilt. In September 1989, one such release was rigidly self-righteous:

> During the course of Anglo-American's existence, I personally did not make one underwriting or accounting entry, and did not make any significant policy decision without advice from inside and/or outside legal counsel. Quite simply, I was extremely careful as a result of the experience I had arising from the Transit maelstrom. I have heard myself accused of a lot of things, but I have yet to hear the charge of stupidity. So what went wrong? Politics.

From the safety of his vantage point in Spain, Miro had exclaimed in another news release, "I view these developments with amusement, disbelief, horror but mostly chagrin." If Miro found travel to be broadening, however, he apparently found incarceration to be downright instructive for it was a far different Carlos I. Miro who appeared before Rep. Dingall's congressional investigations subcommittee.

It was a perfect media moment for Dingall, as a newly chastened Miro testified,

> No one more than I would like to rewind the clock and undo the irresponsible actions, and violations of the law, undertaken by myself and my colleagues which with the benefit of hindsight I truly regret; particularly as those actions caused harm to policyholders and others. So I

sincerely appreciate the opportunity to at least partially mitigate the damage we caused by assisting the subcommittee in its efforts to shed light on questionable insurance industry practices.[11]

Then, in forty-seven pages of alternately remorseful and self-serving testimony entered into the *Congressional Record*, Miro proceeded to recount the ways he had schemed and strategized to bring about a $35 million insurance failure. For good measure, Miro threw in a handful of insights about how to protect the insurance industry from people like himself. It was a stellar performance that did not sway New Orleans federal prosecutor Robert Boitmann, who subsequently sniffed, "It's like a friend of mine in Chicago says; if he's not sorry to have done it, he sure is sorry to have been caught."[12]

Miro's subsequent guilty plea earned him an eight-year sentence; he is presumably continuing to cooperate with state and federal authorities in their prosecution of other figures involved in insurance fraud.

Miro's associates suffered similar fates; the unfortunate Bill Jackson pled guilty to three counts of mail fraud and his insurance license was revoked by Louisiana. In the first wave of indictments, in addition to Miro, Sheldon Irion, Anglo-American Insurance Secretary-Treasurer Mario Mendiola, and the Irish reinsurance company's accountant and managing director Brian Hynes, were all convicted of assorted federal charges. Kroemer and Stein were indicted but have not yet been tried. They face maximum sentences of forty-five years imprisonment and a $1.5 million fine or twice the loss caused by the alleged fraud. Edwards was never charged. Mijalis remains a well-connected Edwards insider and Edwards won reelection in 1991. After first announcing that he would run for a fifth term as governor of Louisiana, Edwards later decided to leave politics in 1996 at the end of his current term.

Notes

1. Transcript of statement of Carlos Miro to the Subcommittee on Oversight and Investigations, U.S. House of Representatives Committee on Energy and Commerce, May 19, 1993.

2. Ibid.

3. From interviews with Carlos Miro, and from numerous published sources.

4. Report of the Subcommittee on Oversight and Investigations of the U.S. House of Representatives Committee on Energy and Commerce, February 1990.

5. Interview with Edwin Edwards.

6. Transcript of the Subcommittee on Oversight and Investigations of the U.S. House of Representatives Committee on Energy and Commerce, April 1989.

7. Ibid.

8. Statement of Carlos Miro to the Subcommittee on Oversight and Investigations of the U.S. House of Representatives Committee on Energy and Commerce, May 19, 1993.

9. From a statement by Miro's landlord to the *Dallas Morning News.*

10. Statement of Carlos Miro to the Subcommittee on Oversight and Investigations of the U.S. House of Representatives Committee on Energy and Commerce, May 19, 1993.

11. Ibid.

12. Interview with Robert Boitmann.

7

The Crisis Continues

By 1990 there was a virtual stampede to closure on the issue
of the insurance crisis. Regulators, congressional investigators, insurance industry officials, and assorted media types
around the nation joined in a ritual of relief and resolution.
America's insurance crisis, they agreed, was ended. Only
one-tenth the proportion of the savings and loan collapse,
it had been largely contained by the end of the 1980s. It
had been painstakingly exposed and brilliantly prosecuted
and now it was out of sight, out of mind, and out of gas
as a headline grabber.

Five years after Rep. Dingall's subcommittee drew
capacity crowds at the insurance industry hearings, there
was one last 1993 media spasm when Carlos Miro emerged
from prison to engage in a creative *mea culpa*. The headlines
from Miro's appearance were mostly drawn from his
description of political corruption and management larceny.
Scant notice was paid to his assertion that he could replicate
his carefully crafted criminal corporation again, any day he
chose to do so.

State insurance regulators, notoriously nervous about

196

all the media mucking about, were competing with each other from coast to coast as they declared victory and departed the battlefield. Insurance industry officials, seriously buffeted by the previous decade's crisis of confidence, were relieved to conclude that the crisis had finally entered the "clean up" stage. And the major American media, notorious for its short attention span, were anxious to be off to some new feeding frenzy down the road.

The only difficulty with sounding the "all clear" signal was that it was dangerously false. Of the Sinister Seven, those states in which half the insurance company failures occurred (New York, California, Pennsylvania, Texas, Illinois, Florida, and Louisiana), only New York appeared to be emerging from the siege. Within the twelve months immediately preceding the completion of the manuscript of this book, major insurance company failures were reported in Alabama, Arizona, Arkansas, California, Connecticut, the District of Columbia, Florida, Hawaii, Illinois, Kansas, Kentucky, Louisiana, Michigan, Mississippi, Missouri, New Jersey, North Carolina, Oklahoma, Pennsylvania, Tennessee, Texas, and Vermont. Many of these failures involved companies that operated in all fifty states. It is simply premature to declare an end to this crisis, no matter how mightily we may wish to do so. In short, the crisis continues, primarily because we have treated some of the symptoms but left several root causes untouched.

One of California's highest-paid insurance industry lobbyists, Clay Jackson, was sentenced to more than six years in prison for racketeering and mail fraud. The $2-million-a-year lobbying legend was indicted along with his codefendant, former State Sen. Paul Carpenter, but Carpenter fled the country, purportedly to seek improved medical care abroad.

California's first elected insurance commissioner, John Garamendi, felt sufficiently secure in his clean-up efforts to mount a full-time campaign for governor. Garamendi had succeeded the hapless former commissioner Roxani Gillespie, who had done everything but put out the welcome mat for insurance thieves. Her legacy of regulation required Garamendi to mount a 1992 spurt of seizures of offshore insurance schemes, closing fourteen companies with assets ranging from none to $1.1 million. Garamendi operated a gargantuan thousand-employee department with a $93 million annual budget.

Unfortunately, a bare handful of California criminals fell into the net, hundreds of thousands of dollars were thrown into the wind by lush-living insurance department administrators while victimized consumers were getting nothing, and $1.7 million was simply looted by Garamendi's department from the assets of failed insurance companies.[1]

Even with a $93 million budget, largest of any state insurance regulator, Garamendi couldn't keep up. On July 1, 1993, his chief investigator gathered employees from around the state for a giant "mail processing party" at the Insurance Department headquarters in Los Angeles. For three days, senior investigators just opened the mail, sacks of unopened letters, consumer complaints, regulatory agency reports, and related correspondence reaching back to the day Garamendi took office.

Key Garamendi administrators literally helped themselves to the remaining assets of failed companies, grabbing equipment for themselves, appropriating furniture and other items for use by the state, or selling items among themselves at prices they set for each other. The department's conservation division cavalierly commingled funds from various failed companies, invested and lost money on high-risk stocks, and even allowed Merrill Lynch to invest hundreds of millions in assets from failed companies without ever inquiring about what fee they were paying for that service. Faced with evidence of such misdeeds, including lavish "employee lunches" and benefits, Garamendi eventually conceded that the remaining funds should have gone to small policyholders and creditors of the companies, not to fuel the insurance department's own lifestyle. He undertook some minimal efforts at an internal clean-up.[2]

The policyholders and creditors frequently got nothing, not even timely information about the status of their claims, while insurance department functionaries were dining on the companies' remains.

The United Bonding Company is a perfect example. The Indiana company was seized by state insurance regulators in 1971. Less than two years later, checks were prepared for claimants but never sent. It has been so long, no one now remembers why not. Each year, the California Insurance Department billed the Indiana insurance commissioner for services rendered on behalf of California claimants, although apparently the "services" consisted of preparing that statement.* The United Bonding funds represented a kind of internal, petty cash fund for the California insurance department. Had United Bonding's remaining funds been invested in 1971, even at minimal interest, creditors would now be looking at $2 million. Today, no one is sure what remains of the United Bonding estate.

---

*Each state insurance department is entitled to bill the state where an insurance company is "domiciled" (in this case Indiana) for services rendered in the liquidation of the company on behalf of the state's residents (in this case California).

Such charges, along with claims that well-placed law firms were receiving astronomical fees while victimized policyholders were getting nothing, were a significant factor in Garamendi's unsuccessful attempt to gain the Democratic nomination for governor as a populist, a "man of the people." Garamendi had served fourteen years in the state legislature and lost two statewide races prior to being elected insurance commissioner. The proposal to make that post elective, Proposition 103, was the only one of five insurance reform plans to win favor with the voters in 1988.

Insurance commissioners' appetites for advancement were bipartisan and bicoastal in 1994, as Florida commissioner Tom Gallagher was denied the Republican gubernatorial nomination in favor of "Jeb" Bush, son of former President George Bush. Incumbent Gov. Lawton Chiles won reelection.

Unmarried millionaire Gallagher may be one of the most eligible bachelors in America. In his second term as insurance commissioner, he was best known either for decorating his office in Ralph Lauren wallpaper immediately after winning election to the $94,000-per-year job, or for wrestling some $100 million from Metropolitan Life for deceptive sales practices. Gallagher also filed charges against eighty-seven agents of MetLife, the nation's second largest life insurer, asserting they sold life insurance policies to customers who believed they were buying retirement plans. Other states soon followed suit, literally, and MetLife's practices came under close scrutiny around the nation.

Gallagher also barred insurance companies from deserting Florida in the wake of Hurricane Andrew in 1992. It was a move that was probably illegal but bought the state sufficient time to pass legislation limiting the number of insurance customers companies could cancel and to establish a state insurance plan for people who couldn't find coverage in the regular insurance market.

Minor Florida insurance frauds continued, including one classic pyramid scheme, operated by American Family Benefits Group, Inc., of Orlando, in which the company solicited members for a $99 fee that entitled them to commissions when they brought in new members. Benefits were to include a $70,000 life insurance policy that did not exist. Insurance regulators in several states became aware of the scheme and the Louisiana Insurance Department issued a cease-and-desist order. The investigation continued in 11 other states.

A Miami post office box was the conduit for applications and payments sent to Gerald Thornton's Mid-Atlantic Representative Association, Ltd., its premium finance company, First Premium Services, Ltd., and a worthless British Virgin Islands insurance company. Applications and premium payments were shuttled overnight to the Turks and Caicos Islands. By the time he was stopped in October 1993, Thornton had taken in $1,696,420 in truck insurance policies and had exactly $52 left. The Thornton case mainly involved action by Louisiana Insurance Commissioner James H. Brown, Jr., whose staff uncovered the scheme. Brown and his staff worked with regulators from the British Virgin Islands and the Turks and Caicos Islands. Thornton was convicted and sentenced to 3.5 years in jail and fined $7,000.

Problems continued for Blue Cross/Blue Shield companies in the 1990s as well. Mississippi Insurance Commissioner George Dale was indicted in January 1994 for taking a payoff to hide management problems at Mississippi Blue Cross/Blue Shield. Dale was also indicted for collecting some

$100,000 in campaign contributions from insurance companies, diverting the monies to his own use, and failing to report the funds as required by law. Both indictments were dropped, at least for the moment, by federal authorities who sought the right to bring future charges after further investigation. Prosecutors filed motions saying that the original indictments no longer "adequately encompass the nature and scope of defendant Dale's conduct now being discovered." Dale responded, "It's a witch hunt and I'm still it."[3]

Mississippi Blue Cross had been under investigation for some time. It also operated Louisiana Blue Cross after the previous Louisiana operation collapsed. Eventually Louisiana closed the Blue Cross operation there, company president Aaron Johnston was indicted, and a new Louisiana board and management was established.

At that time, there were sixty-nine Blue Cross-Blue Shield companies operating in the United States, providing insurance to 68 million Americans. The U.S. General Accounting Office (GAO) charged that eleven of the plans were in serious financial trouble. After two years of hearings, a U.S. Senate report in 1994 found "a very distrubing pattern . . . (including) poor management, extravagant expenditures and not enough interest in detecting health care fraud." Among examples uncovered by Senator Sam Nunn's Permanent Subcommittee on Investigations: The Maryland operation took sixty-four people to the Olympics and paid $300,000 for a sky-box at Oriole Stadium; New York's Empire operation maintained two sets of books; the Ohio operation paid its executive $1 million per year and spent an additional $2 million on sky-boxes at two stadiums; several states' operations were floundering, and several state Blue Cross-Blue Shield executives resigned under fire while the national spokesman for the various state associations was paid total compensation in excess of $1 million annually, a cost eventually passed through to individual policyholders. Key to the Blue Cross-Blue Shield system's profitability is a long-standing federal tax break in return for which the various state operations are supposed to offer equal rates to policyholders. In fact, the GAO study found, only one-third of policyholders were offered equal rates, and forty-five of the sixty-nine companies successfully avoided taxes on $1.5 billion in resources using the tax breaks. The national organization's executive, Bernard Tresnowsky, challenged those conclusions and said the reports were full of "serious misunderstandings or errors."[4]

By early 1994, twenty people had been convicted and sentenced in Louisiana and another ten were awaiting trial.

But prosecution of what was potentially the state's largest insurance failure had barely begun.

The Plundering of Southshore

Southshore Holding Corporation lasted only two years, a period from 1989 to 1991, but cost policyholders and investors well over $200 million. The Louisiana inspector general charged that Southshore officials looted millions of dollars in premium income and valid assets, exchanging them for worthless or negligible assets when they took control of Midwest Life Insurance Company, Public Investors Life Insurance Company, Fidelity Fire and Casualty Insurance Company, and Public Investors Inc.[5]

[continued on page 207]

ORGANIZATIONAL CHART
DECEMBER 31, 1989

SOUTHSHORE HOLDING CORP.
11/1/89* (LA)**

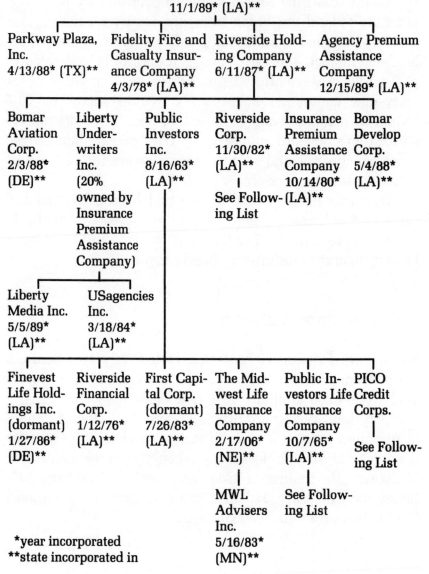

Parkway Plaza, Inc. 4/13/88* (TX)**	Fidelity Fire and Casualty Insurance Company 4/3/78* (LA)**	Riverside Holding Company 6/11/87* (LA)**	Agency Premium Assistance Company 12/15/89* (LA)**

Bomar Aviation Corp. 2/3/88* (DE)**	Liberty Underwriters Inc. (20% owned by Insurance Premium Assistance Company)	Public Investors Inc. 8/16/63* (LA)**	Riverside Corp. 11/30/82* (LA)** See Following List	Insurance Premium Assistance Company 10/14/80* (LA)**	Bomar Develop Corp. 5/4/88* (LA)**

Liberty Media Inc. 5/5/89* (LA)**	USagencies Inc. 3/18/84* (LA)**

Finevest Life Holdings Inc. (dormant) 1/27/86* (DE)**	Riverside Financial Corp. 1/12/76* (LA)**	First Capital Corp. (dormant) 7/26/83* (LA)**	The Midwest Life Insurance Company 2/17/06* (NE)**	Public Investors Life Insurance Company 10/7/65* (LA)**	PICO Credit Corps. See Following List
			MWL Advisers Inc. 5/16/83* (MN)**	See Following List	

*year incorporated
**state incorporated in

ORGANIZATIONAL CHART
DECEMBER 31, 1989

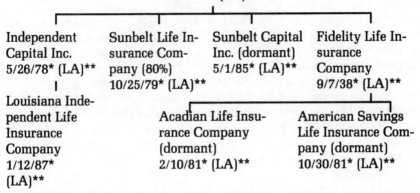

Public Investors Life Insurance Company
10/7/65* (LA)**

Independent Capital Inc. 5/26/78* (LA)**

Louisiana Independent Life Insurance Company 1/12/87* (LA)**

Sunbelt Life Insurance Company (80%) 10/25/79* (LA)**

Sunbelt Capital Inc. (dormant) 5/1/85* (LA)**

Fidelity Life Insurance Company 9/7/38* (LA)**

Acadian Life Insurance Company (dormant) 2/10/81* (LA)**

American Savings Life Insurance Company (dormant) 10/30/81* (LA)**

*year incorporated
**state incorporated in

ORGANIZATIONAL CHART
DECEMBER 31, 1989

PICO CREDIT CORPORATION SUBSIDIARIES

1) Public Investors, Inc. DBA MPress Printing
2) Public Investors, Inc. DBA PICO Credit Corp. of Baton Rouge
3) Public Investors, Inc. DBA PICO Credit Corp. of Houma
4) Public Investors, Inc. DBA PICO Credit Corp. of Lockport
5) Public Investors, Inc. DBA PICO Credit Corp. of Monroe
6) Public Investors, Inc. DBA PICO Credit Corp. of Ruston
7) Public Investors, Inc. DBA PICO Credit Corp. of Shreveport
8) PICO Credit Corp. of Calcasieu, Inc. (inc. 4/6/70, State of Louisiana)
9) PICO Credit Corp. of Jena, Inc. (dormant) (inc. 4/6/70, State of Louisiana)
10) PICO Credit Corp. of Lafayette, Inc. (inc. 12/8/86, State of Louisiana)
11) PICO Credit Corp. of Lake Charles, Inc. (dormant) (inc. 4/19/67, State of Louisiana)
12) PICO Credit Corp. of Many, Inc. (inc. 5/10/65, State of Louisiana)
13) PICO Credit Corp. of New Orleans, Inc. (inc. 8/2/88, State of Louisiana)
14) PICO Credit Corp. of New Iberia, Inc. (inc. 10/20/87, State of Louisiana)
15) PICO Credit Corp. of Slidell, Inc. (inc. 3/10/88, State of Louisiana)
16) PICO Mortgage & Credit of Lafayette, Inc. (inc. 6/20/85, State of Louisiana)
17) PICO Mortgage & Credit of Metairie, Inc. (inc. 5/20/85, State of Louisiana)
18) PICO Credit Corp. of Kenner, Inc. (inc. 8/19/88, State of Louisiana)
19) PICO Credit Corp. of Mandeville, Inc. (inc. 2/9/89, State of Louisiana)
20) PICO Credit Corp. of Harvey, Inc. (inc. 2/20/89, State of Louisiana)
21) PICO Credit Corp. of Alexandria, Inc. (inc. 3/20/89, State of Louisiana)
22) PICO Credit Corp. of Winnsboro, Inc. (inc. 3/20/89, State of Louisiana)

ORGANIZATIONAL CHART
DECEMBER 31, 1989

RIVERSIDE CORPORATION SUBSIDIARIES

1) Beth Corporation (80%) (inc. 10/11/83, State of Louisiana)
2) Gimel Corporation (65%) (inc. 6/19/84, State of Louisiana)
3) UNO Corporation (65%) (dormant) (inc. 2/12/83, State of Louisiana)
4) Riverside Insurance Services, Inc. (dormant) (inc. 9/23/82, State of Louisiana)

The failure of Public Investors cost hundreds of small investors and policyholders their insurance annuity benefits—in many cases their life savings. By the time it collapsed, thoroughly plundered, it had $635,000 in assets against $65 million in liabilities.[6]

Louisiana Insurance Commissioner Doug Green had allowed a series of questionable transactions including one of the most notorious cases of "property flipping" ever seen in America. Parkway Plaza, was an unfinished twenty-one-story office condominium in San Antonio, Texas. It was first sold, on December 14, 1988, by the Federal Savings and Loan Insurance Corporation (FSLIC) to Hickory Development, Inc., for $1.5 million, with another $2 million in outstanding liens. Hickory was an in-house corporation of a real estate firm controlled by a Southshore principal, and thus began the incredible escalation of the value of Parkway Plaza, without its ever being completed or the first tenant attracted.

On November 30, 1989, Jackson arranged the sale of Parkway Plaza for $3 million, to a new company, Parkway Plaza, Inc., which he conveniently headed. This sale included a $500,000 vendor's lien in favor of Hickory. Still unfinished, the property had now doubled in claimed value.

On December 8, 1989, Parkway Plaza, Inc., sold the building to Public Investors, Inc., for $10 million. That sale consisted of $3 million in Fidelity Fire and Casualty stock and $7 million in cash. The cash went from Jackson's Parkway Plaza, Inc., to Southshore Holding Corp., which Jackson also headed.

On December 15, 1989, Public Investors sold the building to Insurance Premium Assistance Corporation (Southshore's profitable premium finance operation), which forgave the $10 million in alleged debt.

On December 18, 1989, Insurance Premium Assistance Corporation sold the building to Fidelity Fire and Casualty, which forgave $10 million in alleged debt. Fidelity now carried the building as a $10 million asset on its annual report to the Louisiana insurance commissioner.

On April 1, 1990, Fidelity sold Parkway Plaza to Southshore for a $10 million promissory note. Southshore promptly exchanged the promissory note for ownership of the Young Ranch in Colorado. The ranch had been appraised at less than $750,000 but Fidelity, its new owner, valued it at $13.6 million and reported it to have a market value of $15.2 million.

April 3, 1990, Southshore sold Parkway Plaza to Concorde Capital, Inc., a Nevada shell company owned by a Jackson associate, for a $15 million promissory note.

That same day, Concorde sold Parkway to Midwest Life for $17 million in cash. That amount included $2 million Midwest had already advanced to pay off liens on the property ($500,000 of which went to Jackson's Hickory Development Co.). Concorde used $1.05 million to buy the Young Ranch and $6 million to pay an outside loan. The remaining $7.8 million went to Southshore.

June 14, 1990 arrived and events demanded rapid additional flipping of the property. On this day, Midwest sold Parkway Plaza for $17 million to three companies that were not even in existence, and listed the sale as a mortgage asset even though it was not completed until September of that year.

One year later, the three companies (Nineteen Story, Inc.; Top Rise, Inc.; and Keller Properties, Inc.) used a convenient escape clause to cancel their purchase of the property, but by then the deteriorating Parkway Plaza still had not been completed or occupied and probably never could be without significant repair. Nonetheless, it had ballooned in value, through insider trading, from $1.5 million to $17 million in transactions that drained money out all along the way.

In the same spiral of transactions, the Young Ranch had been allowed to be listed as a $13.69 million asset on the books of Southshore, substituting for the previous Parkway Plaza listing, an arrangement approved by the deputy Louisiana insurance commissioner. Interestingly, the same appraisal company, Appraisal Group, Inc., of Miami, Florida, valued the Young Ranch at $15.2 million and Parkway Plaza at $26 million, highly optimistic appraisals, to say the least.

As with other instances during the decade of the 1980s, the staging of this elaborate ploy was primarily to pump up the admitted assets of the main Southshore company so it could continue in business, living off premium finance income, as it heaved in an ocean of red ink at all other units of the operation.

Southshore had been created from the skeleton of a previous holding company, Bomar Investment Company, later called Riverside Holding Company. Bomar had originally bought Midwest Life in 1987 using worthless Public Investors Life stock and vastly overstated Alliance Life stock as collateral. The proud, old company had been around since 1906 and was licensed in twenty-nine states. Southshore had been lauded as a white knight when it came to save Riverside, a deal facilitated by Hunter Wagner, a prominent Louisiana Republican operative, along with Jerry Willis, chairman of Insurance Commissioner Doug Green's transition team, who had previously advised Champion Insurance.

Fidelity Fire and Casualty, one of the Riverside companies, was insolvent by the end of 1988. Its major asset, at least in terms of staying in business, was that it had Jerry Willis on its payroll. That relationship was very helpful in getting Commissioner Green to grant a full year for it to gather additional capitalization. An examination of Public Investors Life (PILICO) showed that it, too, was insolvent, but again Green took no action. Part of Bomar's plan to rescue Fidelity involved selling the entire operation, although the plan Green approved made no provision for dealing with the insolvency of PILICO. Hunter Wagner and Bernard Mason owned Financial Associates, Inc., which, in turn, owned 22 percent of the stock of Southshore. Wagner was also employed in another capacity as a public relations advisor and lobbyist for Southshore and made commissions from Southshore for deals he arranged.

When Green was indicted for public bribery, a secret session was held at the Petroleum Club in New Orleans. At that meeting, troubled insurance companies that had received favorable treatment from Green decided to raise money purportedly for Green's reelection but actually intended for his criminal defense. They created, in effect, a "Doug Green Defense Fund." Southshore, through itself and a dozen aliases and associates, began funneling money to the Green effort.

Like all else in life, nothing was for free. The quid pro quo was that Green would name the companies' own nominee as his next deputy insurance commissioner. That was a particularly crucial choice because if Green were convicted the deputy commissioner would succeed him. Southshore's choice was Hunter Wagner and, at a meeting at the Holiday Inn on Siegen Lane in Baton Rouge, Green finally offered Wagner the position. Green, in turn, secured a position with a Southshore affiliate for his brother, Donald, who was later convicted in the same bribery case.

When Green was convicted, Wagner did, in fact, assume the office but almost immediately State Inspector General Bill Lynch, a former crusading capitol newspaper reporter, and Attorney General Billy Guste, met with Wagner. They strongly suggested Wagner recuse himself from all South-shore dealings and make that decision public. Wagner did so and retired State Supreme Court Chief Justice John Dixon was appointed ad hoc commissioner solely to handle the Southshore matter as liquidator. When Jim Brown was finally elected commissioner, it took court action to get the liquidation moved back to the Insurance Department's regular—more experienced and far less costly—staff, where the investigation and various litigations continue to this day. They pointed out Wagner had been on Southshore's payroll as a consultant and his signature was on a $2.9 million loan document between Southshore's Midwest Life and Lake Lots, Inc., owned by Jefferson Parish District Attorney John Mamoulides. In 1990, Midwest Life had sold off nearly $40 million in conservative assets and put about half the money in companies owned or controlled by Southshore's owners.[7]

The acquisition required a public hearing, purportedly held December 15, 1989. John Fontenot, department attorney, served as hearing officer. The department was represented by Tom Bentley, Green's assistant at the time and a man who later went to prison as part of the Green case; Malcolm Ward, later censured as a certified financial examiner; and powerful Baton Rouge lawyer Frederick Tulley, who still represents the Insurance Department. No transcript or tape exists of the meeting, but it was at this time that Tulley and the others accepted Parkway Plaza as a $10 million asset.[8]

The huge network of some fifty Southshore subsidiaries

became known in 1991 when newspapers in Louisiana, Texas, Arkansas, and Florida reported that Midwest Life and Public Investors were in deep trouble. The Nebraska Department of Insurance, which supervised Midwest Life, was already taking steps to control that company's manipulation by Southshore. The Texas Insurance Department began a similar review, eventually going to court to seek the right to review Midwest's books. By then, Nebraska had suspended Midwest and the company had moved its operations to friendly Louisiana. Texas required Midwest to post an additional $5 million cash to continue to do business in that state. Louisiana exerted no such regulatory review.

Southshore subsidiary Fidelity Fire and Casualty, formerly Public Investors Fire Insurance Company, was the cash cow. By 1990, a third of its assets consisted of the Parkway Plaza building. Fidelity wrote the same high-risk business as Champion. Its premium income rose from $7 million in 1988 to $26 million in 1990. Because the Parkway Plaza building was so overstated on its reports, Fidelity was actually insolvent from the day it was acquired by Southshore. Nevertheless, because of its ability to generate large premium volume, yeoman efforts were exerted to hide that fact and to prop up Fidelity's life-support systems. Southshore stripped $7 million from Public Investors and diverted it to Fidelity in December 1989. Midwest Life also ponied up some $7 million to keep Fidelity alive.

Some 466 shareholders in PILICO and Midwest Life joined in a suit against the state, alleging the state protected the interests of property and casualty insurance buyers through use of the state's Insurance Guaranty Fund but that stakeholders in the two life insurance companies were not similarly protected. The suit may eventually reach $10 million as additional defendants join the action. The action also says the state was guilty of regulatory mismanagement by allowing Southshore to loot the assets of its subsidiaries. The plaintiff's group was named "PICO/Midwest Action Group, Inc."[9]

Fidelity's (and Champion's) policies were marketed through USAgencies. The policies were financed through the Insurance Premium Assistance Company (IPAC) and the Agency Premium Assistance Company (APAC), which were really one and the same. The idea was that the premium finance company would lend the premium amount to the customer, pay it to Fidelity, and then collect from the customer on a monthly basis at interest rates of up to 100 percent. In practice, while the finance companies collected from the customers, Fidelity rarely got paid. Meanwhile, the IPAC premium finance notes were bought by Southshore or Jackson's Coastal Loans Acquisition Company. The APAC notes were sold back to Fidelity, USAgencies, and U.S. Premium Corporation. Those companies then reduced the amount APAC owed them for payments APAC had collected on policies.

IPAC was both a premium finance agency and a limited function financial institution, that quasi-bank entity under Louisiana's quaint law. Under that structure, IPAC could issue certificates of deposit. Unfortunately, when finally challenged, the certificates were unsupported and therefore ultimately worthless. IPAC issued $28.5 million in such certificates of deposit to PILICO. Upon challenge, IPAC simply dumped the certificates and issued an equally worthless two-year debenture in the same amount. Had the debenture not been included in PILICO's assets, the company would have entered the 1990s insolvent.

The unfortunate Parkway Plaza and its wildly over-priced counterpart, the Young Ranch, were only the tip of the corporate iceberg when its came to Southshore's far-flung real estate speculations. The balmy climes of Florida became a locale of choice for Southshore's principals. First, they created Master Holding 98, Inc., which they sometimes called Master 98 Holding, Inc. On September 13, 1990, Midwest Life Insurance Company transferred $8,323,670.69 to a Master 98 account. These funds were used to purchase first mortgage notes from Master Holding 98, notes with principal balances of $8,871,448.10. This little transaction came at a time when Midwest Life was in such a precarious financial condition it had no business speculating in real estate to begin with.

Even worse, the mortgage notes came from the Grant Street Bank in Denver. Grant Street was an entity created to sell off the bad loans held by Mellon Bank. Master 98 bought these poor-quality, nonperforming loans at a big discount, as much as fifty cents on the dollar. Master 98 then immediately turned around and pledged the notes at their original face value in return for the cash taken from Midwest Life. The Southshore principals also arranged for Midwest to transfer some quality automobile loans it had previously purchased to Master 98. In return, Midwest got a promissory note from Master 98, secured by the poor-quality loans.

In the savings and loan scandal, this kind of transaction was sometimes called "trash for cash." The traditional question regulators ask when they see obviously one-sided deals of this kind is "Why didn't the victim company properly investigate the collateral?" The answer to that question, regulators and prosecutors suggest, is obvious: Midwest did know because the entire transaction was handled at the Southshore corporate level, where both Midwest and Master 98 were run. Essentially the owners were buying from themselves, fleecing Midwest and draining off mountains of cash in the process.

A similar arrangement was structured with 98 Holding Inc. (not directly related to Master Holding 98). Southshore principals Robert Shamburger and Gary Jackson had an option to purchase 100 percent of 98 Holding. Then Midwest Life transferred $2.6 million to the trust account of the Florida law firm of Commander, Legler, Werber, Dawes, Sadler and Howel. In return, Midwest got a $2,575,000 promissory note from 98 Holding, signed by vice president Peter Bos.

Bos was chairman of the Bos Group, Inc., a holding company controlling more than sixty corporations, including the Sandestin Corp. The Bos Group was owned 50 percent by 98 Holding, 45 percent by Bos, and 5 percent by Bos Group president Leon Murphy. Sandestin Corp., which was in bankruptcy at the time of this loan, effectively controlled the Sandestin Beach Resort and much of its undeveloped land in South Walton County, Florida.

Using the Midwest cash, 98 Holding bought back three Sandestin Corp. promissory notes. Birmingham, Destin Partners received $2,239,68. Relgel Holding, Inc. got $102,810. Comlaw, of which law firm partner Mitch Legler is president, got $102,810. Midwest eventually got paid for the note after Sandestin Resort was sold but lost $200,000 in the deal.

Midwest loaned Online Investment Corp. $900,345.33 on April 4, 1990. The same day, Online's president, Kenny Ross, gave Midwest a promissory note for the same amount, secured by assorted mortgages Online said it owned totaling $932,500. One of the mortgages, dated the same day, was for $92,500 and was signed by Ross personally. The entire debt was eliminated when the mortgages were replaced by stock in American British Enterprises.

Online Investment Corp. also got $200,000 from Midwest for purchase price deposit on The Tops'l Beach and Racquet Club. Online never bought the property but simply assigned its option to Midwest. Midwest then sold the option to purchase the club for $5 million to L'Spot Corp., for a promissory note signed by Kenny Ross, president. The same day, that obligation was assumed by Tops'l Management, Inc., executed by president Kenny Ross.

So far, Midwest had lost the option and the $200,000 but that was not enough. In August 1990, Midwest loaned three L'Spot subsidiaries $2 million each to purchase the Tops'l Beach and Racquet Club. The three, Overlook Corp., Technology Building, Inc., and Sands Tops'l Corp. each gave a $2 million promissory note to Midwest for security. The very busy Kenny Ross signed yet again, this time as president of Overlook Corp.

Midwest wired $5.8 million to various Florida bank accounts, money which, together with the original $200,000, made up the purchase price. By now, Midwest had surrendered its $5 million purchase option to a third party and then loaned the third party $6 million with which to exercise the $5 million option. Given such astute financing management, Midwest's failure was inevitable. The Louisiana Insurance Commissioner finally sold the property in 1994 for $8.7 million, making a $2.5 million profit on the transaction, which he proudly contrasted to the Federal Resolution Trust Corporation which was, at the same time, selling some of its seized properties for dimes on the dollar.[10]

Similarly, under the rule of Southshore, Midwest wound

up carrying on its books a whole host of insanely overstated common stock. Midwest claimed its common stock in Fidelity Fire and Casualty was worth $7,722,000. Fidelity's major asset was the Young Ranch. If the ranch were added at its true value, Fidelity was insolvent and its stock was worth nothing.

Midwest showed $4 million in common stock of American British Enterprises, Inc. (ABE), on its June 1990 quarterly statement. Essentially, Midwest claimed each share was worth $1.38. Actually, the par value was $.001 per share, the company had been dormant prior to 1989 and lost $47,845 that year, meaning it did not meet even the minimal requirements for investment. American British Enterprises, then known as Conoil Exploration, Inc., had lost its capitalization drilling for oil at a $40,000 loss back in 1982 and had been dormant until discovered, renamed, and reorganized just in time for the Midwest transactions. ABE, with $211 in the bank, had obtained a subsidiary, Interstate Drilling Company, from Southshore principal Shamburger in April 1990, which promptly lost another $129,059. ABE then reemerged as Reserve Energy and Capital Corporation, which proudly indicated $10.2 million paid-in capital reserves and Kentucky mineral reserves worth $10.3 million, which were later described as nearly worthless. In an effort to have the ABE stocks included as an admitted asset, the Louisiana insurance commissioner was told that more than 110,000 shares of stock had been traded for prices ranging from $1.25 to $1.50 per share. Actually, there had been only one transaction, an insider deal at $1.00 per share, solely for purposes of "making a market," creating the illusion of activity.

Midwest Life also claimed an asset of $5.1 million in common stock of a theater company called Little Prince

Productions. This stock had been a contribution to Midwest by Southshore to pump up its assets. The insurance examiner later reduced its value to $877,000 but Little Prince was lame, generating no income at all, and its stock was probably worthless.

In short, the Louisiana inspector general asserted that $111,859,408 had been drained by Southshore, mostly from Midwest, but also from Fidelity Fire and Public Investors. It was a particularly cruel irony that Midwest had been charged almost a million dollars for management fees during the time it was being looted. To Midwest's innocent policy-holders, so cruelly victimized, paying Southshore for its services must feel like being held up with one's own pistol!

In 1993, Louisiana Insurance Commissioner Jim Brown filed suit against twenty-five people from seven states. They included Southshore principals, former Bomar/Riverside principals, business associates, and Brown's own predecessor, Douglas D. Green. The suit was unique in that it was filed in federal court as a civil action under the RICO, racketeering and organized crime, statutes. Brown acted in his official role as liquidator for various Southshore companies. He sought treble damages in each case. For Midwest Life that amounted to treble $63 million; for Fidelity Fire, treble $23 million; and for Public Investors, treble $36.5 million. Some of the defendants Brown was unable to locate; others, like Green, were already in prison. All of the defendants are under indictment and most of the cases have yet to come to trial.

The Louisiana Legacy

Southshore was certainly the largest but by no means the lone remaining insurance calamity facing Brown. In fact, he had already identified sufficient insolvencies to stretch into the beginning of the next century. One of the more interesting ones began to unfold in early 1994, when Louisiana filed suit against the former president of the state senate, Michael O'Keefe, and his son-in-law, Eric Schmidt, and others for looting Physicians National Risk Retention Group, with resultant losses that could top $40 million.

Physicians National first opened for business in Louisiana in 1987 under the administration of then-Insurance Commissioner Sherman Bernard, to whose unsuccessful reelection campaign it contributed mightily. Physicians National followed the classic pattern for disaster: it was undercapitalized from the day it opened, then bravely proceeded to sell medical malpractice insurance as much as 60 percent more cheaply than its competitors. When you're losing money on every sale, the only reasonable approach is to make it up in volume! So Physicians National developed a nationwide reputation for insuring every medical professional, no matter how poor his or her previous experience. That open door policy resulted in $20 million a year in premiums. Inevitably, it also resulted in huge court judgments that the company lacked the reserves to pay.

The crisis came just at the time Louisiana was between insurance commissioners. Perhaps among insurance commissioners would be more accurate. Commissioner Green was in prison; his predecessor, and Sherman Bernard, was counting the days until he too would be indicted. Green's successor, interim commissioner Hunter Wagner had resigned to manage a bridge. Darrell Cobb, the newest interim commissioner, was inexperienced at his new job and now faced restructuring a complex, nationwide insurance outfit that was about to collapse.

Then along came Michael O'Keefe, one of the most complicated figures in Louisiana public life. He came from a fine family, which included a former mayor of New Orleans and a secretary of the navy. In the state senate, O'Keefe had been nicknamed "the Spider" because his political machinations purportedly left no tracks. Someone obviously found some tracks because his twenty-four years in public office were followed by eighteen months in prison after he was convicted of swindling his own business partners out of $900,000.

That apparently struck Cobb as perfect preparation for the world of insurance ethics because, in short order, O'Keefe was on the scene at Physicians National and his son-in-law was the company's new president. Immediately thereafter $15.4 million went south, literally, to a Bahamian company, Builders and Contractors Insurance, all with the blessings of Cobb and state officials. Those funds were supposed to provide coverage for any new claims that might be filed before the expiration of the remaining 2,500 policies issued by Physicians National. Of course, this left existing claimants entirely unprotected but somehow in the changing of cash nobody thought to consider that.

Now, obviously a Bahamian company needs an associate on the scene in New Orleans to handle the day-to-day claims management responsibilities. It didn't have to look far at all to find Associated Insurance Consultants of New Orleans—Eric Schmidt, president and principal stockholder, and son-in-law of Michael O'Keefe. Cutting up the company's cadaver proved highly profitable for Schmidt. He struck a deal with Physicians National by which he would receive 90 percent of the company's profits. Apparently it occurred to no one at the Louisiana Insurance Department that the best way to guarantee big profits under such a lucrative arrangement would be to deny payment of legitimate claims. In any event, Schmidt quickly earned $1.6 million in fees and another $3.2 million in profits.

O'Keefe credits "good claims management" and "luck." That's not how the original directors of Physicians National see things. They've filed a federal racketeering suit to recover some $15 million they believe was looted by O'Keefe, Schmidt, and others. O'Keefe claims innocence about the structuring of the deal; "I didn't understand any of the things they were doing. I'm not an insurance man." Cobb now says if he had it to do over again he wouldn't.

The founder of Physicians National, who actually is an insurance man, thinks he knows why this turned out to be such a good deal for Schmidt and company. First, Builders and Contractors avoided any liability for claims that had already been filed by terms of the agreement. Second, he thinks any doctor with a history of medical malpractice was immediately cancelled to lower future claims. O'Keefe says none of that is true. The facts are made more difficult to ascertain because the final contract establishing the agreement has disappeared.[11]

Cobb says he only approved the agreement after Baton Rouge lawyer Johnny Moore assured him the state and policyholders would be protected. Moore represented the state insurance department in the liquidation of Physicians National. He had previously, for a time, represented the principals of Champion Insurance at the time of their indictments. Moore was arrested and charged with allegedly stealing $527,000 from Physicians National as this story unfolded and has since been unavailable for comment. The Insurance Department's consultant who structured the arrangement remembers O'Keefe as proposing most of the details. O'Keefe now claims not to remember that.[12] What is not in question is where the money went and who made the profits, and it clearly was not the policyholders of Physicians National. In October 1994, the Louisiana Insurance Department paid over $11 million in early settlement of claims filed against doctors and other health-care professionals who had been insured by Physicians National.[13]

Even as that story was developing, Louisiana insurance regulators released the results of their examination of Louisiana Blue Cross and Blue Shield, the state's largest health insurer. It found that $20 million had been diverted out of company funds for purposes such as a $5,000 country club membership, $5,577 for meals at one of New Orleans's most exclusive restaurants, $18,675 to pay for a single board meeting at New Orleans's Windsor Court Hotel, and $2,042 for an oriental rug for the president's office.

Louisiana Insurance Commissioner Brown instituted new management of the company including a new president, P. J. Mills, former legislator, insurance and banking executive, and chief of staff to Gov. Buddy Roemer, and a new board that included the widow of Brown's former law partner.

The department moved to revoke the license of a Shreveport insurance agent, Jimmy Garrard, who had simply copied the motor vehicle report forgery scheme first devised by former Insurance Commissioner Green when, as a college student, he began to work for John Eicher. Garrard's system was simple: he requested motor vehicle computer reports for prospective customers, regenerated the reports on his own computer removing speeding tickets and drunken driving convictions, and then insured the customers at lower rates than they deserved, pocketing the difference. Garrard was only unmasked when the insurance company writing the policies, Midland Risk Insurance Company, lost one of the reports, obtained another directly from the state Department of Motor Vehicles, and discovered it didn't match.[14]

Much of the early part of the 1990s was consumed with disposing of the few remaining assets of failed Louisiana insurance companies. A historic downtown New Orleans headquarters of one company was sold for $2 million, and a fleet of luxury vehicles from various companies—including a Jaguar and a Mercedes Benz limousine convertible—brought in another quarter million dollars. Getting tough with insurance companies delinquent in filing financial reports earned another $400,000 in fines and late fees.

Perhaps the crowning achievement of Brown's early tenure was his proposal for an $11.6 million sale of Automotive Casualty Insurance Company. The company had previously been declared insolvent, meaning it would normally have simply been liquidated and closed. Brown's unique system was to restructure the company—his people called it "New Co."—and run it while searching for a buyer. The result was that nearly $9 million in assets were returned to the estate of the former company prior to the sale plus the $11.6 million sale price, all of which would go to the state guaranty association. The previous owners of Automotive Casualty objected, claiming the company was never insolvent to begin with and should have been returned to them or they should have received the proceeds of any sale.[15]

*   *   *

As the 1990s approach the halfway mark, the fanfare of failure still reverberates throughout the industry. Clearly, American consumers face a continuing crisis in which there are fewer insurance companies from which to choose, particularly so for high-risk customers; rates continue to increase; and the crisis in consumer confidence has by no means been resolved. Consumers have witnessed all of the shadow and none of the substance of real, meaningful reform and they anxiously await action.

Notes

1. From interviews with staff members of California's Insurance Commissioner's Office; see also reports in the *Sacramento Bee*, the *Los Angeles Times*, and other papers in the area.

2. Ibid.

3. Federal court documents.

4. General Accounting Office report on Blue Cross-Blue Shield operations, 1994; transcript of testimony before the U.S. Senate Permanent Subcommittee on Investigations, 1994; Report of the Subcommittee, 1994.

5. Report of the Inspector General, State of Louisiana, December 11, 1991.

6. Ibid.

7. Interviews with Louisiana Insurance Department staff, interview with Inspector General Bill Lynch, in addition to published reports in the *Baton Rouge Morning Advocate* and the *New Orleans Times-Picayune*.

8. Ibid.

9. District court documents, Alexandria, Louisiana.

10. Press release from the Louisiana Insurance Department.

11. Interviews with Louisiana Insurance Department; interview by former State Sen. Michael O'Keefe. There were also published reports in the *Baton Rouge Morning Advocate,* the *New Orleans Times Picayune,* and various wire service reports.

12. Ibid.

13. Information supplied by the Louisiana Insurance Department.

14. Report of the Louisiana Department of Insurance.

15. Information obtained from interviews with members of the Louisiana Department of Insurance; additional information was provided by court transcripts.

8

Fine Tuning the Future

Based on what we have learned about the decade of greed and incompetence, the ultimate question remains: "Should government act to fundamentally alter the way the American insurance industry operates?" A pure, free-market economist might argue that the system is inextricably self-correcting; the weak, poorly managed, or criminal operations ultimately fail. That of course is true. But the problem with the paradigm is that, while we are standing around waiting for them to fail, all manner of innocents suffer. The victims range from the insurance consumers who buy from these companies on the strength of their having gained state authority to operate, to well-managed insurance companies that lose business to these buccaneers and then pay extra to the state guaranty funds to compensate for their collapse, to the state taxpayers who bear the eventual burden for each failure.

As a matter of public policy and basic fairness, there is a general consensus that government should not stand idly by and allow another $10 billion insurance industry failure. The real question then becomes, "If insurance reform and strengthened regulation is necessary, should individual states or the federal government be in charge?"

The Case for the States

State regulators argue they are closest to the problem and thus best positioned to exercise direct, cost efficient control of insurance companies operating within their respective jurisdictions. They also point to their respective records in cleaning up the wreckage left in the wake of more than five hundred insurance company failures in recent years. There is some truth to that assertion. Some states have compiled impressive records for managing the costly cleanups. One of the better examples of the new breed of state insurance commissioners is Louisiana's James H. Brown, Jr. A former state senator and two-term Louisiana secretary of state, Brown was a high-powered lawyer before being elected Insurance Commissioner based on his pledge to clean up the state's insurance mess. So serious was the problem that Brown took his oath of office early, a practical necessity since his elected predecessor was in prison. Brown capitalized on the consensus for change to hustle through his state's legislature a number of key reforms and increased funding for his department.

It will cost Louisiana at least $1 billion to clear the wreckage from what may eventually total eighty insurance company failures. So weakened were the reserves of the state's guaranty fund it was able to pay only 30 cents on the dollar toward claims against insolvent property and casualty companies for many months, a problem that has since been partially corrected, partly by the $60 million or so that Brown has recovered by digging among the remains of the failed companies. Brown's recoveries included an exclusive Florida resort, a Colorado hunting lodge, a short-line railroad in Missouri, a virtual fleet of luxury automobiles, and the only motel in President Clinton's hometown.

The recovery was neither quick nor cheap. Brown says it takes about three years from the time he starts collection activity until he sees some money. In the meantime, he will have spent about $12 million in legal fees for asset-recovery suits in every state and twelve foreign nations and another $3 million in outside liquidators. To his credit, Brown has moved much of the liquidation and recovery activity inside his department, where it can be operated considerably more efficiently. One of the great scandals surrounding the insurance crisis has been the resultant feeding frenzy in many states where "insider attorneys" suck up the few remaining assets of failed companies at exorbitant hourly fees, leaving virtually nothing behind for the claimants whose interests they were supposed to protect.

Some other states have adopted professional, aggressive reform and recovery programs run by top-flight insurance commissioners. Texas's J. Robert Hunter, formerly head of the National Insurance Consumers Organization, is a good example. Arriving in time to clean up the worst of the Texas mess, Hunter now supervises thirty-five companies in either supervision or conservation status. Under Texas's unique law, the names of those companies cannot be revealed to consumers or anyone. Hunter's liquidation oversight division oversees twenty-eight special deputy receivers who are liquidating another eighty-seven insurance companies. Other respected state regulators include New York's Salvatore Curiale and Missouri's Jay Angoff. Curiale steered through the New York legislature a package of bills including workers' compensation reform that resulted in an average rate reduction of 5.3 percent in 1994. New York began producing an annual consumer automobile insurance guide, stiffened criminal penalties for filing false insurance claims, required insurance agents to take approved continuing education courses in order to keep their licenses, improved the state's supplemental uninsured motorists law and proposed a continuing series of legislative proposals to increase insurance company solvency and protection of consumers.

The record of competence and commitment does not, by any means, extend to every state. Some insurance commissioners went straight to jail, others are under indictment or have left office in disgrace. Most state regulators lack the staff and financial resources to effectively monitor the far-flung insurance company empires they theoretically control. Despite a budget the size of some Third World nations, the California insurance department can't even seem to open the mail the same year it is received.

As part of the research for this book, each state insurance commissioner was asked questions that would yield information consumers should have a right to know in judging the effectiveness of their state's insurance regulation. These questions included:

- The number of insurance policyholders whose coverage was cancelled or non-renewed because of the insolvency of their insurance company between 1983 and 1993 (the period of this study).

- The total dollar value of civil and criminal recovery by the Insurance Department during that period.

- The number of criminal prosecutions in insurance-related cases during those years.

- The number of troubled or "watch list" companies currently under supervision.

- Specific proposals for insurance reform proposed or supported by the state's insurance commissioner.

One year later, the results of this request for basic information from each state's insurance commissioner are these:

- New York sent a comprehensive response with copies of legislation, annual reports, and consumer publications, but had no idea how many policyholders were left in the lurch, how many criminal cases were filed or against whom, or how much was recovered from failed companies.

- Alabama had no information either, although it knew nine companies were still in liquidation and two in receivership. It claimed to be working for a Fair Claims Practices Act.

- New Jersey sent a postcard saying it would reply in the near future. One year later, the near future has not yet arrived.

- Nevada said it had neither the budget nor the personnel to answer the letter.

- Florida had none of the information either but suggested a visit to Tallahassee, saying that "with considerable time and diligence" one could locate the facts somewhere in its files.

• No other state responded to the questions.

The point is that it is imperative to have such information if a state is to effectively protect consumers or administer regulatory reform legislation. There must be a baseline of data from which to begin. If a state insurance regulator has no clue how many policyholders have had coverage cancelled, it is impossible to know how many people in the state were unable to find affordable replacement insurance or how many now have no insurance at all. When insurance regulators have no idea how much money was recovered from failed insurance companies, is it any wonder no one can find out where that money went? If state insurance commissioners have no idea how many criminal prosecutions are pending, how secure can consumers be that the same insurance crooks have not simply moved down the street and opened for business again under new company names?

The state insurance commissioners have their own fraternity, the National Association of Insurance Commissioners. This country club for insurance commissioners holds fancy dress balls around the country and issues a toothless, voluntary "certification" program of minimal regulation standards.*

---

*When a state insurance department seeks to become certified (accredited) it is reviewed by an independent team of auditors selected by the NAIC. They assure not only that the state complies with the laws and regulations contained in the NAIC accreditation standards but with various regulatory and organizational practices that are also part of the standards. The recommendation is passed on to the NAIC committee on financial regulation standards and accreditation, which makes the final decision. There is an annual review and a formal, on-site five-year review of each accredited state. Thus there is considerable leeway in how various standards are enforced and applied in various states.

It also runs a kind of "early warning system" designed to alert individual commissioners that an insurance criminal from somebody else's jurisdiction is about to set up shop in their state. Eighteen states do not meet the association's minimal standards, although every state has made at least some effort to strengthen its regulatory abilities.

The Case for the Feds

Most experienced observers of insurance regulation have pretty well given up on the ability of frequently inept, generally impoverished state authorities to protect consumers from insurance fraud. These experts believe the pattern of fraud is so pervasive that only the federal government can effectively regulate the insurance industry. Similar concerns led to passage of the federal Occupational Safety and Health Act, federal air and water standards, and national civil rights laws.

State authorities, of course, scoff at that claim, saying if you like the way the federal government saved you from the savings and loan and bank corruption, at a price tag that has long since passed $150 billion, you'll love federal control of the insurance industry. Nonetheless, federal control may soon become the only game in town.

When it comes to national insurance reform, the principal player is Rep. John Dingall, a Michigan Democrat. Dingall has become to insurance reform what Rep. Henry Gonzalez, D-Texas, is to banking reform. In fact, the two aging Roman Catholics share a moral passion for their missions. As he approaches seventy, critics say Dingall is growing increasingly abrasive and isolated, after a forty-year congressional career that has so far earned him a pension worth more than $2 million.* Nevertheless, Dingall's position as chairman of the House Committee on Energy and Commerce has provided an excellent vantage point from which to view the nation's crazy-quilt pattern of insurance regulation. When he made himself chairman of his own subcommittee on oversight and investigations, Dingall guaranteed himself a place on the evening news while the insurance corruption headlines were hot. Some suggest his interest in insurance reform seemed to flag once the television cameras moved on to other subjects, and he has now become a Clinton administration point man for national health insurance.

But the fact remains that only two important pieces of insurance reform legislation emerged from the thousands of hours of congressional testimony and pages of posturing on the subject, and both were sponsored by Dingall. The first was HR 1290, the Federal Insurance Solvency Act of 1993. Dingall's bill would establish a Federal Insurance Solvency Commission to oversee the financial soundness of the insurance industry. The commission's role would be to investigate insolvent insurers that hold federal certificates of solvency to determine the cause for their failures and to study the insolvencies of other insurers. The legislation would create a database of persons convicted of insurance crime, administratively disciplined for insurance-related activity, or who have served as senior officers or directors

---

*Congressional pensions are based on length of service plus additional public service at all levels (i.e., military, local government, and so on).

of insolvent insurers or reinsurers. This is information that state authorities do not now possess.*

The commission would establish national standards for interstate insurance operations and issue a federal certificate of solvency to companies that meet the criteria. It would also prohibit individual states from regulating the financial condition of such companies. There would be a blue ribbon category of "highly capitalized," federally certified insurers who would, thereafter, be virtually exclusively regulated by the federal government and not by individual states. The bill would also provide for federal certificates for reinsurers, and regulate financial institutions operating reinsurance trust funds, including foreign banks operating in the United States.

The commission would have exclusive control over mergers, acquisitions, and transactions involving federally certified insurers and reinsurers and shared power in cases where a holding company has both federally and state-certified insurance or reinsurance operations under its control. The bill would also create a National Insurance Protection Corporation, a nongovernmental, nonprofit corporation to provide timely payment against losses and continuation of coverage in the event of insolvency of federally certified insurers. This fund would be the national equivalent of the states' individual guaranty funds, with member insurance companies contributing to the fund. The commission would serve as receiver for liquidation or rehabilitation purposes for any failed federally certified insurer.

---

*Many states do not have statutes barring persons who are convicted of crimes or sanctioned by insurance regulatory agencies from developing an insurance company within their jurisdiction.

The bill would also create a National Association of Registered Agents and Brokers, essentially a national registration center and clearinghouse for interstate insurance producers. It would also establish a Federal Insurance Regulation Advisory Committee.

Essentially, the bill would create a two-tiered system of certifying insurance companies, as in banking, in which there are federally chartered and state chartered banks and savings institutions. The bill could well represent the first step in a federal takeover of the licensing of insurance companies and insurance agents. Presumably the federal commission would have sufficient staff and resources to finally get a handle on some of the more egregious holding company violations, "rent an asset" schemes, slipping across state borders to avoid prosecution, and the like. It might also bring some sense to the criminally complex structure of false-front offshore reinsurance companies that have plagued the American insurance industry for years.

The second important piece of Dingall legislation was HR 665, the Insurance Fraud Prevention Act of 1993, introduced as part of the omnibus crime bill. This bill basically restates the statutory language that makes bank fraud a federal crime. The problem for prosecutors, up until this point, has been that state laws against insurance fraud were either nonexistent or pathetically weak, forcing some states to prosecute insurance crimes under arcane computer fraud statutes, while federal statutes were insufficient, meaning most federal insurance crimes were prosecuted as mail fraud cases, leading criminals who were filing false reports to use courier services in order to avoid the mails.*

The bill makes it a federal offense to knowingly, with intent to deceive, make a false statement or report, or to materially overvalue land, property, or security in connection with regulatory reports. It would make it a federal crime to embezzle or misuse funds or property while serving as an insurance company officer, agent, director, or employee; to make a false entry in any report; or to use threats or force to obstruct justice in any insurance investigation affecting interstate commerce.

Insiders' Opinions

Both pieces of legislation would go a good distance toward fulfilling recommendations from persons on the inside of the insurance crisis who have reason to know what needs to be done. Federal prisoners serving time for their roles in insurance failures have suggested a variety of improvements to the present scofflaw system. Former Louisiana insurance commissioner Sherman Bernard believes increased qualifications should be required for people wishing to operate insurance companies. Bernard says that people with simple insurance sales backgrounds are not sufficiently qualified to control the growth and operations of insurance companies; they are too sales-oriented to set appropriate limits for their own companies.

---

*The federal government is prevented from regulating the insurance industry. The McCarran Act acknowledges the states' rights to regulate insurance.

Carlos Miro suggested to congressional investigators a number of important steps that should be taken to protect consumers from people like him. Miro said it would not be difficult for him to find figureheads to operate companies on his behalf, except that he would hesitate to do business with them because they would have to be "out-and-out crooks to do business with Carlos Miro." He recommended, however, that regulators take a closer look at beneficial, not just nominal, shareholders, "shadow" directors, "silent" partners, consultants, and intermediaries. He pointed out that a person could derive all the benefits from a company through commissions without actually showing up as an owner at all. He also recommended that managing general agents be outlawed or treated as branch offices, making the insurance companies responsible for their actions. Miro further recommended independent actuarial as well as financial audits, saying most insurance companies set their own reserves without scrutiny and pay little attention to the triennial examinations because they are relatively cursory. Miro said investments should be in real money, not land or speculative stocks from which capital would not be readily available to pay claims. He also decried the present "letter of credit" system of security for foreign reinsurers, saying such security should be in posted, U.S. funds.

Finally, Miro said insurance companies should be judged on a "risk to capital" system, not the present "surplus to premium" system, which allows a company like Transit, with only $40 million in capital, to leverage itself into a $4 billion deficit, a hundred times its net worth. Miro correctly noted that banks can't lose more than they lend and can't lend more than they have, but insurance companies stand to lose many times their total assets and premium income, as Transit proved.

How Can You Protect Yourself?

How can you protect yourself from unwittingly buying insurance from a sham company? How can you protect yourself from buying useless insurance? How can you protect yourself from being mistreated by your insurance company?

You can never be entirely safe but you can take meaningful action on your own behalf. It isn't easy and you have to do it for yourself; you can't rely entirely on someone else to protect you. But the results are worth the effort. After all, your family spends as much as 15 percent of its income on all forms of insurance. This year, Americans will spend almost $500 billion on all kinds of insurance.

You can protect yourself before the sale by understanding what insurance is all about, what kind of insurance you need and how much of it you need. There are some excellent books, written in basic English any consumer can understand, that will help you in this task. One of the best is *Winning the Insurance Game,* by Ralph Nader and Wesley Smith. New York's elected consumer advocate, Mark Green, called it "the best consumer-friendly insurance book ever written."

Taking time to think, to compare prices and coverages, is an important step. No smart shopper would buy the first car he or she sees without reading *Consumer Reports* or comparison shopping for features, costs, and rates. Yet all kinds of shoppers who know better will insure their new car, on which they may still owe $20,000 or more, with the lowest-priced company they can find, never asking about the soundness of that company or the reputation of its agent. The same applies to health, homeowners, life, and all other insurance coverage. When your mother told you, "If it looks too good to be true, it probably is," she was absolutely right!

Before You Buy

There are two kinds of insurance buyers: One buys with crossed fingers, hoping the coverage will never be needed. The wise consumer, on the other hand, buys carefully, only after reviewing all the facts and then with a jaundiced eye toward what will happen if the need for claims payment ever arises. Sadly, that is the moment when most consumers discover they don't have the kind of coverage they believed they were buying or they have no insurance at all. Simple steps taken before the purchase can protect you from future financial misfortune in many cases.

1. Decide what insurance you need and how much you can afford to pay. Think about what the chances are that you may suffer loss and how much you are willing to pay for protection from loss. Remember, the costs for the same coverage may vary by hundreds of percent so shop around for the best, most responsible deal. Rethink your needs as your situation in life changes.

2. Don't buy insurance you don't need, or more than you need. Many customers have a number of duplicate policies protecting against the same thing, such as a number of inexpensive life insurance policies. Only when their survivors attempt to file a claim do they discover there is fine print in the policy called "Coordination of Benefits," which means they can only collect from one policy and they have been paying premiums to the other companies for nothing.

3. Shop and compare. Rates vary widely for the same coverage. Many companies have discounts for which you may qualify but you won't know if you don't ask. Examples are nonsmokers discounts, discounts for homes equipped with smoke alarms, and so on.

4. Take your time. Make no promises; sign nothing until you have shopped around. If the insurance representative says this policy is only available right now, say goodbye!

5. Get another opinion. Ask friends, neighbors, coworkers, and relatives for the names of companies with whom they have had good or bad experience.

6. Don't succumb to high pressure or intimidation. Beware of the salesman who drops names of important insurance customers or who sells policies based solely on his or her religious affiliation. When you ask questions about the coverage, don't just take the word of the salesperson. See where it says so in the policy—and if you can't understand the policy, you have a right to a written explanation in plain English.

7. Know who you are dealing with. Every hustler with a briefcase is not necessarily a licensed insurance salesman. Ask to see his or her insurance license and call your state insurance commissioner to see how many complaints have been filed against that company. Your Better Business Bureau also maintains such information, but you should check with both sources before buying anything.

8. Check the stability of the company. Probably the easi-
est reference book to understand is *Best's Insurance
Report,* which is published annually and should be
available at your public library. If you have an accounting background and fancy yourself especially astute
in insurance matters, *Best's Report* also lists some of
the more than 100 individual ratios used to determine
the rating of each company in specific categories.

Tracking the Paper Trail

Remember that buying insurance protection is only the first
step. You must also be prepared to demand payment in the
event you need to file a claim. For your protection, you need
to create a paper trail to prove what you bought and to
show that you paid for your policy.

1. Where is your policy? It is frightening how many
otherwise bright consumers have absolutely no idea
where their insurance policies are. Many cannot even
remember the name of their agent or the insurance
company that issued the policy. Some paid by money
order and have no proof of payment. What chance
do you think they have in the case of loss? Start an
insurance file, put it someplace safe, and keep
everything relating to insurance in that file. Keeping
the file in a safety deposit box is not always a good
idea unless you have another copy of every form
somewhere else. *In the event of your death, the safety
deposit box may be sealed and not available to those
who need that information.*

2. Always get a receipt for the payment. This and a copy of your application should be the first items in your file. Read the application carefully and make sure it is the kind of coverage you believe you bought and that all information is correct. It should clearly identify the name of the insurance company and the effective date of your coverage.

3. Always get a copy of the policy or, in the case of health insurance, a certificate of insurance. Read the policy carefully. Make sure you understand all the fine print. Most policies have a "free examination period" during which you can refuse the policy and get your money back. Some states have a three-day waiting period before any major financial transaction becomes final. You can cancel before the three days are up and owe nothing. Be sure you have resolved any questions or problems with your policy before that period expires. Remember, the law assumes you knew what you were buying, so *the responsibility is yours.*

4. You should almost always receive your policy within thirty days of payment. If yours hasn't arrived by then, call your agent and demand a written explanation of delay. This is one of the most common areas of fraud, so accept no excuses. If you're not satisfied, contact your state insurance commissioner at once.

5. Why trade? Think carefully before buying a replacement policy, whether it is sold by a new representative who says it is "just as good" as what you already have or by your present salesperson who just happens

to be changing to a new and "better" company. Be especially careful about letting your old policy lapse before a new one becomes effective.

6. Know the penalties for withdrawing money from a life insurance policy or an annuity plan or for cancelling any insurance policy. If you have an annuity or an insurance policy as an investment, keep all letters, brochures, and annual reports from the company and read them for important changes and other information.

Automobile Policies

Most states now require proof of automobile insurance or liability bonds for all drivers. Heavy fines and sometimes imprisonment can result from failure to provide such coverage. Consequently, the question of whether you need such coverage has probably already been answered for you, if you drive. Here are some important tips that can help you select an insurance carrier:

1. Buy from a reliable agent. Ask for the agent's license and call your state insurance commissioner to discover the number of complaints against the agent and the company he represents. Remember, a good deal on insurance is not a good deal at all if you cannot collect on the policy.

2. Shop around. You can save a lot of money by comparing companies. Sometimes an insurance policy is so cheap it sounds too good to be true. And it probably is.

3. Make sure you're buying the right kind of insurance. Most companies look at your recent driving record to determine how much you will pay. If you're being asked to pay extra, demand to see the copy of your driving record upon which that decision is based. If the information is wrong you have a right to correct it.

4. As with all policies, make sure you have proof of payment, that you read and understand the application, that you are provided proof of insurance to carry in your vehicle,* and that you get your policy promptly. If any of this doesn't happen, it should send a warning signal to you immediately.

Life and Health Policies

For most consumers, life and health insurance are among the most important protections in which they will ever invest. There was a time when employers routinely provided health insurance, and sometimes life insurance, but last year one million persons lost their health insurance coverage either through changing jobs, retirement, or because their employers simply quit providing it. Employer-paid life insurance is becoming increasingly rare. Consequently, you need to be able to do the comparisons and study to protect yourself when you are paying for your own coverage.

---

*In most states that require automobile coverage you have to be able to present such a proof of being insured in the event of an accident.

1. Which insurance policy should you buy? There is no easy answer because the decision depends on your own individual needs. *Term insurance** is useful if you are young and want to make sure a spouse and children would be taken care of if you died prematurely. For young people it is often fairly inexpensive. It does not provide the long-term cash value of *whole life insurance.** If you do purchase whole life insurance, make sure you will be able to afford the premiums over a long period; it can be quite expensive if allowed to lapse in the early years. If you are a disciplined consumer, you may want to buy term insurance and invest the savings between that and whole life on your own; you'll probably get a better rate of return. But such a plan only works if you have the discipline to keep making those monthly investments.

2. When is enough insurance enough? There are life insurance salespeople on every corner who will gladly sell you all the coverage you can pay for. That is very different from *all the coverage you need.* Generally, your needs are these: (a) cash for immediate needs, the costs of final illness, burial, taxes, and debts; (b) readjustment money—giving your survivors some breathing room while they decide the important questions about their future; and (c) replacement income to maintain your family's standard of living without your paycheck. Beyond that, additional insurance coverage can be a costly and sometimes unnecessary investment.

---

*See the Glossary for definitions of these terms.

3. The same considerations about policies and agents apply here except that it is even more important that *your beneficiaries know exactly where you keep your insurance file.*

4. If you allowed your life insurance policy to lapse, it is often possible to reinstate it by paying the premiums you missed, plus interest, and proving that you are still insurable. Is that a better deal than just getting an entirely new policy? Frequently it is because the cost of reinstatement will be based on your age at the time the policy was purchased; a new policy would be based on your present age. Similarly, terms on policy loans from the original policy may be offered at a more attractive interest rate than on a new policy.

5. Deciding on the purchase of an *annuity** depends on what others sources of retirement income you already have. Remember that the penalty or surrender charge if you cancel an annuity in the first few years can be quite costly in many cases.

6. Just because your beneficiaries collect from your life insurance policy does not mean they will lose full Social Security payments because life insurance benefits do not count as earned income.

7. COBRA is the federal continuation of benefits requirement for most organizations with twenty or more employees. It lets you keep the group health insurance you had with your former employer for eighteen

---

*See the Glossary for definitions.

months or more, although you have to pay the premium. It does not help if your company goes out of business, though, since it is tied to your employer's policy, not to any particular insurance company.

8. If a person dies and the insurance policy cannot be found, send a self-addressed, stamped envelope to the American Council of Life Insurance, 1001 Pennsylvania Avenue, Washington, DC 20004, and ask for a *policy search form.* A search should be undertaken at least ninety days after you make the formal request.

9. If your policy was issued by a company you can no longer locate, call the Insurance Consumer Helpline, toll free, 1-800-942-4242. The helpline will reply, giving you names of companies which have merged, changed names, or have gone out of business.

Homeowners' Policies

Since your home is probablly the single most expensive investment of your life, finding the right insurance protection for that investment is worth the time and trouble.

1. The same rules of consumer safety apply as in the other types of insurance already described.

2. There are various types of policies, each discussed in the Glossary, but you are basically buying protection against three kinds of losses: (a) fire, windstorm, and other *physical damage*; (b) theft of *personal property*; and (c) *liability* for injury or damage

resulting from your negligence or the negligence of a family member covered by the policy (e.g., someone slips on your ice-covered front steps).

3. Homeowners usually buy insurance based on replacement cost, not market value. That is, you need to be insured for an amount which would allow you to replace your house at today's cost, not for what you could get for you house if you sold it. Many policies require you insure for 80 percent of replacement cost.

4. Some states do not require insurance companies to offer coverage to everyone who applies. Laws about how much notice you must be given before your policy lapses also vary widely from state to state. Many states also provide a FAIR plan* to provide availability of at least minimum coverage for homeowners. Your state insurance commissioner can tell you if it is available where you live.

5. Regardless of where you live, a home safety inspection including smoke alarms and carbon monoxide alarms is a good idea. So are fire drills, especially for children.

6. Take photographs of items in each room or make a video tape recording room-by-room. This and a complete inventory will be very important if you suffer a loss. Your insurance agent may be able to provide you with a form for such an inventory.

---

*See the Glossary for definitions.

Complaints

No matter how effective your state insurance commissioner may be, that department cannot help if you don't report a problem. Most disputes can be resolved promptly by contacting your agent. Keep a written record of when you called and with whom you spoke. If you are not satisfied, you are entitled to complain to your state insurance commissioner. If you don't get prompt, courteous satisfaction, tell your agent you are going to make a complaint and then do so. The number for each state insurance commissioner can be found in the Appendix. Call promptly to report improper denial of claims, unreasonable delays in settling claims, illegal cancellation or termination of policies, misrepresentation by a broker or agent, misappropriation of funds paid to an agent or broker, or premium disputes.

What information will you need to make such a complaint? All the information you have carefully maintained as part of the insurance file, suggested earlier in this chapter.

Some Tips for Older Persons

The elderly are especially vulnerable to unscrupulous insurance operators. Here are some special tips just for your protection:

1. Be especially careful of nursing home, Medicare supplement, or "extra protection" policies. Some are worthwhile; many others are worthless. *Consumer Reports* and other such objective sources are available in your library to rate the value of such offerings.

Take time to research before you buy and don't be rushed into a hasty decision.

2. Be cautious with radio, television, and mail advertising, even though they feature a paid spokesman whom you admire.

3. Use a good local agent to help you decide what to buy, preferably an agent who has also helped your friends or relatives.

4. Be careful about replacing old policies with new ones. Frequently there are waiting periods or exclusions that might leave you without coverage when you need it most. *Read the fine print,* or have someone you trust read it for you. Ask questions. It is your right to do so.

5. Buy only one good Medicare supplement policy. Buy the best you can afford but avoid buying several, because they are frequently duplicative and often only one will pay.

6. Tell a friend or relative whom you trust, or your attorney, where your insurance file is kept.

Ultimately, your protection as an insurance consumer is likely to be no better than the quality of your state insurance commissioner. But every insurance commissioner can tell you whether or not you are dealing with a licensed, reputable company. Most insurance commissioners will tell you whether the agent or the company has had any serious complaints registered with the insurance department office in the past year. You owe it to yourself to ask before you buy.

The lessons I can impart from a decade of dealing with thousands of honest, sincere, and qualified insurance agents as well as the notorious pirates in pinstripes described here are that the cheapest coverage is not always the best bargain and the glossiest brochures do not always represent the best product.

Know your insurance needs. Be alert and aware of the insurance options available to you. But most of all, don't take anything on face value. Check it out for yourself!

Appendix 1

Consumer Resources

A. M. Best Company
Ambest Road
Oldwick, NJ 08858-9988
(212) 439-2200

Consumer Insurance Interest
   Group
9321 Millbranch Place
Fairfax, VA 22031
(703) 836-9340

Consumer Reports
101 Truman Avenue
Yonkers, NY 10703-1057
(914) 378-2000
Fax (914) 378-2900

Federal Emergency Manage-
   ment Agency
Federal Insurance
   Administration
500 C Street SW
Washington, DC 20472
1-800-638-6620

Insurance Information Institute
110 William Street
New York, NY 10038
(212) 669-9200

Insurance Services Office, Inc.
175 Water Street
New York, NY 10038
(212) 487-5000

National Association of Insurance Commissioners
12 Wyandotte Place
120 W. 12th Street, Suite 1100
Kansas City, MO 64105
(816) 842-3600

National Association of Life
  Underwriters
1922 F Street SW
Washington, DC 20066
(202) 331-6000

National Association of Professional Insurance Agents
400 N. Washington Street
Alexandria, VA 22314
(703) 836-9340

National Insurance Consumer
  Organization
414 A Street SE
Washington, DC 20003
(202) 547-6426

Appendix 2

State Insurance Commissioners

Alabama
James H. Dill,
Commissioner of Insurance
135 S. Union Street
Montgomery, AL 36130-3401
(205) 269-3550
Fax (205) 240-3194

Alaska
David Walsh,
Director of Insurance
333 Willoughby Avenue
Juneau, AK 99811-0805
(907) 465-2515
Fax (907) 465-3422

Arizona
Susan Gallinger,
Director of Insurance
3030 N. 3rd Street, Suite 1100
Phoenix, AZ 85012
(602) 255-5400
Fax (602) 255-4722

Arkansas
Lee Douglas,
Commissioner of Insurance
1123 S. University Avenue
Suite 400 University Tower
    Bldg.
Little Rock, AR 72204-1699
(501) 686-2900
Fax (501) 686-2913

California
John Garamendi,
Commissioner of Insurance
45 Fremont Street
San Francisco, CA 94105
(415) 904-5410
Fax (415) 904-5889

Colorado
Joanne Hill,
Commissioner of Insurance
1560 Broadway Suite 850
Denver, CO 80202
(303) 894-7499
Fax (303) 894-7455

Connecticut
Robert R. Googins,
Commissioner of Insurance
State Office Building
Box 816
Hartford, CT 06142-0816
(203) 297-3802
Fax (203) 566-7410

Delaware
Donna Lee H. Williams,
Commissioner of Insurance
841 Silver Lake Boulevard
Dover, DE 19901
(302) 739-4251
Fax (302) 739-5280

Florida
Tom Gallagher,
Commissioner of Insurance
Plaza Level 11, The Capitol
Tallahassee, FL 32399-0300
(904) 922-3100
Fax (904) 488-3334

Georgia
Tim Ryles,
Commissioner of Insurance
Seventh Floor, West Tower
2 Martin Luther King, Jr. Drive
Atlanta, GA 30334
(404) 656-2056
Fax (404) 656-7628

Hawaii
Linda Chu Takayama,
Commissioner of Insurance
Box 3614
Honolulu, HI 96811
(808) 586-2790
Fax (808) 586-2806

Idaho
Harry C. Walrath,
Director of Insurance
700 S. 10th Street
Boise, ID 83720
(208) 334-4250
Fax (208) 334-4398

Illinois
Stephen F. Selcke,
Director of Insurance
320 W. Washington
Springfield, IL 62767
(217) 782-4515
Fax (217) 782-5020

Indiana
John F. Mortell,
Commissioner of Insurance
311 W. Washington Street,
Suite 300
Indianapolis, IN 46204
(317) 232-3520
Fax (317) 232-5251

Iowa
David J. Lyons,
Commissioner of Insurance
Lucas State Office Building
Des Moines, IA 50319
(515) 281-5705
Fax (515) 281-3059

Kansas
Ronald L. Todd,
Commissioner of Insurance
420 SW 9th Street
Topeka, KS 66612-1678
(913) 296-7801
Fax (913) 296-2283

Kentucky
Don W. Stephens,
Commissioner of Insurance
229 W. Main
Frankfort, KY 40602
(502) 564-3630
Fax (502) 564-6090

Louisiana
James H. Brown, Jr.,
Commissioner of Insurance
Box 911
Baton Rouge, LA 70821-0911
(504) 342-5900
Fax (504) 342-3078

Maine
Brian K. Atchinson,
Superintendent of Insurance
State House Station #34
Augusta, ME 04333
(207) 582-8707
Fax (207) 582-8716

Maryland
Dwight K. Bartlett III
Commissioner of Insurance
501 St. Paul Place
Baltimore, MD 21202-2372
(410) 333-6300
Fax (410) 333-6650

Massachusetts
Linda Ruthardt,
Commissioner of Insurance
470 Atlantic Avenue
Boston, MA 02210-2208
(615) 521-7777
Fax (615) 521-7772

Michigan
David Dykhouse,
Commissioner of Insurance
611 W. Ottawa
Lansing, MI 48933
(517) 373-9273
Fax (517) 335-4978

Minnesota
Jim Ulland,
Commissioner of Insurance
133 E. 7th Street
St. Paul, MN 55101
(612) 296-4026
Fax (612) 296-4328

Mississippi
George Dale,
Commissioner of Insurance
Box 2306
Jackson, MS 39205
(601) 359-3569
Fax (601) 359-2474

Missouri
Jay Angoff,
Director of Insurance
Box 690
Jefferson City, MO 65102-0690
(314) 751-4126
Fax (314) 751-1165

Montana
Mark O'Keefe,
Commissioner of Insurance
Box 4009
Helena, MT 59604
(406) 444-2040
Fax (406) 444-3497

Nebraska
William H. McCartney,
Director of Insurance
941 "O" Street, Suite 400
Lincoln, NE 68508
(402) 471-2201
Fax (402) 471-4610

Nevada
Teresa Rankin,
Commissioner of Insurance
1665 Hot Springs #152
Carson City, NV 89710
(702) 687-4270
Fax (702) 687-3937

New Hampshire
Sylvio L. Dupuis,
Commissioner bInsurance
169 Manchester Street
Concord, NH 03301
(603) 271-2261
Fax (603) 271-1406

New Jersey
Samuel F. Fortunato,
Commissioner of Insurance
20 W. State Street CN 325
Trenton, NJ 08625
(609) 292-5363
Fax (609) 633-3601

New Mexico
Fabian Chavez, Jr.,
Superintendent of Insurance
PERA Building
500 Old Santa Fe Trail
Santa Fe, NM 87504-1269
(505) 827-4500
Fax (505) 827-4734

New York
Salvatore Curiale,
Superintendent of Insurance
160 W. Broadway
New York, NY 10013
(212) 602-0429
Fax (212) 602-0437

North Carolina
James E. Long,
Commissioner of Insurance
Box 26387
Raleigh, NC 27611
(919) 733-7349
Fax (919) 733-6495

North Dakota
Glenn Pomeroy,
Commissioner of Insurance
State Capitol 5th Floor
Bismarck, ND 58505-0320
(701) 224-2440
Fax (710) 224-4880

Ohio
Harold T. Duryee,
Director of Insurance
2100 Stella Court
Columbus, OH 43266-0566
(614) 644-2658
Fax (614) 644-3743

Oklahoma
Catherine J. Weatherford,
Commissioner of Insurance
1901 N. Walnut
Oklahoma City, OK 73105
(405) 521-2828
Fax (405) 521-6652

Oregon
Kerry E. Barnett,
Director of Insurance
440 Labor and Industries
   Building
Salem, OR 97310
(503) 378-4271
Fax (503) 378-4351

Pennsylvania
Cynthia M. Maleski,
Commissioner of Insurance
1326 Strawberry Square, 13th
   Floor
Harrisburg, PA 17120
(717) 787-2317
Fax (717) 783-1059

Rhode Island
Sheldon Whitehouse,
Commissioner of Insurance
233 Richmond Street, Suite 237
Providence, RI 02903
(401) 277-2246
Fax (401) 277-6098

South Carolina
John G. Richards,
Commissioner of Insurance
1612 Marion Street
Columbia, SC 29201
(803) 737-6160
Fax (803) 737-6205

South Dakota
Darla L. Lyon
910 E. Sioux Avenue
Pierre, SD 57501-5070
(605) 773-3563
Fax (605) 773-5369

Tennessee
Elaine A. McReynolds,
Commissioner of Insurance
500 James Robertson Parkway,
   5th Floor
Nashville, TN 37243-1135
(615) 741-2241
Fax (615) 741-4000

Texas
J. Robert Hunter,
Commissioner of Insurance
Box 149104
Austin, TX 78714-9104
(512) 463-6169
Fax (512) 475-2005

Utah
Robert E. Wilcox,
Commissioner of Insurance
3110 State Office Building
Salt Lake City, UT 84114
(801) 538-3800
Fax (801) 538-3829

Vermont
Elizabeth Rowe Costle,
Commissioner of Insurance
89 Main Street
Montpelier, VT 05620-3101
(802) 828-3301
Fax (802) 828-3306

Virginia
Steven T. Foster,
Commissioner of Insurance
1300 E. Main Street
Richmond, VA 23219
(804) 371-9694
Fax (804) 371-9873

Washington
Deborah Senn,
Commissioner of Insurance
Box 40255
Olympia, WA 98504-0255
(206) 753-7301
Fax (206) 586-3535

West Virginia
Hanley C. Clark,
Commissioner of Insurance
2019 Washington Street E.
Charleston, WV 25305
(304) 558-3394
Fax (304) 558-0412

Wisconsin
Josephine W. Musser,
Commissioner of Insurance
Box 7873
Madison, WI 53707-7873
(608) 266-3585
Fax (608) 266-9935

Wyoming
John P. McBride
Commissioner of Insurance
122 W. 25th St.
Cheyenne, WY 82002
(307) 777-7401
Fax (307) 777-5895

Glossary

Accident Only Coverage: An insurance policy that only covers losses due to an accident.

Actual Cash Value Replacement Cost: The cost of replacing or repairing damaged property with property similar in age and condition to that which was damaged.

Actuarial Audit: An examination by an insurance actuary to determine whether revisions should be made to the level of reserves or in required premiums based on the company's past experience and its estimated future claims.

Actuary: The insurance professional responsible for the calculation of probabilities. Duties include estimating reserves, setting premiums, establishing dividend rates, assisting in development of new policy products, and providing statistical information for rate-setting on insurance, annuity and retirement products.

Adjuster: The insurance company representative who first determines its policy obligations after a claim is made.

Adjustable Life: A relatively new form in which the policyholder may increase or decrease coverage by changing the amount of premium payments or the period of the policy.

Agent: The licensed insurance professional who sells for insurance companies, usually paid on commission for such sales.

AmBank: One of the financial institutions with which Champion Insurance maintained an account, the bank whose monthly statements were replicated and forged.

Annuity: An investment in which you pay premiums now with the promise of receiving an income later.

Appeal Bond: A sum required to be posted before a judgment may be taken to a higher court on appeal.

Arbitrage: A term loosely applied to the portion of the investment industry involved with mergers, acquisitions, leveraged buy-outs, junk bonds, and corporate takeovers.

Arbitration: A nonjudicial hearing in which disputing parties present their side of the dispute to a neutral party, the arbitrator, who then renders what is usually a binding decision. Nonbinding recommendations are usually rendered by mediators.

Assigned Risk Pool: Insurance provided as a matter of law to drivers who would not otherwise qualify. Each insurer in a state participates in the pool, charging a rated premium as part of the pool.

Assumed Reinsurance Arm: An assumed reinsurance arm is an operating division which takes on reinsurance coverage from other companies in addition to writing its own direct insurance coverage.

Bad Faith: A form of tort in which an insurance company breaks its contract to treat its insureds in good faith.

Basic Hospital Expense Coverage: An insurance policy promising to pay some portion of your hospital room and board and sometimes other expenses of hospitalization.

Basic Medical Surgical Coverage: An insurance policy promising to pay for costs of a physician for surgical operations and sometimes for other medical professionals and costs.

Beneficial Shareholders: A person or entity that gains the benefits of holding a share of stock without actually appearing on the stock certificate as owner of record.

Beneficiary: The person entitled to receive the proceeds of a life insurance policy.

Binder: An agreement between the consumer and the insurance agent in which insurance coverage is provided before the actual policy is issued, usually done only in property and casualty insurance sales.

Book of Business: An insurance company's aggregate policies, often referred to by the types of insurance policies the company offers.

Breach of Contract: The wrongful failure of an insurance company to pay what it is legally required to pay under the policy.

Basic Homeowners' Insurance Coverage: A standard homeowners policy that protects your home and personal property from damage done by fire or lightning, windstorm or hail, vandalism, theft, vehicle and aircraft damages to your property, riots, glass breakage and comprehensive liability.

This coverage may be expanded by broad form coverage, which increases coverage or by special form policies that cover other structures and virtually all risks.

Broker: A licensed agent not affiliated with a specific insurance company who helps consumers select the right policy and cost. Usually paid on commission for such sales.

Bulk Reinsurance: The total of reinsurance assumed (accepted by others), reinsurance capacity (the retention limit), and reinsurance ceded to others.

Cancellation: Termination of an insurance policy.

Carrier: Another term for an insurance company.

Cap: Maximum payment which may be made under a specific insurance policy.

Cash Managers: The persons within an insurance company responsible for properly receiving income and determining how it should be divided, i.e., reserves, operations, etc.

Cash Value Life Insurance: Life insurance that gains financial worth during its existence.

Casualty Insurance: Protection from economic losses due to unexpected and unpredictable occurrences and protection from monetary damages assessed for negligence and other forms of liability to other parties.

Certificate of Authority: A statement issued by any state insurance commissioner allowing a company to offer specific types of insurance for sale within that state. Sometimes a similar statement given by an insurance company to its agents.

Claim: A formal request for benefits made by an insured against an insurance company based on the policy.

Collision Insurance: A policy which pays for damages to your car resulting from an accident whether or not you were at fault. The amount of payment depends upon your deductible.

Commercial Liability: Protection against damages resulting from actions of the company, such damages being either in the present (direct) or in the future (contingent).

Comparative Negligence: In some states, an aspect of personal injury law in which an injured person's damages from an accident are reduced by the percentage by which the accident was his or her fault.

Comprehensive Insurance: For automobile coverage, a policy that pays for damages that did not occur because of a wreck, minus the deductible. For homeowners' insurance, the most expensive kind of coverage which protects against every peril except earthquake and flood.

Condominium Insurance: A relatively new form of policy which insures only the interior of a condominium, not the structure, similar to tenants' insurance.

Conservatorship: In many states, the process of operation of a insurance company that has been seized by the state insurance commissioner while it is being liquidated, often after rehabilitation of the company has been unsuccessfully attempted.

Consultant: In the insurance industry, usually an independent advisor, generally an insurance agent.

Contingency Fee: A fee arrangement in which a lawyer receives a specified percentage, plus costs, only if the attorney wins the case. This allows access to the legal system to persons who might not otherwise be able to afford to bring legal actions.

Contributory Negligence: In some states, an aspect of personal injury law that prevents an injured party from collecting any damages if he or she was even partially responsible for causing the accident.

Conversion Rights: The right contained in an insurance policy or provided as a matter of law which allows a person to convert from one form of coverage to another, usually seen in term life insurance policies, allowing them to be switched to whole life.

Coordination of Benefits: A provision contained in some policies which limits the amount an insured can receive under more than one policy, usually by setting a maximum amount payable on a certain type of coverage or by providing benefits may be paid only on one policy.

Copayment: The portion that the insured must personally pay for coverage under certain policies, usually found in fee-for-service health insurance policies.

Coverages: The type of loss for which the insurance company will pay.

Credit Accident, Sickness, or Life Insurance: A special type of insurance available when you make a loan or participate in other credit transactions. This policy pays your creditors while you are sick or disabled or in the event of your death. The payment goes directly to the creditor. It is generally not required and usually very expensive. A basic term policy provides the same protection at lower cost in most cases.

Debenture: A bond secured only by the general assets of the government or corporation issuing it.

Damages: The injury or financial loss someone suffers, after which that person has the right to sue those responsible.

Declarations: On automobile policies, the policy number, the insured's name and address, a description of the insured vehicle, the name of any other person with a financial interest in the vehicle (the loss payee), and the kinds of limitations of coverage under that policy.

Decreasing Term Insurance: A kind of term life insurance policy in which the benefits go down each year but the premiums do not increase.

Deductible: The amount of money the insured must pay under a policy before the insurance company is required to make any payment. Generally, the higher the deductible, the lower the insurance premium.

Defendant: The person who is sued in a lawsuit.

Definitions: In automobile insurance, the "fine print" defining the meaning and application of terms used.

Depreciation: The decrease in property value due to age and condition.

Deregister: The process by which a company voluntarily surrenders its right to sell stock under the rules of the Securities and Exchange Commission. It may retain state authority for sale and other rights.

Disability Insurance Protection: A policy providing for weekly or monthly benefit payments while the individual is disabled from accident or injury.

Dividend: Payments made by a mutual insurance company to policyholders or their policies as a result of company earnings.

Elimination Periods: In disability policies, long-term policies, and hospital policies, this may refer to the number of days at the beginning of each disability or confinement the policy will not cover. Generally, the longer each elimination period, the lower the premium.

Endorsements: Forms attached to your policy that change the policy to fit your specific needs.

Excess Liability: Basically an umbrella policy which reimburses losses above the specific limits of a separate policy.

Exclusions: In an automobile policy, a list of certain situations in which the policy will provide no coverage.

Exclusive Agent: A agent who sells for only one insurance company.

FSLIC: The Federal Savings and Loan Insurance Corporation, the savings and loan equivalent of the Federal Deposit Insurance Corporation, which provides insurance protection up to $100,000 for each account.

Face Amount: The amount to be paid under a life insurance policy in the event of death.

FAIR: Fair Access to Insurance Requirements. A federal program providing property and casualty insurance in areas where private carriers are concerned about environmental or economic problems. Several states have enacted their own versions of this legislation.

Fair Claims Procedures Act: A consumer-protection act passed in various forms in some states which sets out the rules for proper handling of insurance claims by companies and adjusters.

Family Income Plan: A combination insurance plan covering an individual, usually the principal wage earner, with whole life or endowment and decreasing term insurance. Often bought by couples with young children.

Fault System: The traditional method of determining who must pay for damages in an automobile accident based on who was at fault.

FDIC: The Federal Deposit Insurance Corporation.

Federal Liability Risk Retention Act: A federal risk retention program which allows insurers to operate in a state in which they are not licensed.

FEGLI: A group life insurance program for federal employees in which both risk and income are reinsured to private carriers.

FELA: Federal Employees Liability Act, which provides workers' compensation insurance to federal employees.

FIA: The Federal Insurance Administration, which runs various programs such as FAIR.

Forgery Affidavit: A notarized statement in which a victim swears that monies properly belonging to him or her have been unlawfully taken by some other party. Often required before a bank or other institution will reimburse the rightful owner of the funds.

Front-Loaded Fees: Various costs charged to a consumer at the time a policy is sold, an important source of additional revenue for large-volume insurance operations.

Fronting Fee: Essentially a commission one insurance company pays to the insurance company that cedes it insurance coverage it has written or assumed.

Fronting Proposal: The sales proposal setting forth the commission schedule and other inducements to establish a reinsurance agreement.

General Damages: Noneconomic losses suffered in a personal injury case, often called pain and suffering. Not allowed in all states.

Group Health Insurance: Coverage provided to a large number of persons under one contract, usually at a lower rate than individual health insurance.

HMO: Health Maintenance Organization. An organization that provides health care services directly to its members for a fixed monthly fee.

Holding Company: A corporation organized for the purpose of owning and holding the stock of other corporations.

Hospital Confinement Indemnity: A policy that pays a fixed amount for every day of hospitalization.

INBR: Losses Incurred But Not Reported. In the process of loss reserving, a category covering losses that an insurance company must assume to have occurred but which have not yet been reported.

Incentives: Inducements, monetary or otherwise, provided by one party to encourage specific actions by another.

Individual Health Insurance: The opposite of group health insurance, in which only one person or members of one family are covered under one policy.

Insurance Commissioner: The person, usually elected, with responsibility for licensing and regulating the activities of insurance companies authorized to do business within a specific state.

Insurance Examiner: The employee of a state insurance commissioner who reviews the policies, procedures, and financial stability of insurance companies operating in that state.

Insurance Fraud: The crime of obtaining or attempting to obtain benefits from an insurance company through knowingly giving false information or withholding crucial information.

Interlocking Group Companies: Companies that may appear to be independent but are actually owned and/or controlled by the same person or persons and operated to benefit each other or the owners. In insurance company fraud cases, usually pierced by SBE, "Single Business Entity," suits brought by regulators.

Intermediary: In insurance, a broker who, for a commission, negotiates contracts of reinsurance for the reinsured.

IRIS: Insurance Regulatory Information System. A series of cooperative programs operated by state insurance commissioners whereby information about troubled companies is shared and procedures are standardized.

Joint Venture: An arrangement in which two or more entities arrange to share responsibilities, costs, and profits in a certain project or projects.

Layering: The process of covering all or part of a contingent loss with several policies.

Leveraging: In insurance, the system that allows companies with very limited capital to use reinsurance and manipulated assets and reserves to wind up with possible exposure many times their ability to manage or to pay.

Liability Coverage: In automobile policies, this policy pays for another person's property or bodily injury losses if the policy holder is responsible.

LFFI: Limited Function Financial Institutions. In Louisiana, companies that were, for a time, allowed to perform all the duties of banks except the offering of checking accounts. Most were directly tied to insurance companies. No new LFFI charters have been issued in several years.

Lloyd's Plan Companies: In the United States, a voluntary, unincorporated association of individuals in which each individual assumed a certain portion of the liability under each policy issued. The groups generally required lower capitalization to start than other insurance companies, usually operated through a common attorney-in-fact whom they appointed and usually had less regulatory supervision in most states.

Long-Tailed Claims: Claims for which the resultant cost will likely continue for many years; workers' compensation insurance claims are a typical example.

Long-Term Care Coverage: Policies that pay for skilled, intermediate, and custodial care in a nursing home. The definitions of such care vary widely by policy.

Looping Procedure: In insurance, the policy of an insurance passing its exposure on to another which did the same in a circular pattern, often eventually resulting in the first company finally insuring itself at the end of the chain.

Loss: Damages caused to someone because of an injury, property destruction, or some other incurred liability.

Loss Reserves: Reserves established to estimate the pending loss which must eventually be paid, including all categories of losses.

Major Medical Expense: A policy designed to cover the high cost of serious accidents and injuries.

Market Conduct Study: That portion of some states' insurance company audits which reviews how promptly and appropriately the company's claims are paid and how decently it conducts itself in the state's insurance industry.

McCarran Act: Federal legislation that protects insurance companies from being charged with anti-trust violations so long as they are regulated on a state level. It also allows pooling of insurance rate information and operation of rating bureaus.

Medicaid: A state and federal program providing medical aid to the aged, blind, disabled families with dependent children, and to needy children. For qualifying persons it eliminates the need for other health insurance.

Medical Payments: In automobile insurance, this policy provides coverage to the policyholder and passengers regardless of who is to blame for an accident.

Medicare: A federal health care program for persons over 65 and those receiving Social Security disability benefits.

Medicare Supplement Insurance: Policies that purport to pay costs that Medicare does not cover, valuable only after very close scrutiny.

Modified Life: A life insurance plan in which premiums are very low in the early years of the policy but increase later.

Mortality Charges: The base rates upon which costs of life insurance policies are calculated.

Mutual Insurance Company: An insurance company owned entirely by its policyholders in proportionate shares.

Negligence: Damages caused where one person breaches the duty of reasonable care to another person.

No-Fault Insurance: A system of automobile insurance in which significantly limited benefits are paid to the insured whether or not he or she caused the accident.

Nominal Shareholders: Those persons whose names actually appear as owners of record of shares of stock in a corporation.

Non-Admitted Assets: Insurance company assets that cannot be counted toward net worth under statutory rules such as monies agents owe the company for advances against future commissions, furniture, and the like.

"Off the Manual" Sales: Sales of insurance policies at discounts below the published or manual rate. Prohibited by law but sometimes done in the case of large-volume, highly competitive cases.

Office of Financial Institutions: The state agency, by that or similar title, that regulates the licensing and conduct of banks, savings and loans, and other financial institutions that are chartered by a state, rather than federally.

Peril: Any possible cause of loss such a fire.

Physical Damage: The section in an automobile policy describing the benefits payable if the automobile is damaged.

Plaintiff: The person who brings a lawsuit.

Pools: A group of insurers who jointly underwrite a class or classes of risk, sharing in premium income and claims payment costs on a pre-determined basis. Also groups or organizations that self-insure against contingent losses.

Preexisting Conditions: A condition an insured already has when a policy is purchased.

Preferred Risk: A person with lower risk of loss than the average.

Premium Finance Notes: Contracts signed by a buyer of insurance, usually automobile insurance, in which the cost of the premium plus a substantial interest charge is to be paid to a private finance company, often affiliated with the company that sold the insurance policy; a major source of revenue to such companies.

Premium Rebates: Refunds of collected premiums, usually made by an insurance company directly to its selling agent in addition to the commission.

Proof of Loss: A written statement from the policyholder to the insurance company regarding a claim; a first step in the settlement procedure.

Property Flipping: The illegal process of a group of individuals or entities selling a property back and forth among themselves numerous times so that the property is eventually inflated in value.

PPO: Preferred Provider Organizations. An arrangement in which an employer or insurance company makes a contract with selected hospitals and doctors to provide services at discounted rates.

Punitive Damages: A cash award to a plaintiff over and above monetary damages, usually given where intentional misconduct is shown; not allowed in all states.

Rate: The cost of a unit of insurance from which the total premium is calculated.

Rating Bureau: An organization, supported by insurance companies, that provides information on statistics, rates, and other data.

Reinsurance: Sharing of risk too large for one insurer by ceding part of the risk to another company (the reinsurer).

Reinsurance Pool Participant: See Pool.

Renewal: The provision in each policy that defines the terms of renewal and states the company's right to change premium rates. Such terms include noncancellable, guaranteed renewable, conditionally renewable, and nonrenewable provisions.

Rental Reimbursement: A provision providing if an insured's car is damaged by a covered peril or accident, the company will pay for a rented car, with specified limitations.

Reserves: A liability established in order to pay for future claims.

Retroceding: Passing along once-ceded insurance to yet another reinsurer, a process sometimes repeated many times in looping arrangements.

Rider: Extra coverage available on health or life insurance policy.

Risk: The chance that a loss will occur.

Risk-to-Capital System: A system whereby the financial stability is judged on its aggregate risk compared to its paid-in and total capital. This is a much more conservative system than the surplus-to-premium system that is more frequently used by regulators. That system more generously compares surplus (the difference between total admitted assets and total liabilities) to net premium written (which subtracts all the ceded reinsurance), thus allowing companies to significantly overextend.

Salvage and Subrogation Account: A ledger account to receive repayments for losses caused by a third party.

Scheme of Arrangement: The British system for dissolution of failed insurance companies.

Self-Dealing: An arrangement, similar to insider trading, in which affiliated companies transact business among themselves to their mutual benefit.

Settlement Work: The process of an insurance company's negotiating a compromise settlement of a disputed claim.

Shadow Director: A person whose involvement as director conceals a secret arrangement with another.

Silent Partner: A person whose equity or working interest in an organization, not necessarily restricted to a partnership, is withheld from public knowledge by counter letter or other artifice or by simple silence.

Social Security: A federal program paying benefits for long-term or permanent disability in addition to traditional retirement benefits.

Special Damages: Actual out-of-pocket damages suffered by the injured party in a personal injury lawsuit.

Specified Disease or Accident Coverage: Policies that cover only a specific accident or disease such as cancer.

Statutory Insolvency: The determination established by law that reveals an insurance company to be unable to meet its current obligations as they come due.

Surplus-to-Premium System: See Risk-to-Capital.

Syndicates: A pool formed by several participants to share risks and benefits of a particular venture.

Staff Actuary: See Actuary.

State Guarantee Fund: A fund established in virtually every state by which every insurance company operating in that state pays a specified percentage of premium to the state fund. Those proceeds are then used to pay claims against failed insurance companies to the extent possible.

Stock Insurance Company: A company that has issued stock and is owned by its stockholders; opposite of a mutual company.

Surety Bond Agreement: A guarantee made by a person or company through which the guarantor agrees to make a specified payment in the event the subject fails to perform.

Subsidiary: A company or entity controlled by another.

Surplus Lines: A form of insurance that is not offered by a company admitted in the applicant's state. In such an instance, the insurance agent may purchase insurance from a non-admitted company.

Term Insurance: Insurance restricted to a specified period of time or until a certain age. Generally does not build cash value and is less expensive than whole life insurance.

Third Party Coverage: Insurance to pay damages to third parties in which the insured was negligent.

Tort: A civil wrong, except breach of contract, which results in suit.

Umbrella Liability: Protection over the limits of other existing policies.

Undercapitalized: Lacking sufficient or statutory capital to allow for prudent operation of an insurance company.

Underwrite: The risk selection, evaluation of applications for insurance, and the degree of resultant risk to which the company would be exposed in the event such policies are issued.

Unlicensed Carrier: A carrier unlicensed to write insurance in a specific state.

Uninsured/Underinsured Motorist Coverage: A provision that pays benefits if the insured is hit by a driver with no insurance or too little insurance to pay for all the damages.

Universal Life: A policy that allows the consumer great flexibility in selecting terms and conditions and changing them when appropriate.

Variable Life: A type of cash value policy in which the owner may choose to invest in stocks, bonds, or money market funds.

Waiting Period: The amount of time that must elapse after the policy takes effect before coverage begins; usually applies only to illness.

Whole Life Insurance: A type of cash value policy that stays in effect for the lifetime of the insured or until it lapses.

Workers' Compensation Insurance: A system that varies from state to state which provides medical care and disability payments for injured workers. It is paid for by employers.

Zone Audit: Under the National Association of Insurance Commissioners system, a program in which various states participate in the audit of an insurance company and agree that all states will accept the results of the audit. The audit team is normally led by the insurance commissioner in the state where the insurance company is domiciled.

Index

283